THE
PREACHING
OF PAUL

A Study of ROMANS

THE PREACHING OF PAUL

OF PAUL

A Study of ROMANS

R. Hollis Gause

ISBN: 0-87148-719-5

DEDICATION

TO MY BROTHER

VALDANE JAMES GAUSE

AND HIS WIFE

NELLIE BLANTON GAUSE

with gratitude for their love
in the family and in the Lord

CONTENTS

OUTLINE 9

INTRODUCTION 11

Chapter 1
SALUTATION AND PROPOSITION 19

Chapter 2
THE SINFULNESS OF MAN 29

Chapter 3
THE NATURE OF JUSTIFICATION 51

Chapter 4
THE NATURE OF SANCTIFICATION 75

Chapter 5
THE HOLY SPIRIT AND HOLINESS 95

Chapter 6
ISRAEL AND GRACE 123

Chapter 7
THE PRACTICE OF HOLINESS 165

Chapter 8
CONCLUSION 203

OUTLINE

COMMENTARY ON ROMANS

INTRODUCTION

I. SALUTATION AND PROPOSITION

    A. Salutation (1:1-7)
    B. Prayer and Concern (1:8-13)
    C. Paul's Debt (1:14, 15)
    D. Proposition (1:16, 17)

II. THE SINFULNESS OF MAN

    A. The Revelation of God to the Gentiles (1:18-20)
    B. Sinfulness and Judgment (1:21-32)
    C. Conscience and Judgment (2:1-16)
    D. The Law and Judgment (2:17-3:7)
    E. Universal Conviction of Sin (3:8-20)

III. THE NATURE OF JUSTIFICATION

    A. Justification and the Righteousness of God (3:21-26)
    B. Justification and Old Testament Witnesses (3:27-4:8)
    C. Justification and Circumcision (4:9-15)
    D. The Seed of Abraham in Faith (4:16-25)
    E. The Results of Justification in the Heart (5:1-11)
    F. The Transmission of Sin and Righteousness (5:12-21)

IV. THE NATURE OF SANCTIFICATION

    A. The Crucifixion of the Old Nature (6:1-7)
    B. Holiness and Faith (6:8-14)
    C. Enslavement to Holiness (6:15-23)
    D. Freedom From the Law (7:1-6)
    E. The Law and Moral Accountability (7:7-13)
    F. Personal Struggle With Sin (7:14-25)

V. THE HOLY SPIRIT AND HOLINESS

    A. Freedom From Condemnation (8:1)
    B. The Law of the Spirit of Life (8:2-4)
    C. The Spiritual Mind (8:5-11)
    D. The Spirit of Holiness (8:12-14)
    E. The Spirit of Adoption (8:15, 16)
    F. Heirs of the Kingdom of God (8:17-22)
    G. The Spirit's Witness of the Kingdom (8:23-27)
    H. God's Provisions for the Believer (8:28-39)

VI. ISRAEL AND GRACE

    A. Paul's Compassion for Israel (9:1-3)
    B. Israel's Advantages (9:4, 5)
    C. The Israel of Promise (9:6-12)
    D. God's Promise and God's Sovereignty (9:13-21)
    E. Vessels of Wrath and Vessels of Glory (9:22-29)
    F. Israel's Failure (9:30-10:4)
    G. The Righteousness of the Law and the Righteousness of Faith (10:5-13)
    H. The Word of Faith (10:14-21)
    I. The Remnant of Israel (11:1-10)
    J. The Blessing of the Nations (11:11-16)
    K. The Olive Tree (11:17-25)
    L. The Fulfillment of God's Purpose (11:26-32)
    M. The Doxology (11:33-36)

VII. THE PRACTICE OF HOLINESS

    A. The Bases of the Practice of Holiness (12:1, 2)
    B. The Practice of Holiness in Relation to Other Members of the Body of Christ (12:3-8)
    C. Manifestations of Love (12:9-21)
    D. Subjection to Civil Authority (13:1-7)
    E. The Debt of Love (13:8-14)
    F. Problems of Conscience (14:1-12)
    G. Instructions for Harmony (14:13-23)
    H. The Example of Christ (15:1-6)

VIII. CONCLUSION

    A. The Blessings of God for Gentiles (15:7-13)
    B. Paul's Ministry and Plans (15:14-33)
    C. Personal Greetings (16:1-16)
    D. Warnings About Evil Teachers (16:17-20)
    E. Additional Greetings (16:21-23)
    F. Doxology (16:24-27)

INTRODUCTION

"The greatness of the Epistle [to the Romans] is seen in the importance of its subject matter, the comprehensiveness of its reasoning, the breadth of its outlook, and the vigor of its style."[1] The book before us is the longest of the epistles of Paul. It is also the most comprehensive statement of his theology, and its organization has probably set the pattern of the development of Christian systematic theology. This book, however, is not a "systematic theology" in the sense in which we have come to use the term. This is a personal and official letter of the apostle Paul to a church (or groups of believers) that he had never visited, but in which he had many acquaintances (Romans 16).

We do not know what prompted Paul to deal with the subjects that are in this epistle. We have no record or hint of correspondence between him and the Roman believers. We have no reports of error in doctrine or in practice. There are no challenges to his apostleship. In writing this epistle Paul felt free to discuss issues of Christian doctrine applicable in all circumstances and in all ages.

In the commentary we will designate Romans 1:16, 17 as the proposition of the book. The kernel of that statement is "The just shall live by faith" (Romans 1:17b; Habakkuk 2:4). For Paul this is the essence of grace, and grace is the essence of the plan of salvation and its application to men. In order to show the nature of grace Paul must establish the doctrine of the glory of God and the doctrine of the unworthiness of man in sin. He does this in Romans 1-3 in which he shows the sinfulness of both gentiles and Jews. His descriptions of the work of God and his references to the law of God set forth the glory of God as the "incorruptible God" (Romans 1:23). The glory (holiness) of God lies at the foundation of Paul's doctrines of sin and grace.

With this foundation established, Paul applies the doctrine of grace to the experiences of salvation: justification, sanctification, life in the Holy Spirit, and adoption (Romans 4-8). Then Paul applies the doctrine of grace to the identity of the people of God. The people of God are the seed of Abraham according to promise. As Paul applies the doctrine of grace to the issues of sin and salvation, he applies the doctrine of grace to the identity of Israel. In that way he can extend the same promises to gentiles that are extended to Israel and on the same basis—grace. This is the subject matter of Romans 9-11. One should not look on these chapters as a parenthesis. They are integral to the entire book, and the doctrine of grace.

In Romans 12:1 through 15:6 Paul deals with life in grace. He applies the principles of grace to worship, obedience, the functions of ministry, responses to abuse and injustice, the role of government and citizenship, and the relationship of believers to each other in differences of conviction. It is possible to take these chapters and turn them into a listing of "rules of behavior." These rules of behavior are there, but they are there as the outworking of the grace of God—transformation by the renewing of the mind (Romans 12:1, 2).

In the closing portion of this book Paul explains his ministry, and gives us some insights into the ambitions that moved him to certain decisions. He is especially concerned to show his relationship to the gentiles in the fulfillment of his apostleship. In the salutations we see Paul in personal relations. These relations deny the stereotype of Paul as harsh, distant, and impersonal. He was deeply and emotionally involved with many people; Romans 16 gives us a short list of those people who meant so much to the Apostle.

THE CHURCH AT ROME

Though we use the term "the church at Rome," we should not think of this group in a modern sense. It is clear that there was no one founder of the church in the imperial city. It had grown up without apostolic presence in the city. In Romans 16 there are at least three specific groups referred to. There was a church in the house of Priscilla and Aquila (Romans 16:5). A group of brothers is mentioned in 16:14. Romans 16:15 mentions the saints that were with Philologus, Julia, Nereus and his sister. So the church at Rome probably consisted of small groups meeting in homes and other places. There is no hint of association with synagogues, though this cannot be ruled out dogmatically.

It would be difficult to determine whether the majority of the believers in Rome were Jews or gentiles. The subject

matter of the book and appeals to the Scriptures (We designate them the Old Testament.) certainly show that the believers in this city knew the traditions of the Jews. There is every
indication that they knew those traditions and respected them
(Romans 7:1). The appeals that are made, however, can be
accounted for in a well-informed gentile Christian congregation.

There are also issues that indicate gentile concerns. Paul is
anxious to assure gentiles that the promise to Abraham includes
all nations (Romans 3:17-31). In Romans 9-11 Paul deals with
the salvation of Jews and gentiles. In Romans 14:1 through
15:6 Paul deals with issues that must have arisen from the
presence of gentiles and Jews in the same believing body.

On balance one could argue for a predominance of Jews or
gentiles by the evidences of content. Realistically, we must say
the argument would not be conclusive. Paul's sense of the
fulfillment of his apostleship to gentiles is a bit more indicative.
His salutation (Romans 1:1-7) shows that Paul was fully
confident in assuming authority to instruct the Roman church.
Paul expresses a desire to have fruit among the Romans as
"among the other gentiles" (Romans 1:13). In his closing
comments he indicates a determination to come to visit them
and spend some time with them (Romans 15:14-33; cf.,
Romans 1:11-13). With these considerations we must also note
Paul's determination not to build on the foundation of another
man (Romans 15:20). Paul was fully aware of the distinction
of his apostleship as the apostle to the uncircumcision (Galatians
2:8). It is not likely that he would have assumed the authority
over the Roman believers that he did unless this body of
believers was considered to be a gentile church.

The church at Rome consisted of people of great maturity.
Their close association with Paul (as shown in the greetings in
Romans 16) would help explain this situation. The extent of
their maturity is indicated by the weighty matters that take up
this book. The duty he imposes on them to receive the weaker
brothers and to restrict their own conduct for the sake of the
weaker is a duty of maturity (Romans 14:1-15:6). The immature cannot tolerate this kind of duty. Paul does instruct the
immature in this section, but the weight of the instruction
goes to the stronger.

THE ORIGIN OF THE ROMAN CHURCH

We have no biblical record of the establishment of the church in Rome. The only biblical indication of its presence in New Testament times is this book, and the presence of believers from Rome who met Paul as he went to Rome as a prisoner (Acts 28:12-16). Paul's quick association with Aquila and Priscilla in Corinth probably indicates they were believers in Christ when they were forced out of Rome, but this cannot be asserted dogmatically (Acts 18:1-4).

Two characteristics of the times may help us understand how the church originated in Rome. The first is the practice of Jews and Jewish adherents (such as the gentiles, proselytes and "god-fearers") to go to Jerusalem at festival times. The second is the freedom and frequency of travel in the Roman Empire.

Luke tells us there were "devout men from every nation under heaven" at Jerusalem on the Day of Pentecost (Acts 2:5, *KJV*). By the expression "under heaven" Luke usually means the Roman Empire. He also mentions that there were visitors from Rome, "both Jews and proselytes" in Jerusalem at that time (Acts 2:10, 11; *KJV*). As a result of the outpouring of the Holy Spirit and the preaching of the gospel, about three thousand received Christ and were baptized (Acts 2:41). It is entirely reasonable some of these converts were residents of Rome. When they returned to Rome after their pilgrimage to Jerusalem, they would proclaim their message of Christ. Even though these people may not have known each other when they were in Jerusalem, their rallying point in Rome would be the lordship of Jesus Christ. Under these circumstances groups of Christian believers could have been formed. Our purpose in developing these possibilities is to show one possible route for the developing of the church at Rome.

Travel throughout the Roman Empire was easy for that day and it was frequent. Roman authority had unified the empire. Trade and military routes had opened up the means of travel. Paul used them frequently in his travels as an Apostle. Frequently others traveled with him. We have noted the arrival of Aquila and Priscilla from Rome in Corinth. They traveled with him to Ephesus; they received Apollos in Ephesus as he made his way to Corinth (Acts 18:18-28). We see Paul greeting them in Rome in Romans 16:2-5.[2] Paul's travels carried him to the important cities along the travel routes of the Roman Empire. He ministered both among the Jews and among the gentiles. It is reasonable to think many of the people who were converted under his ministry were from Rome; they would return there after with their new found faith. Such people would have the rallying point of their faith in Christ, and also their mutual acquaintance with Paul. This again represents a reasonable explanation for the formation of the church in Rome. It is further enhanced by the number of Paul's acquaintances and fellow workers in the city (Romans 16).

In all probability both avenues of planting and growth took place in Rome. This view will help explain the problems that have arisen in the question of the makeup of the church in Rome. Many of these people would be well schooled in the traditions of Israel. If they were frequent visitors in Jerusalem, they would have heard of the Christian movement even before the Day of Pentecost. Many people of the congregations there would also know Paul. They would have associated with Paul and would have been instructed by him. They would be prepared for the heavy theological material in this epistle.

There is a third view of the founding of the church in Rome that we should note. It is the view that the church in Rome was founded under the ministry of the Apostle Peter, that he became the first bishop of the church in Rome, and that he spent the last quarter century of his life there in this ministry. There are many reasons not to accept this view. Through reliable tradition does place Peter in Rome at the time of his death, evidence is lacking for his having spent such a long time in Rome. He was prominent among the Apostles in Jerusalem as late as the Jerusalem Council (Acts 15:6-11). This would place him still in Jerusalem less than 20 years from the time of his death. According to Paul it was the agreement of the church that Peter's special area of ministry was among the circumcised (Galatians 2:6-10). Peter's name is significantly absent from the list of Paul's greetings in Romans 16. He is not mentioned among the brothers who met Paul as he traveled to Rome (Acts 28:11-16). He is not mentioned in any references to Paul's imprisonment in Rome. It is the opinion of this writer that the four Prison Epistles (Ephesians, Philippians, Colossians and Philemon) were written from Rome. There is no mention of Peter in this series of letters. True, these are arguments from silence, but the significance of his silence can hardly be doubted. We cannot forget Paul's determination not to enter into the fruits of other men's labors or to build on their foundation (Romans 15:17-20; 2 Corinthians 10:15-18). It is not likely he would have presumed to take the oversight of the believers in Rome if he had known the church to be the fruit of Peter's labor. This view seems to conceive of the church at Rome as a single unit, but the references to the believers there seem to indicate small groups meeting in houses and other places of convenience.

AUTHORSHIP AND OCCASION OF WRITING

The writer of this book identified himself by name and by office, Paul the Apostle. The personal references in the epistle confirm the genuineness of this book as Pauline. His emphasis on his apostleship to the gentiles fits the picture of Paul presented in other parts of the New Testament. The acquaintances mentioned by the author agree with what we know of Paul in other books of the New Testament.

It is almost pointless to talk about subject matter, vocabulary, style of writing, and so forth, because our ideas of Pauline subjects, vocabulary and style of writing are shaped predominantly by this epistle. We should note, however, that this epistle agrees with other acknowledged Pauline books in these matters. It is possible to develop unified concepts of all of these. The epistle to the Romans fits that pattern.

The acceptance of this book as from the pen of the Apostle Paul goes back to the earliest evidences. There are reflections of this book in Clement of Rome (A.D. 30-100), the epistles of Ignatius (death c. A.D. 116), Justin Martyr (A.D. 100-165), the epistle of Polycarp (A.D. 69-155) and Marcion (died A.D. 165). (Note[3]) These authors (with the possible exception of Marcion) and epistles accept the book as it was written. They all accept it as Paul's epistle to the Romans. In modern studies there is no significant question of the authorship of this book. Those who have raised this question have come from a radical school of thought and study. Even the most liberal scholars today accept the Pauline authorship of Romans.

We have noted the question of Romans 16, whether it was a part of the original letter. As we have noted, there is insufficient evidence to support this view. However, even those who separate Romans 16 from the rest of the epistle tend to identify it as Pauline in origin.

In our attempt to discover the occasion for the writing of this book we must look into the book itself since we have no historical data outside this epistle. It seems clear that Paul was writing because he had been foiled in his plans to visit the Roman believers (Romans 1:8-13), and to tell them of his continued plans to visit them (Romans 15:23-32). He also uses the occasion to commend Phoebe to the believers in Rome, though that was hardly the reason for writing.

Though Paul does not charge the Romans with any corruption in doctrine or practice, he was clearly concerned that they understand the doctrine of grace. He may have been troubled by the fact that the church had grown to this point without apostolic presence among them. If so, he does not indicate it. In Romans 16:17-19 he gives a general warning about corrupt teachers, but he does not press the point as if they were among the Romans. From all of these considerations we conclude that Paul wrote this epistle as his comprehensive statement of his message. He calls it "my gospel." What is written here is what Paul preached.

A comparison of material in Romans 15:23-33 with 1 Corinthians 16:1-4, 2 Corinthians 8 and 9, and Acts 20:1-5 will help us in determining the date of the writing of this epistle. In Romans 15:23-33, Paul tells the Roman believers that he is traveling to Jerusalem with an offering made up from the gentile churches for the poverty stricken saints in Jerusalem (v. 25-27). So, at the time of this writing the collection has been made and Paul is prepared to deliver it. At the time of the writing of 1 Corinthians the offering has not been completed; Paul instructs the Corinthians on the procedure for preparing for his visit to them and the completion of the offering there (1 Corinthians 16:2, 3). At the time of the writing of 2 Corinthians the offering was still not complete, but Paul indicates that Titus and others would come to complete the collection (2 Corinthians 8:16-24). This correspondence took place on Paul's third missionary journey, which was conducted between A.D. 54 and 58. During this time Paul spent three years in Ephesus. Near the end of that time he decided to go to Jerusalem by way of Macedonia and Achaia. He proposed to go to Rome after that (Acts 19:21, 22). After his departure from Ephesus, he went to Greece and stayed there about three months (Acts 20:1-4). During this stay in Greece Paul wrote the epistle to the Romans. This would date the writing about A.D. 57.

INTRODUCTION

END NOTES

[1]H. C. Thiessen, *Introduction to the New Testament* (Grand Rapids: Eerdmans, 1948), p. 219.

[2]There are scholars who feel Romans 16 was not a part of the epistle to the Romans as Paul wrote it. The arguments for this view are subjective and interpretational. It is argued that the benediction in Romans 15:33 signals the end of the epistle. This idea fails to take into account other instances in which Paul interjects similar sayings (liturgical elements) when he does not intend to close an epistle. Note the following: Romans 11:33-36; 15:5, 13; 16:20; Philippians 3:1; 4:8. The separation of Romans 16 from the rest of the book has no textual evidence to support it. It is characteristic of Paul to close his letters with personal greetings. If the epistle to the Romans closes at 15:33, it is uncharacteristic for Paul. This would leave the book without personal greetings. We acknowledge that Ephesians is a Pauline book that does close without such greetings, but the reason for this closing is probably the fact that Ephesians was intended to circulate to several churches.

[3]Thiessen, op. cit., p. 220.

CHAPTER ONE

SALUTATION AND PROPOSITION

ROMANS 1:1-17

SALUTATION
1:1-7

Paul's greetings at the opening of his letters are significant. He used a letter (epistle) format, which was in common use in his day; it was used in virtually all legal, government, business and personal correspondence. Paul makes significant changes in the format because of his special purposes. He makes his openings distinctly Christian. His salutation to the Roman believers is contained in 1:1-7.

In this greeting Paul identifies himself, his message and his Lord. He identifies himself by name, by his relationship to Christ, and by his office: "Paul a bondslave of Christ Jesus, called an apostle separated unto the gospel of God" (v. 1). By the word "bondslave" *(doulos)* the apostle places himself at the most subservient level—a servant bound by debt to a master who has absolute authority over him. By placing himself at the absolutely lowest level of bondage he places his Master at the absolutely highest level of lordship. In testifying to his own servitude he testifies to Christ's sovereignty.

In identifying his office Paul is called an apostle. The call being divine word made Paul what it called him to be. Paul's calling in Christ identified him as an apostle (Acts 9:15, 16). So his calling in Christ through regeneration cannot be distinguished from his calling as an apostle of Christ.

The term apostle may be used in a general sense of any believer who goes out under the commission of Christ. It is seldom used in that sense in the New Testament. Paul never uses it of himself in that sense. The predominant use of the word "apostle" in the New Testament is a designation of special ministers of Christ. An apostle was one who had seen the resurrected Lord; that is, he had seen Christ in the flesh after the resurrection. An apostle was also one who had received his commission and knowledge of the gospel directly from Christ and not from man or tradition. Paul consistently uses these credentials of himself in order to defend his authority. He did not need to defend his apostleship among the Roman believers, but he did feel that need in writing to the Galatians (Galatians 1:1-5) and to the Corinthians (1 Corinthians 9:1, 2; 2 Corinthians 11:1-5). The early Christian church acknowledged Paul's apostleship, placing it on a level with that of Peter (Galatians 2:7-10). Paul wrote this epistle in the fulfillment of his servanthood to Christ and of his apostleship.[1]

Paul's apostleship also identified his message; he had been separated unto the gospel of God. His special relationship to the gospel was as a proclaimer of the gospel to the gentiles (Galatians 1:15, 16; 2:7, 8) and most particularly in areas where none had preached the gospel before (Romans 15:15-21). The identity of the message lies in the nature of the word "gospel" (evangelion) and its origin. The term "gospel" identifies the content of Paul's message; it is the message which announces salvation in Christ. It is the message which had God as its Author; it is out from God. This gives the message the authority that Paul assumes everywhere and states specifically in Romans 1:16, 17.

This is the gospel God promised beforehand through the prophets. In Galatians, Paul describes the promise God made to Abraham as the gospel preached before to Abraham (Galatians 3:8; cf., Genesis 12:3). The subject matter of the prophets' preaching was Jesus Christ and His sufferings, and they preached this gospel by the Spirit of Christ who was in them (1 Peter 1:10, 11; 2 Peter 1:21). It is appropriate to say that gospel promise and preaching began in the Old Testament. Paul speaks of the Old Testament as the "Holy Scriptures"; he is clearly designating the authority of these writings as the authority of the gospel that is out from God and, therefore, Scripture.[2]

The content of the gospel which Paul emphasizes here is the description of God's Son, who is here described in terms of His humanity, His deity, His titles, and His works. In these descriptions Paul gives us a full picture of his doctrine of

Christ. It is significant that Paul's detractors never (in the New Testament records) attacked his doctrine of Christ. In fact neither his trinitarianism nor his Christology was attacked. It would appear that what he taught in these areas was not controversial. He often, as here, enunciates these beliefs especially his Christology. Paul supports his doctrine of Christ by citing the Scriptures (1 Corinthians 15:1-3) and by citing creeds and hymns of the early Christian church (1 Corinthians 15:1-3; 1 Corinthians 12:3; Philippians 2:5-11). It is safe to say that this doctrine of Christ's nature and work was received without controversy in the early Christian community. Controversy developed over these teachings, but at a later stage, and there was controversy between Christians and Jews over these teachings. What Paul states as assumption and greeting in Romans 1:1-4 was the received teaching of the early believers in Christ.

In relation to His human nature, Christ became the seed of David. The phrase "according to the flesh" stands for the entirety of humanness; Jesus was in body, soul and spirit fully man in the line of David. His humanity has a specific point of beginning: namely, the conception and birth in and from the womb of the virgin Mary. So Paul says that He "became" of the seed of David. In His human nature the Son of God stepped into the stream of history and into the lineage of King David, to whom God had made a promise that he would have a son on the throne of Israel forever (2 Samuel 7:12-14; Jeremiah 23:5). The gospel according to Matthew confirms this Davidic lineage (Matthew 1:1-17). Christ's humanness has a temporal beginning point. Under this relationship, He holds the kingly title of "Son of David."

The divine nature of Christ is eternal, having no beginning point. So, Paul speaks of Christ's being declared to be (pointed out as) the Son of God. He is in eternal order the Son of God, but in temporal order He is announced as divine Son. The Agent of the announcement is the "Spirit of holiness,"[3] or the Holy Spirit. The occasion and instrument of this announcement is the resurrection of Jesus from among the dead.[4] The Holy Spirit is not only the Announcer of Jesus as Son of God; He is the One who raised Him from the dead (Romans 8:11). In his sermon at Pisidian Antioch, Paul related the resurrection of Christ with the fulfillment of Psalm 2:7 (Acts 13:33).

In this connection the resurrection of Christ is the point of Christ's coronation. He is established on the throne of his father David as Messiah and Heir of that throne; and He is established at His Father's right hand reigning until His enemies are placed under His feet (Hebrews 1:1-4, 8, 13; Psalm 45:6, 7; Psalm 110:1).

From the opening line of this salutation Paul has used exalted titles of Jesus. These titles reflect His earthly and historical identity (Jesus), His office as anointed of the Lord (Christ = Messiah), His royal lineage as Seed of David, His divine nature as Son of God, and His sovereignty as Lord. The last of these titles is used consistently by Paul to affirm that Jesus is the fulfillment of the *I AM* of Old Testament revelation (Lord = Yahweh). Paul uses each of these designations when he speaks of Jesus. While He was among us in the flesh and known as Jesus of Nazareth and was crucified He was identical with the Person who was raised from the dead and is now seated at God's right hand. When He was among us in the flesh it was appropriate to call Him Lord, God, and Son of God; and His disciples did. Now that He has been raised from the dead and is exalted above principalities and powers and is in heavenly places with His Father it is appropriate to call Him by His earthly and human identity Jesus of Nazareth. So Paul and other New Testament authors mix the so-called human titles with the divine titles and use them both of the earthly mortal manifestation of Jesus and of His heavenly glorious manifestation. These are the identification of one Person in two natures.

This greeting announces the divine nature of Christ from another standpoint; He is the Origin of grace and apostleship. In this work He is equal to His Father. Grace is the free and unmerited gift of God; its central gift is Jesus Christ and in Him salvation. This is a gift that is made jointly and equally by God the Father and His Son Jesus Christ. As joint Giver with the Father of divine blessing, He is equal to the Father in divine nature. In relation to himself Paul acknowledges that his apostleship is a joint bestowal of both the Father and the Son (1:1, 5). In relation to the position of the saints in Rome, Paul affirms that they are the recipients of both the grace of God and the peace of God from both the Father and the Son (1:6, 7).

In addition to their description of Christ, verses 5-7 offer us important insights on the nature of salvation. The aim of the gift of grace is the obedience of faith: that is, the obedience which faith produces. Paul will emphasize justification by faith alone, but he will never tolerate a faith that does not obey. In fact there is no such thing as a faith that does not obey (James 2:18).

Paul applies these benefits first to himself. From Christ he has received grace. The bestowal of grace is a divine right and exclusively so. Grace can be offered only under circumstances of pardon and pardon is a divine function. It is in this same grace and calling that Paul was made an apostle. This also is divine function. By emphasizing these functions Paul affirms the divine nature of our Lord.

It is in this grace that Paul understands obedience. This obedience was for Paul fulfilled in his apostleship to the gentiles. He is the agent for fulfilling the offer of salvation to all nations. This promise had been anticipated in the covenant with Abraham (Genesis 12:3). Paul cannot separate his life in grace from his exercise of his calling. The apostleship and calling are "concerning His name." That this is a divine name is demonstrated in its centrality to, and power in, the message of Paul's apostleship.

The believers in Rome (at least some of them if not most) are examples of the application of grace and peace among the gentiles. Paul shows the effect of their calling in Christ. As the name of Christ was for Paul the saving name, it is the saving name in His proclamation. The Roman believers had been called in that name and by that calling had become the beloved of God (1:7). In their calling they had been made "holy ones" (saints; 1:7). The position of these believers involves the grace of their pardon and the giving of the peace of God. This peace is redemptive peace—the peace of God's reconciliation of man and man's reconciliation with God. These benefits are offered by Paul in this benediction.

In an ordinary letter the salutation is a formality of politeness. Paul has turned its formal structure to a distinctly Christian use and has made it a blessing and prayer for those who would receive the letter. He has also made a significant statement about the book that is to follow. He has set the doctrinal foundation in which he will speak to the Romans.

PAUL'S PRAYER AND CONCERN
1:8-13

Throughout this letter Paul assumes an intensely personal relationship with the believers in Rome. No passage shows this up more than 1:8-15. They were continually in his prayers (1:9, 10). He recalls that their faith is known throughout the world (1:8; Paul uses this expression to define the Roman empire). For this he is overjoyed. One of the objects of his prayers was that he might be given an opportunity to visit the Romans (1:10). His purpose in visiting them was that he might share with them a spiritual gift (1:11). The expression a "spiritual gift" is appropriate to the description of the spiritual gifts that are described in other portions of Scripture (Romans 12:3-8; 1 Corinthians 12; Ephesians 4:7-16). Here he combines two words: "gift" *(charis)* and "spiritual" *(pneumatikos)*. The first emphasizes the grace (unmerited favor) in which the benefit is given. The second emphasizes the Source of the gift, the Holy Spirit. In Paul's relation to such spiritual benefits he is only a minister; he has no sovereignty over the gifts and no authority to bestow them.

Even though we have given attention to the spiritual gifts above, it is not necessary to conclude that Paul has in mind the placing of these spiritual gifts in the Roman church. First, Paul makes it very clear that the distribution of spiritual gifts is the function of the Holy Spirit (1 Corinthians 12:11). Second, we are not to suppose the Roman congregation (or congregations) would be left devoid of spiritual gifts in Paul's absence. Third, Paul seems in this case to be talking about a mutually shared ministry—a ministry in which he would benefit the congregation and they him (1:12). Paul's purpose was to strengthen the Roman believers by ministering to them; this could well be described as a spiritual gift. He also expressed the hope that he would be strengthened by them: "and in this to be comforted in you by the faith that is in one another, both in you and in me" (1:12). For Paul ministry was not a "one-way street." He and the congregation were one, and each ministered to the other. Each one comforted the other and each one contributed to the faith of the other. Such is the biblical order of ministry.

Paul reminds the Romans that he had planned many times to come to them, but in each case he had been hindered

(1:13). His language could be a reference to a divine prohibition, but more probably it refers to hindrance of circumstances. He justifies his wish to come to them by seeking fruit among them as among other gentiles (1:13).

PAUL'S DEBT
1:14, 15

Paul states a fundamental theology of ministry in Romans 1:14, 15—"Both to the Greeks (Hellenists) and to the barbarians; both to the wise and to the ignorant, I am a debtor; so I am eager to preach the gospel to you the ones in Rome." The debt which Paul speaks of is a moral obligation. He does not speak here of a debt in relation to God, but of a debt to those whom he lists. His indebtedness to God is not to be denied (1 Corinthians 3:21-23; 6:19, 20), but this is not Paul's point here. He is under moral obligation to the lost to share the gospel of salvation with them. By the word "Greek" Paul speaks of the people of Greek ethnic and linguistic identity. The Greeks considered non-Greek speakers to be "babblers" or "barbarians." Paul acknowledges these prejudices of superiority in the world (though he does not accept them); he also recognized the haughtiness presumed when men call themselves wise and others unwise. The carnal distinctions by which worldly people divide society and create their own standards of superiority are of no moment in the believers' debt to the lost. Though Paul does not list all the distinctions among men, he does show that he has in mind the universality of the gospel.

Paul expresses emphatically his eagerness to discharge his debt. His readiness to preach the gospel to those in Rome shows that he would regard such a mission as fulfilling the obligation which he mentioned in verse 14. To describe the preaching of the gospel Paul uses the word *euangelidzomai.* This word by this time in the early Christian tradition had become a formal word to describe the gospel of Christ.

PROPOSITION
1:16, 17

Romans 1:16, 17 has been called the proposition of the book of Romans, but it is more than that. It is the proposition of Paul's entire mission and message. This is the statement of Paul's message and it is his chief confrontation with all other religious and philosophical systems.

The opening statement "For I am not ashamed of the gospel" may seem strange in our insulated society in which a profession of Christianity is considered respectable. Paul, however, did not speak from that perspective. He spoke in a pluralistic society in which the profession of Christianity marked one for rejection and ridicule. So this is a bold statement and it is an open challenge to all other religious messages. The connection between verses 14, 15 and verses 16, 17 shows that Paul was aware he was coming against all religious systems known among Greeks, barbarians, wise and unwise. Rome probably had as many altars, images and shrines as Athens, if not more. In this statement Paul is saying two things. First, he was not embarrassed to proclaim this despised message in the midst of all sorts of opposing messages. Second, he was not fearful that the claims of this message would in any way be refuted. None of its announcements of judgment and none of its promises would fail. Beyond this, "Paul means that he glories in the gospel and counts it a high honour to proclaim it."[5]

The content of the gospel is specific. Its basic proclamation is the story of Jesus Christ: His life, death, bodily resurrection, ascension and return. Such a message would be ridiculed in both Jewish and pagan circles. Salvation by the death of another is despised by the pride of man. Salvation by the death of an accursed man as the Jews viewed the death of Jesus would be rejected; it is a stumbling block. The claim of facts (especially such claims as the bodily resurrection, the ascension, and the physical return of one who is God) would be rejected as mythological by sophisticated Greeks and Sadducees. Such claims would be offensive to those who despise the body and regard it as a hindrance to the soul (as is the case with most pagan religious-philosophic systems). Paul analyzes these attitudes in 1 Corinthians 1:18-31.

The apostle was bold to make this proclamation because he took the message of the gospel to be divine word. "It is the power of God for salvation to everyone who believes" (1:16). It is the quality of a divine word that it accomplishes what it says. Divine word is not dependent upon another medium for the fulfillment of its decree; the fulfillment lies in the character of the word itself.[6] The gospel is no less divine word than the decree of creation which fulfills its own command. So the gospel's announcement of salvation is the giving of salvation.

The gospel applies salvation in the relationship of faith; this gospel is God's power for the purpose of salvation by faith. Herein is another element of despisal by the world. A salvation by faith would be scorned by those who attempt to elevate man in the works-righteousness of merit. Salvation by faith scorns the concept of merit in human achievement. A salvation by faith sets aside the values which men attribute to status represented in birth or bloodlines. Men who assume their superiority to other men on the basis of birth and bloodline are offended by a redemptive system that counts such as worthless (cf. John 1:11, 12). This message of salvation is to the Jew first and also to the Greek. This statement tells us that the gospel is universally applicable. The order of salvation—to the Jew first and also to the Greek—is not an order of merit, but the order of revelation. Paul will later apply this order to the order of responsibility and judgment (Romans 2:9).

Paul was not afraid to proclaim this Word as the saving Word. He was not ashamed of its content, though it was despised by its detractors. He was not fearful that its promises would fail. In fact, the Word of God is not, in the first place, a book or a letter; it is, in the first place, a Person, Jesus Christ, the Son of God (cf. John 1:1, 18). The same is true of the gospel; it is a Person, Jesus Christ, the Son of God (1 Corinthians 1:23, 24, 30, 31).

Salvation must deal with the righteousness of God; it cannot deal with relativity in righteousness as man-made systems do. So it is in the gospel that the righteousness of God is being revealed. Righteousness so defined is out of God as its Fountainhead, Standard, and Giver. It is in harmony with the law of God because it issues from the Lawgiver. Such righteousness is not discoverable by human search and insight. It is the subject matter of revelation (cf., 1 Corinthians 2:6-10; Isaiah 64:4). This righteousness is revealed "out of faith unto faith." It is the faith which is from Christ and has as its object its own origin, Jesus Christ (cf. Galatians 3:22). The sense of the statement is that the revelation and reception of the righteousness of God is by faith alone.

This message is based in Scripture: "Just as it stands written, 'The righteous shall live by faith' " (1:17; Habakkuk 2:4; cf., Galatians 3:11; Hebrews 10:38). The term "the righteousness" means the ones who are righteous in God's sight. They are righteous in His sight on the basis of His judgment and declaration; this is a judicial concept and is consistently applied in Scripture to the declaration of righteousness. It also anticipates right behavior in the sight of God. Holiness in position calls for holiness in nature and practice. All of these concepts of righteousness are included in a right relationship with God.

The instrument of the receiving of righteousness is faith. So the claim of the righteousness is a faith claim on the part of man; it is not and cannot be an achievement on the part of man. Faith cannot be simply a faith claim; it must also be a way of living. It is more than believing this or that; in fact it is more than believing a person even if that person is God. Faith is a pattern of living in relation to God. This pattern of living affirms as true what God has said; it makes a personal application of God's Word to oneself, and it is a personal commitment to faithfulness in relation to God. Both the concept of righteousness and the concept of faith will be developed by Paul in the subsequent portions of Romans.

CHAPTER ONE
END NOTES

[1]John Murray, *The Epistle to the Romans*, (Grand Rapids: Eerdmans, 1968), pp. 2, 3.

[2]"The Old Testament background of the New Testament use of *euangelion* is found in the LXX of Isaiah xl-lxvi (especially Is. xl.9, lii.7, lx.6, lxi.1) where this noun or its cognate *euangelidzomai* is used of the proclamation of Zion's impending release from exile." F. F. Bruce, *The Epistle of Paul to the Romans*, (Grand Rapids: Eerdmans, 1978), p. 72.

[3]"The Spirit of holiness is the regular Hebrew way of saying 'the Holy Spirit'; and Paul produces here the Hebrew idiom in Greek." Ibid., p. 73.

[4]"But Christ's resurrection is denoted by a phrase which hints at the future resurrection of the people of Christ; . . . (cf., 1 Corinthians xv. 20-23)." Ibid, p. 74.

[5]Ibid., p. 79.

[6]This is beautifully illustrated in the record of creation. In each case where "God said" the immediate result was that what God said occurred: light (Genesis 1:3), the firmament (Genesis 1:6, 7), the gathering of the waters (Genesis 1:9, 10), the earth's bringing forth grass, and so forth (Genesis 1:11, 12), the establishment of lights in the heaven (Genesis 1:14, 15), the bringing forth of moving creatures in the waters (Genesis 1:20-22), the earth's bringing forth the beasts (Genesis 1:24, 25), and God's creating man in His own image (Genesis 1:26, 27).

CHAPTER TWO

THE SINFULNESS OF MAN

ROMANS 1:18-3:20

The climax of this section of our study is Romans 3:20—"Therefore by the works of the law shall no flesh be justified, for through the law is the knowledge of sin." In order to come to this conclusion and to show how he arrives at it, Paul moves through an intricate series of reasons to show that sin is the common factor that exists among all men, Jew and gentile. He begins this series of reasons by describing the sinfulness of the pagans; this is the subject of Romans 1:18-32.

THE REVELATION OF GOD TO THE GENTILES
1:18-20

In this section Paul is dealing with the evidences of the revelation of God to those who do not in their traditions possess the law of Moses. In this observation Paul will show that his assessment of their sinfulness is justified. God is revealing Himself to mankind (1:18-22). The language of this section is important and has often been misunderstood. This language is the material often used to define a so-called *general revelation,* with the implication that the material universe inherently testifies to the nature of God. A careful study of the language will show revelation is always God's act and is not inherent in anything material. God as personal God makes Himself known; He uses various devices as instruments of His voice, but revelation is always the direct act of God. It is also always an encounter with God for salvation or judgment.

Paul's opening statement is, "For the wrath of God is being revealed from heaven upon every impiety and unrighteousness of men who are suppressing the truth in unrighteousness

29

(1:18). This is a supernatural revelation. The passive voice verb is a commonly used device to ascribe action to God without using the name of God. This revelation has its origin in heaven; it is not earthly and the human nature and environment are not capable of discovering or offering this knowledge (1 Corinthians 1:21). This revelation is described with a present tense verb; so, it is not a revelation that simply occurred once in the ancient past. It is a revelation that is continuously present.

The subject of this revelation is the wrath of God. Paul speaks here of wrath as a righteous attribute of God. In judgment wrath testifies to God's righteousness and holiness. This wrath is being manifested against every form of irreverence; idolatry is especially in mind in this word. The wrath of God is also being directed against every form of immorality among men; here Paul speaks of moral corruptions such as he will list later.

The objects of this wrath are those men who hold the truth in unrighteousness; they are in the process of suppressing the truth. It is clear that Paul understands that such men do know the truth and that they are suppressing it. This passage does not look on such men as innocent. Paul returns to this thought and elaborates on it in 1:21-25.

The instruments of this revelation are the things that God has created (1:19, 20). The reason men may be accused of suppressing the truth is that "which is known of God is evident to them because God has revealed [it]" (1:19). God has used the created things to show this knowledge (1:20). This revelation declares the invisible things of God, and they consist of God's everlasting power and divine nature (translated in the King James Version as "godhead"). These aspects of God's nature have been revealed since the foundation of the world ("from the creation of the world," 1:20).

The purpose of this revelation is to render those who are guilty of suppressing the truth defenseless: "in order that they should be without excuse" (1:20). Their defenselessness lies in the fact that "when they knew God, they did not glorify Him as God and they were unthankful" (1:21). In this statement Paul demonstrates what he has just said. The presupposition is that these men had had an experience of knowing God in some level of truth. Paul does not assert that they had received a full revelation of God. He does say that what they had seen they rejected. They knew God as God and not as myth or idol. When they knew God, they gave Him none of the glory appropriate to His nature. They did not render worship at all, and they were not even thankful. Thanklessness is here treated as moral default, and it is. This sinfulness provoked a trajectory of sinfulness that would intensify until man would wallow in his depravity. That is Paul's next step in reasoning.

SINFULNESS AND JUDGMENT
1:21-32

There is a progression in judgment commensurate with the degeneration of man's response to God. From verse 21 Paul describes man's degeneration as a step-by-step descent into moral corruption. With each step there is a divine response, and that response is in the form of judgment. The judgment takes the form of intensifying the moral and physical distortions of the nature of man. God judged sin and continues to judge sin by imposing even greater sinfulness upon the sinner.

The first step in this progression of judgment is God's response to man's unthankfulness. When men refuse to give thanks to God, God makes them to be empty in their reasoning. Man's reasoning capacity is the very faculty in which men of philosophic interest regard themselves as strong. It is this faculty that God brings under judgment. The form of judgment is that their foolish heart was darkened. Each verb used in this statement (1:21) is a passive voice verb ("They were made to be foolish . . . and their foolish heart was darkened."). This is a typical Hebrew way of ascribing the action to God.

The word which we have translated "empty" means to be rendered futile; in this case the futility is revealed in their reasoning. Their reasoning does not arrive at the knowledge of God. So Paul describes their hearts as foolish: that is, void of understanding. This is a spiritual condition which is consistently used in Scripture to describe those who deny God (cf. Psalm 14). God judges such moral default with even greater darkness.

But man even in this condition of judgment continued to regard himself as wise: "while they continued to regard themselves as wise, they were made foolish" (1:22). Their actual condition stands in absolute contradiction to their view of themselves. Their view of themselves is that they were wise; God has made them insipid—void of understanding. While they call themselves wise they become more and more corrupt. This lack of understanding and deepening corruption are direct results of God's judgment.

The next step in man's rebellion against God takes the specific form of idolatry; they changed the glory of God into images. This is especially offensive in the light of the following considerations. First, God is incorruptible; His glory is higher than any imagery can depict and greater than any physical temple, altar or image can contain (1 Kings 8:27; 1 Chronicles 16:25-29; 2 Chronicles 2:6; 6:18). Second, every form of idolatry is forbidden by terms of the first two commandments of the decalogue (Exodus 20:3-6). Third, these men substituted the images of corruptible things for the glory of the incorruptible God. God will not give His glory to another, nor will he allow it to be done without bringing judgment upon the idolater (Exodus 20:5, 6; Isaiah 42:8).

The incongruity of this exchange is evident to all mankind. This incongruity is that God by nature is incapable of being corrupted. Because He is infinite He cannot be reduced to any limited form. Because He is unchangeable He cannot be represented by any element that is capable of changing or being changed. Because He is sovereign He cannot be reduced to an element that is subject to another.[1] The exchange that men made was to offer images of corruptible things as if they represented the nature and glory of God. Paul names these images: corruptible man, birds, four-footed beasts and reptiles. In these Paul runs the gamut from the nature of greatest dignity to the beasts and reptiles. "The threefold classification of animals (cf. Genesis 1:20-25) and the terms 'glory', 'image' and 'likeness' (RV. cf. Genesis 1:26) suggest that Paul's account of man's wickedness has been deliberately stated in terms of the Biblical Narrative of Adam's Fall."[2] All of these forms are corruptible and corrupt. To reduce God to the image of a man is just as much an attack on the glory of God as to reduce Him to the image of a serpent. The sin cannot be measured in terms of the dignity or indignity of the image; the sin lies in the fact that any temporal image of God is a corruption of His nature. So this exchange was by nature presumptuous and blasphemous.

God judged this corruption of His nature by imposing the sentence of corruption on the men who blasphemed His glory in idolatry. God gave them over to the lusts of their flesh in order that they might dishonor their own bodies (1:24). This is God's act of judgment for the indignities that men had imposed on the nature of God. Judgment is never simply a matter of natural and mechanical cause and effects relationships. "This advises us of a principle which is invariable, namely, that retribution is never in operation except on the judgment of God against sin."[3] The indignities are also self-inflicted. As self-inflicted, these corruptions arise out of the nature of man; they proceed from the lusts of their heart. Their aim is the filth of nature that dishonors the body. It imposes on the body a distortion of nature—a use of the body that was not intended by God when He made man, and a use of the body that contorts its nature. So, mankind in these sins dishonors their bodies among themselves. It is clear that Paul is speaking of sexual dishonor. Some would argue that the sexual function does not dishonor the body, and to this we must agree. But it is the biblical position that fornication is an abuse of the body: "The body is not meant for sexual immorality, but for the Lord, and the Lord for the body" (Flee from sexual immorality. All other sins a man commits are outside the body, but he who sins sexually sins against his own body") (1 Corinthians 6:18). Paul's point is that these sins are both moral and physical corruptions of man's nature in the same pattern as man's corruption of God's glory.

The next downward step for man was to exchange the truth of God for the lie. The truth of God is the truth of His being—the truth which He declared of Himself from the creation, even His eternal power and divine nature (1:19, 20). This truth has been rejected in man's turn to idols (1:23). Its corruption is intensified here in the worship and service of the creature instead of the Creator. In describing this sin Paul uses the definite article. In rejecting "the truth" men turned to "the lie," and the lie is the worship of the creature instead of the Creator. This flies in the face of the most fundamental moral obligation, and that is that men are morally bound to glorify God. God ought to be worshiped because of "the truth" that He "is to be praised forever, Amen" (1:25b). By using this expression Paul breaks into a sense of worship; God is forever praised. The "amen" is the affirmation of faith. By worshiping the creature and not the Creator, men are revolting against the judgment and the activity of eternity. They have exalted the lie of time above the truth of eternity.

God has also judged this sin. As the sin reached greater depths of corruption, God sentenced man to great depths of corruption: "on account of this God gave them over to dishonorable passions" (1:26). The preposition (*dia*: on account of) shows that there is a direct cause and effect relationship between man's sins and God's act. Man provoked the judgment of God. This verse is very plain; God is directly active in the judgment and its execution. The greater intensification of this sinfulness is shown by the character of the sins to which men were abandoned. These dishonorable passions distort the moral character and the physical and psychological nature of mankind. The specific sins that are here named are the distortions of homosexuality and the perverted use of sex organs. The sinfulness of lesbianism is first named, and with that the distortion of the body by unnatural uses if involved: "For their women [literally females] exchanged the natural function for the unnatural" (1:26b). Then, Paul names male homosexuality: "For even the men [literally males] when they had left the natural use of the females burned in their lust one for another" (1:27a). The implication is that the perverted use of the female provoked homosexual lust among the males. This homosexual lust produced indecent acts between men and men, and they received appropriate judgment; in fact the judgment was and is morally necessary (1:27b). This judgment has certain physical consequences; one physical perversion produces another. Sin is used to punish sin. We must never imagine, however, that these consequences are not divinely ordered and morally necessary.

The final insult that man imposes upon God and His glory is that he did not consider the thought of God to be a worthy thought for his mind: "Even as he did not consider God worthy to have in mind" (1:28). Man's presumed nobility of mind did not consider God a worthy subject of thought. God judged this sin by bringing the mind of man under the sentence of reprobation—a mind rendered worthless and corrupt. "A reprobate mind is to therefore one, abandoned or rejected of God and therefore not fit for any activity worthy of approbation or esteem."[4] As a result man did those things that are "not convenient;" the phrase refers to anything considered indecent or inappropriate to human dignity. They are out of the order of decency and contrary to the character of mankind. Paul then gives a long list of those things he considers indecent and out of character for man. The list probably needs no amplification, but we should note that Paul describes man as being filled with these indecencies. What is said here of man is applicable both to individuals and to human society. Individual men are depraved and so is the social structure that he dominates.

In terms of application we should understand that when man sins he is not "doing what comes naturally" and he is not "just being human." When a man sins, he is acting contrary to his nature. In this observation, Christian doctrine is infinitely superior to the evolutionary doctrine of human imperfection which is gradually being overcome in the evolutionary process. In the evolutionary view when man sins, he is acting according to his nature; so, there is no moral connotation. If there is no moral connotation, there is no basis for judgment; if there is no basis for judgment, there is no basis for grace.[5]

Verse 32 reaches the epitome of this description of sin: "Although they know God's righteous decree that those who do such things are worthy of death, they not only continue to do these very things but also approve of those who practice them" (New International Version). Though Paul has described these sins as common to man; there is another conclusion that is common to man. In the sensitivities of men these things are condemned. God has left a witness of Himself in the mind and conscience of man that these things correctly call for divine judgment (cf., 2:14, 15). In spite of this sensitivity of conscience, men sear their consciences and continue in the same sins that they know are damnable. They further provoke God by taking pleasure in those who do these sins. There is a companionship of pleasure among those who follow the way of sin. The man or woman who says he or she does not try to influence others to sin is a liar. Sin by its nature desires and requires companionship, whether it is fornication, homosexuality, stealing, lying, or rebelling against parents. Make no mistake; sin is proselytizing.

CONSCIENCE AND JUDGMENT
2:1-16

It is logical that Paul would next deal with the issue of judgment. Paul understands that the moral issues he is dealing with are universal in authority and consciousness. There is no segment of mankind nor any individual man that is not obligated to the morality God has revealed. Likewise, there is no segment of mankind nor any individual man that is without conscience in these fundamental issues of morality. So, Paul proceeds to argue his case for the universality of judgment.

Paul begins this stage of his argument by dealing with men's judgment of other men. The act of judging another places an obligation of conduct upon the one who judges. His conduct must be consistent with the obligations that he imposes on his neighbor. Judging also reveals the level of the moral sensitivities of the one who judges. These are universal principles of judgment and reasoning and are applicable to gentiles as well as Jews. Such reasoning does not depend upon the possession of a written revelation (such as the law of Moses or even the gospel of Christ). This section of the epistle (2:1-16) provides an easy transition from gentile considerations to Jewish.

The act of judging another renders the one who judges inexcusable for his own sins (2:1). The assumption of this verse is that the one who judges also sins. The sentence is emphatic: "Wherefore, you are without excuse, Oh man, everyone who judges." The reason immediately follows: "For that in which you judge another you convict yourself, for the one who judges practices these same things." The truth of this statement does not depend on a proving of the identical behavioral manifestations of sin. Paul knows that there were gentiles of honorable behavior. Many of them would agree with Paul in his denunciation of the debauchery in Romans 1:18-32. They would also assume their superiority. This is the point Paul wants to make. So-called honorable behavior is also full of sin.[6] It is not necessary for Paul to prove the guilt of all those who judge by showing they have committed specific forms of sins already named. Jesus' analysis of lust as the essence of adultery and his analysis of hatred as the essence of murder show that sin is a solidarity (Matthew 5:21-28). James 2:10-12 analyzes the singularity of sin on the basis of the solidarity of the law. The law is not many laws (or for that matter even ten); it is one law as there is one God. So sin cannot be dealt with in terms of guilt for this sin or that sin. Sin stands as a transgression of the nature of God, whose nature is described in His law. So any guilt renders one condemned by his judgment of others.

The assumption of judgment is a correct one: "and we know that the judgment of God is according to truth upon the ones who practice these kinds of things" (2:2). Paul has already demonstrated the evil of these things. He will affirm later that not having the law in written form does not let an offender get by as innocent. The absence of the law does not transform wrongdoing into innocence, and innocence cannot be interpreted as righteousness.

Paul's point is that the judgment against these things is "according to truth" not simply according to the Mosaic law. The base of judgment is broader than the written law; it is the truth of God (cf. 1:18-20). Paul does not limit himself to the categories of sin named in 1:21-32. In reference to sins he uses the phrase "these sorts of things"; it is all inclusive. So the judgment of God is universal. It is against all the practicers of these kinds of sins—both the judged and the judges.

The apostle also wants to show that the very act of judging another under these circumstances is a presumption against God (2:3-6). To judge another while one is guilty of the same kinds of things assumes a personal immunity against divine judgment as if God were a respecter of persons. Such an assumption reasons in this way: "And do you reason in this way, Oh man, who judges the one who practices these things and who does the same things, that you will escape the judgment of God?" (2:3). This is a two-fold rhetorical question. First, the question assumes that the person accosted will answer, "No." This is his defensive answer, because he will admit no such presumption. Second, it assumes that the only truthful answer to the question is "Yes." In this way Paul shows the presumption of the one who judges.

Paul follows with a companion question: "Or do you despise the riches of His goodness, and forbearance and longsuffering, not knowing that the goodness of God leads you to repentance?" (2:4). This question is designed to show that this is indeed the case; such presumption is a despisal of the goodness of God. Here, again, the person is expected to say, "No, I do not despise God's goodness." But the question shows that the real answer is, "Yes, you do despise the goodness of God." The terrible result of such presumption is that it aborts the prospect of repentance. These attitudes ignore the fact that it is God's goodness that leads men to repentance. By judging others for sins which we commit we assume that in our case repentance is not necessary. As long as one thinks that there is no need for repentance, he will not repent. This is a terrible presumption against God because it elevates man's righteousness to the level of God's. This is a despisal of the grace of God that leads us to repentance.

God's judgment is inevitable under these circumstances, and it is intensified by man's presumption: "But according to your hardness and unrepentant heart you lay up for yourself a treasure of wrath in the day of wrath and revelation of the righteous judgment of God" (2:5). These presumptuous attitudes are a condition of hardness of heart. This is an evil condition, and it will not admit the necessity of repentance. The avoidance of repentance in the present time simply lays aside the judgment of God and puts it in a storehouse to be opened at the day of judgment. This is the word picture that Paul paints; it is as if one were storing up a treasure to be opened at some future point of reward. The only problem is that the treasure being put away is a "treasure house" full of the wrath of God. Paul assures us of the certainty of judgment in the phrase "in the day of wrath and the revelation of the righteous judgment of God." A specific time of judgment is in view; it is the day of wrath. It is the act of God to reveal His judgment. The revelation of His judgment is the fulfillment of His own holiness, and it is the fulfillment of His purposes for creation. We conclude that God's righteousness is not fulfilled without a day of judgment. We also conclude that God's plan for creation and for this age is not complete without a day of judgment. At that point God will give to everyone according to his works (2:6). This is a transitional verse. The thought introduced here is completed as Paul shows how judgment operates in relation to those who have the law and those who do not.

God will judge all men by the standards of revelation open to them. Verse 6 has stated the basic fact of judgment, and has shown that such judgment is universal. God will give to every man according to his works. There are fundamental elements of morality that stand in every concept of judgment. First, God will reward patience in good works in seeking glory and honor; the reward is eternal life: "To those who by persistence in doing good seek glory, honor and immortality, he will give eternal life" (2:7, *NIV*). Paul does not suggest here the possibility of human merit as a ground for justification; but morality does call for God to honor those characteristics in the creature that match His holiness. This is fundamental to perfect judgment. Second, God will punish contentiousness, [7] disobedience to truth, and obedience to unrighteousness. Note that these are not the gross and anti-social sins that Paul listed in 1:29-31. They are nevertheless offensive to the holiness of God. The punishment is divine wrath and indignation: "But for those who are self-seeking and who reject the truth and follow evil, there will be wrath and anger. There will be trouble and distress for every human being who does evil" (2:8, 9a, *NIV*). There are no exceptions to this principle of judgment exactly as there are no exceptions to the principle of reward. Almost as if he wished to place an exclamation point at the end of this statement, Paul says, "to the Jew first and also to the gentile" (2:9). In this emphasis the apostle makes two points. First, the principles of judgment are applicable to every segment of mankind—Jew and gentile. The fact that some have the law in written form and some do not does not change the fact that all will be judged. Second, the order of judgment is the same order as the order of salvation which is to the Jew first and also to the gentile (1:16). This is the order of revelation. It is also the order of salvation (Romans 1:16).

What is at stake in judgment is the righteousness of God: "For there is no partiality with God" (2:11). Men perish in relationship to their disobedience to the revelation of God given to them (1:18-20). Sin is not a sin against oneself (as if revelation were intrinsic to man). Sin is always a personal act against God. Revelation is God's gift and it is always His personal act of self disclosure. A violation of that which God reveals about Himself is a sin against God whose word is the revelation of God. It is possible for men to sin who have not received the law of Moses; in fact, it is Paul's purpose to show that all such men do sin. They will be judged: "All who sin apart from the law will also perish apart from the law" (2:12a, *NIV*). So, it is clear that ignorance of a specific form of revelation (such as the Mosaic code) does not spare the sinner from judgment. This ignorance does not make such a person sinless; so, it cannot relieve him of judgment.

The other side of this principle of judgment is that those who have the law and who sin against God under its terms of revelation will be judged by the law: "And whoever has sinned in relation to the law shall be judged through the law" (2:12b). Exactly as ignorance of the law cannot render one guiltless, possession of the law cannot render one righteous. Hearing, reading and possession of the law are of no value before judgment. Obedience alone is of value: "For it is not those who hear the law who are righteous in God's sight, but it is those who obey the law who will be declared righteous" (2:13, *NIV*). Paul has emphasized this aspect of judgment because of the presumption of those who think that the receiving of the law by the Jews grants them salvation. The disobedience that is damning to one person (Jew or gentile) is also damning to another.

In a parenthesis (vv. 14, 15) Paul addresses another mistake that men often make; it is the false assumption that not having the law means a man is entirely ignorant of the law. It is his contention that there is no man totally devoid of the knowledge of the law. Paul has already established this fact in the reasoning in 1:18-2:6. He grants that the gentiles do not have the law, but he points out that they do by nature the things that the law requires (2:14). They as men and in the fulfillment of this nature do the things contained in the law; so they become a law to themselves. They organize their societies and their own systems of accusation and judgment in affirmation of the things contained in the law; so they become a law to themselves. In this they demonstrate the work of the law written in their heart. Paul regards this presence of the law as a spiritual awareness; it is God's witness of Himself in them (cf. 1:19). The specific manner in which this presence of the work of the law is demonstrated is that these societies of the gentiles accuse or excuse one another on the grounds of the law. This is confirmed in their consciences (2:15). Accusation and exoneration are always moral judgments; they may not be accurate in their conclusions, but there is no ground for either except moral obligation. Paul's conclusion is that such societies of men become a law to themselves.

In order to make the connection of Paul's thought we should read verse 16 immediately following verse 13. God will make judgments of sin and righteousness in the day of judgment. These are not temporal judgments and chastisements; they are the judgments of the last day. The hidden things of men are the concern of this day of judgment. The exposure and judgment of evil secrets is certainly intended in this statement. At the same time, it is the function of divine judgment to judge according to truth, not the external appearances which men use: "He will not judge by what he sees with his eyes, or decide by what he hears with his ears; but with righteousness he will judge the needy, with justice he will give decisions for the poor of the earth" (Isaiah 11:3, 4; *NIV*). "Man looks at the outward appearance, but the Lord looks at the heart" (1 Samuel 16:7b, *NIV*). The authority by which Paul predicts this judgment is the gospel of Jesus Christ. The Agent whom God has appointed to judge is Jesus Christ, whom He has raised from the dead (cf. Acts 17:31).

THE LAW AND JUDGMENT
2:17-3:7

Paul now turns his attention specifically to the Jews; his intention is to show that though they have the revelation of the law of God, they also have sinned. Paul's point is *revelation* (whether to the gentiles or to the Jews) will not keep men from sinning. As the gentiles have demonstrated Paul's proposition, the Jews also demonstrate it.

This section opens with a conditional statement that Paul accepts as correct: "And if you call yourself a Jew, and if you rest in the law, and if you know the will of God, and if you being instructed by the law approve the superior things, if you have persuaded yourself that you are a guide to the blind a light to those in darkness" . . . . (2:17-19). The portion cited above is incomplete, but it is sufficient to show Paul understood the status which the Jews had in relation to the law of God. They called themselves Jews; this was a name of superiority as far as they were concerned. They relied on the law and approved the things contained in the law. As we look back on the Pharisaic period, we are inclined to see the law as a burden to the Jews. This is a misunderstanding. They considered the law and their relationship to it as a distinction. They were right to understand that the standards of morality presented in the law were superior to anything produced out of gentile culture. They made their boast in God. This was their claim of privilege, and their evidence of superiority. It was also their ground for excluding others; and when they admitted others into a covenant identity, they gave them second class citizenship.

They prided themselves in having the law. They, therefore, claimed special insights into God's will (2:18). They knew the will of God. They were instructed by the law which is the revelation of God. They considered themselves to be wise in counsel (2:19, 20). This equipped them to guide the blind. They were light in the darkness. They could instruct the foolish and the children. They had the form of knowledge and truth in the law. This is the reason that they could bring themselves to think as they did. So far as God's act of giving the revelation was concerned and as far as the character of the law was concerned, the Jews should have been able to do and be the things that they boasted. Paul does not question the validity of these assumptions, but he does question and condemn their presumptuousness in these matters. However, he will agree that the Jews should be able to claim all covenant benefits. The covenant, however, is in grace and allows none of the boasting common to the form of Judaism against which Paul speaks.

The Jews invalidated their claims by pride and spiritual default. They confused superficial obedience and ceremonialism with the essence of the law and spirituality. The apostle shows the hollowness of the Jewish claims by a very carefully worded statement; they have "the form of the knowledge of the truth in the law" (2:20). His words imply the very ceremonialism and superficiality that he will describe; theirs is not a genuine spiritual experience in knowing the truth. Their relationship to the truth (though it is contained in their law) is nominal. Paul shows this up by a series of rhetorical questions. "Do you teach others and not yourself? Do you preach, 'Thou shalt not steal,' and yet steal? Do you prohibit adultery and yet commit adultery? Do you despise idols and still rob temples [commit sacrilege]? Do you demand obedience and yet dishonor God by violations of the law?" (2:21-23). Paul supplies the answer to these questions by the manner in which he asks them. They were guilty of all the charges implied by the questions, even though they would deny their guilt.

By appealing to an Old Testament passage Paul makes a direct accusation: "For the name of God through you is being blasphemed among the gentiles just as it is written" (2:24; cf. Isaiah 52:5; Ezekiel 36:20). Both of these Old Testament passages were spoken of Israel when she was in captivity for her sins. The prophets lament that the captors of Israel boasted over both Israel and her God. Paul's contention is that the situation for Israel in his day was unchanged from the days of the prophets Isaiah and Ezekiel. The accusation Paul makes here is not simply his; it is God's accusation. In this case the blasphemy from the gentiles was provoked because of the sinfulness evident in the life of Israel even though she did possess the law of Moses.

Such compromises of holiness of life have the effect of invalidating the symbols of the covenant that Israel used and claimed. Circumcision is an appropriate symbol of the covenant if the circumcised keeps the law, but it has no power to transform unholy living into covenant reality: "On the one hand circumcision is of value if you are a practicer of the law; but on the other hand, if you are a transgressor of law, your circumcision has become uncircumcision (that is, as if you had never been circumcised and were by nature a gentile)" (2:25). The circumcised, disobedient Jew is no more in the covenant and has no more privileges before God than gentiles who have never been circumcised.

Paul turns this negative application around and applies it positively to the gentiles: "If the uncircumcised keep the requirements of the law, will not his uncircumcision be credited to him for circumcision?" (2:26). Again, Paul has answered his question by the way he asked it; the answer is, "Yes, it will be." In fact, Paul goes on to indicate that the uncircumcised who keeps the law will be elevated to a judge over the Jews who do not keep the law: "The man who by nature is uncircumcised and who is a fulfiller of the law will judge you who by the letter and by circumcision are a transgressor of law" (2:27). Paul's language shows that the manner in which the Jews were using circumcision and the letter of the law was a transgression of the law. In their presumption they had turned the possession of the law and the practice of circumcision into transgressions. For these sins they stand condemned by the conduct of uncircumcised persons who keep the law in its real nature.

A person's inner nature must be in harmony with the outward symbols of the covenant; if this is not true, there is no covenant relationship: "For he is not a Jew who is one outwardly, neither is circumcision outward in the flesh" (2:28). Paul explains this statement by declaring that Jewishness is a matter of the heart, and circumcision is also a matter of the heart (2:29). This is not a teaching that Paul originated; the first person in Scripture to teach this was Moses: "The Lord your God will circumcise your hearts and the hearts of your descendants, so that you may love Him with all your heart and with all your soul and live" (Deuteronomy 30:6, *NIV*). Paul here speaks of circumcision which is "in Spirit and not in letter." It seems correct to understand the Spirit here as a reference to the Holy Spirit as the divine agent of spiritual circumcision (cf., Colossians 2:11, where true circumcision is ascribed to Christ). Persons who are circumcised in the flesh have fulfilled externally verifiable signs of the covenant; such signs are appraised by men and such people are accepted by men. Those who are circumcised in the heart and by the Holy Spirit are accepted by God; He alone can verify spiritual circumcision.[8]

So far the accusations of the Jews have come down so hard that one might ask the question which Paul himself raises in 3:1: "What, therefore, is the advantage of the Jew, or what is the benefit of circumcision?" The apostle does not wish to be misunderstood as if he despised his own people according to the flesh nor his own Jewishness (cf. Romans 9:1-3; 10:1; 11:1, 2). Paul answers his own question by giving one advantage as the chief advantage for Israel: "They have been entrusted with the oracles of God" (3:2). Paul does give a more extensive list of advantages in Romans 9:4, 5. In the context of the passage before us, Paul's emphasis has been on the modes of revelation God has used among the gentiles and among the Jews. To the gentiles He revealed Himself through the agency of the creature; to the Jews He revealed Himself by His own voice—the oracles of God. The word (*logion*) that Paul uses here is a word used of prophetic utterance, with the understanding that the utterance given is the exact Word of God. He refers to the special revelation of God through law, prophets, and wisdom of the Hebrew Scriptures. The advantages of such a revelation are clear. God's Word is a clear and precise revelation of His nature and will. The tradition of Hebrew Scriptures presents a specific offer of salvation and prescribes worship rites designed to set forth and seal the experiences of redemption to them in covenant. A written code (such as the Hebrew Scriptures) offers a norm of righteousness that was not altered by education, culture, or the abuses of human conscience. So, it is sufficient for Paul to give only one advantage in this context; he has chosen the one advantage most important and most appropriate to the context.

There are still those who would argue with Paul and would deny the advantage means anything in the light of the default of Israel. The unbelief of the creature cannot affect the truth of the Creator. It is a truism, but Israel needed to be reminded that even the covenant people are creatures. Note Paul's answer to this quibble: "For what if some do not believe? Shall their unfaithfulness do away with the faithfulness of God?" (3:3). Paul virtually shouts his answer, "God forbid!"[9] Paul continues his answer by the challenge, "Let God be true and every man a liar!" (3:4). God will remain true and faithful even if every man were damned as a liar. Here Paul reflects David's judgment in Psalm 116:11. He then appeals to another psalm: "So that you may be proved righteous in your words and that you may prevail in your judgment" (3:4; cf. Psalm 51:4).[10]

Paul faces yet another objection to his argument: "And if our unrighteousness commends the righteousness of God, what shall we say? Is not God unrighteous who inflicts wrath" (3:5). This question is also a quibble, and Paul brands it as such: "I speak as a man" (3:5b). This is the false reasoning unbelieving men use, and Paul recoils with another shout, "God forbid!" This kind of reasoning strikes at the very heart of the moral order, which neither the Jews nor the gentiles will allow. If God is unjust, there is no moral order; there is no ground upon which any moral opinion can be expressed. "Paul appeals to the fact of universal judgment and he does not proceed to prove it. He accepts it as an ultimate datum of revelation, and he confronts the objection of verse 5 with this fact.[11] That there will be a judgment of the world is taken as axiomatic among Jews and gentiles.

Paul is deliberately pressing these questions and answers to absurd points in order to show the error in the reasoning involved. Paul's next question takes the matter even further, and it also reflects what some of his detractors were saying about him and the Christian teaching. He forms the question for his antagonists: "If the truth of God has abounded to the glory of God through my lie, why then am I judged as a sinner?" (3:7). The argument is trying to say that if God is glorified for judging me as a sinner, then I have contributed to the glory of God and ought to be commended and not damned. In that case we might as well say, "Let us do evil things in order that good things may come" (3:8b). Paul acknowledges that some accuse him and other Christians of saying this: "as we are slanderously reported and as some say that we say" (3:8a). They are trying to say that this interpretation makes evil a positive force in the evaluation of the manifestation of God's justice. It is not that people were saying that Paul said these things in these words; the claim was that Paul's logic leads to these conclusions. They were claiming this absurdity to be the teaching of Christianity. The apostle's answer to this charge is that such persons deserve the judgment which they are moving toward: "whose judgment is deserved" (3:8c).

UNIVERSAL CONVICTION OF SIN
3:8-20

The apostle has reviewed the response of gentiles to the revelation of God. He has subsequently reviewed the response of the Jews to the revelation of God. The response of both Jews and gentiles was to sin against God. So Paul's question and answer in verse 9 are appropriate: "What then? Are we better? (That is are the Jews better than the gentiles?) By no means! We have already charged Jews and Greeks all to be under sin." Paul's entire line of reasoning has been to show that this charge is true. The Greeks under heathenism have shown the world a finely developed philosophy. At the same time they had developed a society of idolatry, superstition and moral decay. The Jews had taken the written revelation that God gave them and had shown the world how legalistic and mechanical religion can become. This system had left its adherents groping in their basic inner sins.

Paul concludes this section with a collection of Old Testament quotations that sums up the nature of man in sin. The psalmist has declared and now Paul quotes: "There is not one righteous" (3:10; cf. Psalm 14:1). This sinfulness is manifested in the mind and will of man. From the standpoint of the mind (which is fundamentally related to the heart of man), "There is none who understands" (3:11; cf. Psalm 14:2). The Scriptures always deal with the mind and understanding as spiritual matters. To be void of understanding in relation to God is to be sinful. This depravity of mind leads to depravity of will: "There is none that seeks God. All have turned aside; together they have become unprofitable. There is not one that does good; there is not even one" (e:11, 12; cf. Psalm 14:3). The language is emphatic and is designed to remove any doubt about the charge and to claim that there are no exceptions to the charge. The violence of man's heart erupts in the violence, bitterness and anger of his speech: "The throat is a tomb standing opened; with their tongues they have been treacherous, the venom of vipers is under their lips, whose mouth is filled with cursing and bitterness" (3:13, 14; cf. Psalm 5:9; 140:3). Speech is always an index of the heart. "The good man brings forth good out of the good stored up in his heart, and the evil man brings evil things out of the evil stored up in his heart. For out of the overflow of his heart his mouth speaks" (Luke 6:45). It is not possible to be vile and abusive in speech and to be pure in heart. Depraved man's language is a picture of his depraved innermost depths. The violence of the heart also manifests itself in man's physical violence: "Their feet are swift to shed blood; destruction and misery are in their way, and the way of peace they have not known" (3:15-17; cf. Isaiah 59:7, 8; Proverbs

1:16). The venting of their wrath in speech escalates to violence of behavior. Both of these conditions grow out of a depraved heart. It is a mistake to think that explosive speech dissipates anger. It is the product of anger and does not serve as an emotional and spiritual catharsis. It simply sets the stage for physical violence. This passage is an analytic diagram of the origin and end of violence. The epitome of this spiritual description is that "there is no fear of God before their eyes" (3:18; cf. Psalm 36:1). This is the essence of atheism. Such a view does not need to deny God by verbal act; this view denies God in behavior. The entire list of sins in the preceding verses was committed in the sight of God, but on the assumption that there was no God to see; or if there were a God, He did not see. "The fool has said in his heart there is no God" (Psalm 14:1; cf. Psalm 10:11).

The above is a description of total depravity. The Scriptures do not say that all men have done or will at some time commit all these sins. Neither do the Scriptures teach that man—though so terribly depraved—is worthless and no longer bears any aspect of the image of God. The Scriptures do not teach that all men are as violent in sin as they may be. We must understand, however, that man in sin does not control his own sinful behavior (John 8:45; Romans 6:16). On the other hand, when we view man in comparison with the glory of God, this is the biblical picture of man. As viewed by God, the depth of man's sin is so great that it forbids man's entrance into God's presence without being damned. This is man's picture as he faces God's law and His matchless holiness. In man's hatred there is murder. In his ignorance of God there is idolatry, and in all of this there is no room for or understanding of God. This depth of sin forbids man's attainment of righteousness by his merit. We should also point out that this description is not a description of a particularly evil group of men. This is a description of man—even respectable men—in sin.

The climax of Paul's argument is represented in Romans 3:19, 20; this conclusion has been his goal from 1:16. Law does not justify; it condemns. The law speaks to those who are under the law (3:19). In specific terms, this statement speaks to the Jews, or to any who have the law of Moses. At the same time, Paul has shown earlier that even the gentiles have the work of the law of God written in their heart (2:14, 15). In the broad sense of conviction all transgressors are under the law. The law speaks to all transgressors, and its purpose in speaking is conviction: "in order that every mouth may be silenced and that all the world become answerable to God" (3:19b). All men are placed under the same conviction by the same standard—the law of God which is the holiness of God stated.

By removing law as a medium of salvation Paul has removed works as a ground for salvation. This is a universal exclusion, and a universal inclusion. The universal exclusion is that no one can be saved by the works of the law. In making any judgment about the possibility of salvation of anyone, we must be careful not to appear to usurp the authority of God who is the only and final Judge; He judges the secrets of men [2:16]. However, many of our attempts to figure out ways in which the heathen may be saved apart from the gospel of Christ violate the very principles of grace. Those who say that God will not damn a sincere seeker after truth elevate sincerity and seeking to the level of merit. They stand in contradiction to the statement that is before us, and they violate the only way of salvation that is possible—salvation by the grace of God. They create a legalism of conscience, and offer the pagan a works—righteousness based on obedience to a depraved conscience. Paul's statement is, "Therefore, no flesh can be declared righteous before Him by the works of the law" (3:20a). The reason for this is the function of the law: "for through the law is the knowledge of sin" (3:20b). Law is the accusing element in the Word of God and it is the accusing element in the conscience of man. It is a measuring stick and has the same limitations of any measuring stick. It can verify conformity to the standard or it can reveal default from the standard. It cannot supply the standard in that which is being measured. In this analogy the law (whether it is the conscience of those who have not heard the law of Moses or whether it is the law of Moses) can only reveal sin. This is the universal exclusion.

The universal inclusion is the way of salvation. If there is but one standard of exclusion, there is but one standard of inclusion. That standard is the grace of God. The instrument of receiving this grace is faith. Paul's reasoning has come now to offer salvation by grace to both Jews and gentiles. It is this thought that Paul develops in his doctrine of justification, the subject of our next chapter.

CHAPTER TWO
END NOTES

[1]The prophet Isaiah ridicules idolatry on all these counts. A man plants a tree; later the tree which was planted by a man is cut down. With a part of the tree the man makes a fire and cooks his food. With the rest of it he fashions an image: "yea, he maketh a god, and worshippeth it; he maketh it a graven image, and falleth down thereto" (Isaiah 44:15). He even prays to the idol he has made: "Deliver me; for thou art my god" (Isaiah 44:17).

[2]Bruce, op. cit., p. 85; cf. M. D. Hooker, "Adam in Romans 1", *NTS*, VI (1959-60), p. 301.

[3]Murray, op. cit., 1:43

[4]Murray, op. cit., 1:49

[5]Even those evangelicals who embrace the doctrine of "progressive creationism" do not adequately protect themselves on this point. The doctrines of sin and grace are not integral to their doctrine of man and of Christ.

[6]Bruce, op. cit., pp. 86, 87.

[7]Some suggest this word should be taken to mean people who are consumed with selfish advantage. They have the mind-set and ambitions of a hireling. Cf. C. K. Barrett, *A Commentary on the Epistle to the Romans* (New York: Harper and Row, 1957), pp. 46, 47; cf. also Arndt and Gingrich; Murray, op. cit., 11:65, note 15.

[8]There are some aspects of circumcision that are parallel with the Christian sacrament of baptism, but that is not the primary symbolism of circumcision. By its nature and by its applications in Scripture, circumcision is more appropriately applied to the experience of sanctification. Moses speaks of the circumcision of the heart: "Circumcise your hearts, therefore, and do not be stiff-necked any longer" (Deuteronomy 10:16, *NIV*).

[9]The King James Version has chosen this emphatic prohibition in order to express the full weight of Paul's cry. It is not a mechanical literal translation, but it does translate the sentiment. We will use this expression as translation of this Greek exclamation throughout the commentary.

[10]David's great sin with Bathsheba was the context in which David had originally written these words. The default of the king of Israel who served as the type for Messiah did not annul the word of God—neither the law or the promise. The point made in all divine judgments is that God is glorified in judgment because His judgments are righteous. Judgment is a manifestation of the holiness of God exactly as the rewards of grace are manifestations of God's holiness.

[11]Murray, op. cit., 1:99

CHAPTER THREE

THE NATURE OF JUSTIFICATION

ROMANS 3:21-5:21

In the doctrine of grace there are two poles. The first is the issue of God's righteousness. The second is the issue of man's sinfulness. The question of grace is how to bring these two together without compromising the holiness of God or without insuring the damnation of the sinner. The doctrine of grace answers that this is to be done in the provision of forgiveness. We must understand, however, that forgiveness is not simply overlooking or winking at sin. This answer to the sin question would compromise the righteousness of God. Forgiveness must take into account the offensiveness of sin and the unworthiness of the sinner. Forgiveness must provide a satisfaction of the justice of God so that sin comes under the full weight of judgment. At the same time forgiveness must provide a covering for the sinner so that he does not bear the weight of God's wrath in the process of the judgment of his sins. These are the issues which are being addressed in this section of Romans. They are especially under consideration in Romans 3:21-31.

In all of this section there is a special problem for Paul; it is the question whether this doctrine may be substantiated in the Scriptures. If the doctrine of grace (specifically justification) cannot be found in the Hebrew Scriptures (our Old Testament), Paul would have been in violation of his own commitment to the authority of the Word of God. This is the special consideration of 3:21 and 4:1-24.

Justification is an act of divine judgment; it is God's declaration by which He places the believer in the position of forgiveness and righteousness. As in the case of all judicial acts, this occurs in the tribunal of God. It is incongruous to speak of the justification of one who is still in a sinful condition. So justification must deal with the question of the changes that occur in the believer when he is justified before the judgment bar of God. This is the special consideration of Romans 5:1-11.

Since justification is provided through the righteousness of another, there must be a means of transferring the merit from one person to another. It is the question of the transfer of Christ's merit to the account of the believer. This medium of transfer is represented in the unity of the human race, represented typologically in Adam and fulfilled in Christ. This is the special consideration of 5:12-21.

JUSTIFICATION AND THE RIGHTEOUSNESS OF GOD 3:21-26

According to Romans 3:21, 22, the righteousness of God has been manifested and is still evident in the experience and claim of those who believe in Jesus. The term "righteousness of God" is critical in this discussion. Since it is God's righteousness, it is absolute. In fact, it is the ground upon which the law was written. The law is God's Word, and as the word of the personal God, it is true to the character of God. So the pattern of grace and justification must not compromise this absolute with relativity. So, justification must be a manifestation of that absolute righteousness. Therefore, it is a manifestation of righteousness "without the law." Obedience to the law is not its medium of achievement.

The question is: Is this scriptural? Paul answers that it is, and that it has been declared by the law and the prophets. By the expression "the law and the prophets" Paul intends the entirety of the Hebrew Scriptures. So this doctrine of justification is not an innovation for Paul or for Christianity as a whole. It is essential to New Testament theology that it find its origins in the Old Testament. Paul will return to this issue in Romans 4 and show how justification was experienced by the Old Testament saints. Here, he simply notes the law and the prophets are the foundation from which he expands the doctrine of justification by faith.

Paul defines the righteousness of God as "the righteousness of God through the faith of Jesus Christ" (3:22). This formula of faith stands over against the formula of righteousness by the law. Paul's point, though, is that the righteousness of faith is the righteousness of God. God's holiness is fully satisfied (and the law of God stands fulfilled) in the righteousness of faith. Faith, as it is used here and consistently throughout Scripture, consists of both trust and obedience. Trust in God abandons self and commits one's destiny entirely to God. Such faith cannot be distinguished from obedience. Obedience is faith. But the perfection of obedience is not the ground of justification. The supreme qualification of this faith is not its perfection, but the fact that it is the "faith of Jesus Christ." It is faith which is His gift of grace, which has its origin in Him, which is sustained by His power, and which has Him (as He is presented in the gospel) as its object.

The benefit of this faith (namely, justification) is placed upon all those who believe. It is clear that Paul intends this "all" to include gentiles as well as Jews, "for there is no distinction" (3:22b). As law has made all men the same in judgment, grace has made all men the same in salvation.

The reason that there is no difference is stated in 3:23: "For all have sinned and are falling short of the glory of God." In the first verb (*have sinned*) Paul uses a past tense verb (*aorist*). The question here is not whether the individual is now in the practice of sin; it is the question whether he has ever sinned. Paul has demonstrated the sinfulness of all men in the preceding chapters. The second verb (*and are falling short*) is a present tense verb. Here Paul's accusation is that all do continue to sin. He uses a quotation from Isaiah 43:7 where God describes His children as "everyone who is called by my name, whom I created for my glory, whom I formed and made" (*NIV*). None would argue that the man whom Paul described in Romans 3:10-18 is fulfilling the glory which God intends for man whom He made. All men continue to come short of the perfection of God and the goal which God designed man to fulfill. This common factor of sin reduces all men to a single level. There is no difference between Jewish sinners and gentile sinners. In our own day the same could be said of educated and uneducated, sophisticated and unsophisticated, advantaged and disadvantaged, black, white, red or yellow, refined and unrefined. In the presence of God there is only one issue and that is the holiness of God and man's failure of that holiness.

There is another point in which there is no distinction
between men and that is justification: "being freely justified by
His grace through the redemption in Christ Jesus" (3:24).
This is the language of gift and not works, and the language
of grace not law. A fundamental principle of giving is the gift
is never a commentary on the worth or the worthiness of the
recipient. It is always a commentary on the assets and generos-
ity of the giver. So the giving of justification is not a
commentary on the holiness of the receiver, nor does it imply
any kind of superiority of one recipient of the gift over
another. In fact, all classes of men are equalized by the
pattern of justification by grace. So, there is no distinction
between Jew and gentile. God has made one promise to and
one provision for all whether Jew or gentile, for there is no
difference.

The effectual ground of justification is the "redemption that
is in Christ Jesus." The word that is translated "redemption"[1]
carries the connotation of *ransom*. Thayer defines it formally
as "to release by paying a *price*."[2] We often use the term
"ransom" but we should not understand this in the sense of
the payment of criminal ransom or a slave's ransom. It is the
payment of the price of a forfeiture. It is payment made on
behalf of another that relieves him of any obligation or
encumbrance. In spiritual matters, the Scriptures apply this
idea to the release of man from the bondage in sin and the
restoration of his freedom and *righteousness*.[3] Paul speaks of
this ransom as being in the Person of Jesus Christ and in His
blood. For this reason Jesus in His Person is referred to as
being our redemption (1 Corinthians 1:30). He is our redemption both in who He is and in what He does, as the next verse
shows: "Whom God has ordained as atonement, through faith
in His blood" (3:25a). Three words stand out in this statement:
ordained, atonement, and blood. Christ is the ordained of
God for purposes of redemption; He is the only One ordained
of God for this purpose. Paul, has, thus narrowed the way of
salvation to one Person Jesus Christ; this is consistent with all
the rest of Scripture (John 14:6; Acts 4:12). This term also
shows that this is the purpose of Christ's coming that God
might present to the world God's offer of mercy.

The second word we have translated "atonement." The
King James Version uses the word "propitiation"; the New

International Version uses the phrase "a sacrifice of atonement." This specific word appears in the New Testament only here and in Hebrews 9:5 where it is translated "mercy seat"[4] in reference to the holy of holies. The meaning of this noun and related words is that the propitiation (atonement) is a cover to protect the sinner from the wrath of God. It is a cover for sins, but it is a cover that fully satisfies the claims of divine justice against the offender. The cover that is provided consists both of the Person and work of Christ. In His Person, He is the atonement—the covering. In His work He accomplishes the terms necessary to satisfy the judgment of God against the sinner.

For this reason, Paul lays particular stress on the blood of Jesus. The blood of Jesus is the essence of His life (cf. Leviticus 17:11), and it is the symbol of His sacrifice. For this reason faith in the blood of Christ is essential to saving faith. Paul does not imply that faith can be in an impersonal object such as blood. Christ's shed blood represents the sacrifice by which He became the covering for our sins. His blood is His life.

The purpose for this provision for the remission of sins is to demonstrate the righteousness of God through the act of *forgiveness*.[5] God forgives the sins of the past in a proof of His righteousness and forbearance.

This is the marvel of the grace of God; His righteousness is declared in forgiveness exactly as it is declared in judgment. This declaration of God's righteousness occurs in "the present time" (3:26). We are inclined to think of the declaration of God's righteousness as the subject of the age to come, in the fulness of the kingdom of God. However, Paul shows that this aspect of the kingdom is the subject of the present time. God already forgives sins; He has already done it in the blood of Jesus. In the forgiveness of sins, believers already participate in the kingdom of forgiveness (the age to *come*).[6] In this act of mercy, God is already being shown as just and the Justifier of the one who has the faith of Jesus (3:26b). God's righteousness is not only maintained in the act of justification; it is proved by the act of justification. What God demanded of His Son in substitution for the sinner stands as eternal proof that God is perfectly righteous.

In 3:27-31, Paul makes specific applications of this doctrine of justification. These applications deal most particularly with the relationship of justification by faith to the question of merit. In turn, Paul applies this question to the place of Jews and gentiles in God's plan of salvation. Paul employs his familiar dialogue pattern of questions and answers. The first question is, "Where, therefore, is boasting?" (3:27a). The answer is, "It has been shut out" (3:27b). The second question is, "Through what kind of law was it shut out? through the law of works?" (3:27c). Paul's answer is, "Through the law of faith" (3:27d). Until this point in Romans, the word "law" (*nomos*) has been used to refer to the law of God particularly as it has been given in Moses. Here Paul uses the term to refer to a system of relationship with God; we might use the term *principle*. What is the principle on which boasting has been excluded? It is excluded because of the principle of faith.

When Paul says "For we consider a man to be justified by faith without the works of the law" (3:28), he intends to apply the offer of justification by faith to both Jews and gentiles. He uses the term "man" to mean any man who has the faith of Christ. Paul associates the universal offer of salvation with his concept of the universal authority of God: "Is He the God of the Jews only, and not of the gentiles? Yes, [He is the God] of the gentiles also" (3:29). This is the third question in the series. A limited god means a limited law, a limited morality, a limited judgment, and a limited salvation. If we say these things, we actually say that God is nothing; His law is nothing; His judgment is nothing, and His salvation is nothing. God is one (3:30a); by this statement Paul also means God is universal in presence and authority (Deuteronomy 6:4; Matthew 22:34-40). So, as He has authority of judgment over Jews and gentiles, He has authority to justify Jews and gentiles. Here, Paul turns his terminology from the ethnic designations (Jew and gentile) to the religious designations—circumcised and uncircumcised (cf. 2:28, 29). The circumcised are justified by faith; their circumcision has nothing to do with the spiritual experience of being called righteous before God's judgment. Conversely, not being circumcised has nothing to do with whether one will be called righteous by God (cf. 1 Corinthians 7:19; Galatians 5:1, 2). God justifies both circumcised and uncircumcised by the same instrument—faith: " . . . Since there is only one God who will justify the circumcised by faith and the uncircumcised through the same faith" (3:30, *NIV*).

Paul's final question in this dialogue is one he anticipated from his antagonists: "Do we destroy the law through faith?" (3:31a). This is unthinkable, for that would imply that the law and the God who gave it were *evil*.[7] Faith is not a system for circumventing the law or for ignoring its morality. Faith establishes the law; this was Paul's reasoning in 3:25, 26 where he speaks of demonstrating the righteousness of God in the atonement.

JUSTIFICATION AND OLD TESTAMENT WITNESSES 3:27-4:8

The next concern of Paul is to show that the doctrine of justification by faith was the promise to and the experience of Abraham. The fundamental covenant blessing is not the law, but justification. Paul first discusses the character of grace and its confirmation in the Hebrew Scriptures. Paul emphasizes here that he speaks of Abraham in the literal sense, that is as our father (that is, Father of Israel) according to the flesh (4:1). He is not spiritualizing Abraham's identity, for he intends to be taken literally here. He reasons that if Abraham had been accounted righteous because of his works (that is, the works of the law), he would have reason for boasting (4:2), and Paul has already shown that this is excluded (3:27). Paul seems to concede that this possibility for boasting could exist in Abraham's relationship to men, but certainly not before God.

The answer of Scripture to Paul's question in 4:1 is, "Abraham believed God, and it was accounted to him for righteousness" (4:3; Genesis 15:6; cf. Galatians 3:6). Paul is not elevating faith to the level of merit, for that contradicts his entire thesis. Instead, he speaks of faith as the economy of grace in which God, in spite of the believer's ungodliness, declares him righteous.

In explanation of this statement from Moses, Paul explains the economies of works and grace. In the economy of works, reward is a matter of wages and not a matter of gifts: "But to the one who works, the wages are accounted not according to gift, but according to debt" (4:4). The works-wages relationship is a matter of contract; when the work has been done, the wages are due and are subject to demand. It does not matter how little one had to work for a given amount (even minimum work for fabulously large wages); when the work has been done, the wages are an indebtedness, a moral obligation. This has never been God's relationship with man, especially fallen man.

In the economy of grace (gift) the reward is reckoned according to the good will of the giver: "But to the one who does not work but believes on Him who justifies the ungodly, his faith is accounted to him for justification" (4:5). When Paul says "the one who does not work," he does not mean the one who does not obey. (This is the principle of harmony between Paul and James 2:20-24.) The one who does not work, in this case, is the one who trusts God to account as righteous those who are, by personal history, ungodly; He justifies the ungodly. This principle forbids absolutely any appeal to works. If salvation is according to grace, it cannot be by works or grace is not grace (Romans 11:5, 6). Grace operates in an economy of gift; this is a relationship of unilateral covenant and not of bilateral contract.

Justification is, by nature, a gracious act of God, an act undeserved by the sinner. This doctrine and the doctrine of justification by works are mutually exclusive. One is either justified by faith without works or he is justified by works without faith. If one works for justification and is justified by those works (or that work), God is his debtor and is obligated to justify. There is no element of grace in debt. Faith recognizes the sinner's ungodliness, and so depends upon the grace of God to justify the ungodly. This faith—empty-handed so far as merit is concerned—is reward by God's declaration of righteousness.

The first Old Testament authority for this doctrine of justification that Paul cited was Moses, the mediator of the law (Galatians 3:19) and the historian of Genesis. Now Paul cites David, the king and psalmist of Israel, who lived under terms of the law of Moses. David has defined for Paul the character of justification. First, it is a state of divine favor which Paul and David describe with the term "*blessed*."[8] Second, Paul understands David to be describing the very same experience that Paul is in process of explaining and defending; it is to be declared righteous without the merit of the works of the law. Paul cites Psalm 32:1, 2: "Blessed are those whose wickednesses have been forgiven [cancelled], and whose sins have been covered; blessed is the man to whom the Lord does not account sin." In this statement Paul hears David define the forgiveness of sins under three parallel terms: the canceling of sins, the covering of sins [here the concept of atonement, which was understood as a covering for sins and sinners, is appealed to], and the refusal of God to look upon the sinner as chargeable for his sins. This is a thorough description of the nature of justification.

From this description of justification we may draw two conclusions. First, Abraham's justification was the same as the blessedness of which David spoke. Abraham's blessedness occurred prior to the law, and David's occurred under the law. So the law could not have been the ground of the experience. Second, the experience of Abraham and the experience of David are identical with the New Testament experience of justification. In the rest of Romans 4 Paul expands these conclusions.

JUSTIFICATION AND CIRCUMCISION
4:9-15

The question is: "Does this blessedness [of justification] come upon the circumcised or upon the uncircumcised?" For we say that "the faith was accounted to Abraham for righteousness" (4:9). By the appeal of faith Paul shows that justification was available to the ones who believe and circumcision is of no consequence. Paul enforces this conclusion even further by asking the question: When was Abraham justified, before he was circumcised? Paul answers his own question by saying, "Not in circumcision, but in uncircumcision" (4:10). Paul is appealing to the order of history in Abraham's experience. Paul was called in the covenant and given the promise of God in Genesis 12. In Genesis 15 it is testified that Abraham believed God and it was accounted to him for righteousness (Genesis 15:6). The ceremony of circumcision was not established for Abraham and his seed until Genesis 17. From the chronology it is clear Abraham was considered righteous by God long before he was circumcised, before God ever instituted circumcision. This chronological order was also

the ground of Paul's conclusion that circumcision was a sign
of righteousness and was not the ground of *righteousness*.[9] So,
Paul defines this rite as sign and *seal*[10] of the righteousness of
faith which Abraham had while he was still uncircumcised
(4:11). Paul's claim is that it was a fact that Abraham had a
right relationship with God before the rite of circumcision was
ever established. That means circumcision is a secondary
consideration in one's relationship with God. It also means
others can have a right relationship with God without being
circumcised. In terms of the covenant with Abraham this
means that his fatherhood over covenant children is based on
his justification by faith and not on his circumcision. He is the
father of all those who believe (4:11). The covenant is not
simply a rite (or for that matter simply a judicial declaration);
it is a way of life. This way of life cannot be represented by
circumcision. It must be represented by walking in the steps
of the faith of our father, Abraham (4:12). This was the way
Abraham walked before he was circumcised; so, he is the
father in covenant of other uncircumcised people who walk in
the steps of his faith. Paul would allow that circumcision can
still serve the Jew as it did Abraham—as a sign and seal of
justification which had already been established before
circumcision. So, being circumcised does not invalidate one's
justification; circumcision is not an evil thing. It must be
understood in its proper order of experience.

From 4:13 Paul explains and applies the truth that he has
just established. The covenant promise is that Abraham and
his seed would inherit the world (4:13; Genesis 18:18; 22:17,
18). This promise did not come through the law, but through
the righteousness of faith. If inheritance of this promise can
come through the law, "faith has been entirely emptied of its
power and the promise has been cancelled" (4:14). This
conclusion cannot be accepted because Paul has just shown
that Abraham received the promise before the law or circumcision had been given. Besides this, it is not even within the
purpose or the character of law to give a promise, "For the
law works wrath" (4:15a). Law is a judicial instrument and not
a reward instrument. The law does not give the comfort of
promise, but the terror of wrath; for it brings the knowledge
of transgression. In order to show this character of law, Paul
adds "Where there is no law there is no *transgression*"[11] (4:15b).

Paul explains the limitation of the law in Galatians 3:21: ", the law, therefore, opposed to the promise of God? Absolutely not! For if a law has been given that could impart life, then righteousness would certainly have come by the law" (*NIV*).

THE SEED OF ABRAHAM BY FAITH
4:16-25

God so ordered the promise that it should be of faith by grace and not by the works of the law. In this manner the promise comes to all the offspring under grace and not to those children who became children under law only (4:16). By his expression "all the offspring" Paul intends to include believers who were uncircumcised and those who were circumcised—Gentiles and Jews respectively. Paul appeals to the promise made to Abraham in Genesis 17:5: "I have appointed you father of many peoples" (4:17).

The faith that Paul is commending and which he sees in Abraham is particularized faith. Its strength is not the determination of Abraham to believe. Its strength is the understanding which Abraham had of God. He "believed in God who raises the dead and calls into existence those things which do not exist" (4:17b). If we are to be children of Abraham, we must possess and exercise the same kind of faith that he had. The faith of the father and the children must be the same. This provides for the unity of the covenant family. This description of Abraham's faith appeals to two events. The first is Abraham's confidence that God would raise Isaac from the dead (Genesis 22:1-19, especially verse 5; cf. Hebrews 11:17-19). The second is the creation. In creation, God calls all things out of nothing (Hebrews 11:3). It was this concept of God's power that enabled Abraham to maintain the claim of a son even when Sarah was barren and both she and he were old (cf. Hebrews 11:11). Notice Paul does not demand that the child's faith be as strong as Abraham's faith, but that it be the same faith in terms of its concept of God and the promise of *God*.[12]

Now Paul looks at the obstacles to Abraham's faith, which in light of his concept of God were not obstacles. Abraham is said to have "against hope [that is, all natural expectations] believed in hope in order that he might become father to

many peoples according to the saying 'so shall your seed be' "
(4:18). In Abraham's faith the promise of God materialized
the fulfillment. This is the way it had been in the creation;
God spoke and things came into being. Now, God has spoken
again, and the promise of God will produce the son and all
the seed that have been promised. Now Paul tells us how
Abraham's faith worked.

Abraham recognized the deadness of his own body and of
Sarah's womb. First, Abraham was 100 years old. Second,
Sarah was 90, and even in her youthful years she had been
barren. Faith does not deny reality; it does not treat illness
and other aspects of reality as if they were imaginary. (It is a
false faith very much akin to the errors of the Christian
Science doctrine and ancient gnosticism that claims that illness
does not exist or that things exist which do not exist.)
Abraham did not claim that he had a son when he did not
have a son. He did not claim that his body and Sarah's womb
were "alive" when their history showed them to be childless
(Genesis 17:17, 18). The error of this kind of thinking (and it
should not be called faith) is that it places the power of
fulfillment in the mind of the believer and not in the power
of God. It is not what we say about a thing that makes it so; it
is what God says about it. (What God says can overcome
obstacles, but they remain obstacles and they remain realities
until God removes them.) The victory of Abraham's faith is
that these things did not weaken his faith in God. Instead of
being weakened, he was strengthened not by the presence of
the infirmity but by the promise of God: "He gave glory to
God being fully convinced that He who had promised is able
also to do" (4:20, 21). The strength of his faith was his
concept of God. The primary result of Abraham's faith was
not the production of a son, but Abraham's justification:
"Wherefore, it was counted to him for righteousness" (4:22).
His faith put him in right relationship with God; hence his
justification and the birth of the son of promise.

Paul sees this entire history and the promise of justification
(Genesis 15:6) as having been recorded for New Testament
believers (4:23, 24). The records of the Old Testament are not
written with an exclusively historical purpose. They are recorded
for us. Abraham's experience is intended to teach us that
righteousness is imputed to us when we believe, exactly as

righteousness was imputed to Abraham when he believed. The faith required of us is the same as the faith that brought righteousness to Abraham. The only difference in the faith of Abraham and New Testament faith is the perspective in relation to the resurrection of the dead. Abraham believed God could give a son to a barren woman, and that after this son had been given God could raise him from the dead when he had been sacrificed. The faith of the New Testament is that God has already raised Jesus from the dead. Abraham's faith is prophetic faith; New Testament faith is fulfillment faith so far as the resurrection of Christ is concerned.

Paul is very clear that justifying faith now must affirm the resurrection of Christ. In this faith the resurrection of Christ Jesus our Lord is attributed to God the Father (4:24). The concepts of God, His power, and His promise are the same for us as for Abraham. The significance of the resurrection of Christ makes it essential to saving faith: "Who was delivered for our transgressions and raised for our justification" (4:25). This verse describes Christ's atonement provision as a single event which involves both His crucifixion and His resurrection. Christ's death is the answer of judgment for transgression; hence, He was delivered to death as judgment for our sins (2 Corinthians 5:18-21). Christ's death was for our offenses; it was punishment due us but given to Christ because He took our sins. God raised Him from the dead to provide for us justification. Resurrection is God's answer to judgment and His provision for our justification.

THE RESULTS OF JUSTIFICATION IN THE HEART

The climax of Paul's line of reasoning since Romans 1:16, 17 is represented in 5:1-11. So, this section opens with "therefore." As a consequence of his prior arguments Paul can state his conclusion: "Therefore, having been justified by faith we have peace with God through out Lord *Jesus Christ*" (5:1). In summary, we should describe the nature of justification. It is a judicial act of God; it occurs in the tribunal of God, where all accusations of transgression must be settled either by forgiveness or judgment. As a judicial act, this act changes the relationship of the believer to the law of God and to God the Judge. It is a declaration that the believer has a right relationship with God. He is no longer under wrath, but under God's pleasure. Justification is an act of imputation; in it God places the account of Christ over the record of the sinner's account. God imputes the righteousness of Christ (both the judicial fulfillment of God's wrath in His death, and the obedient fulfillment of all God's nature and law in the perfect life of Christ) to the believer. God looks upon the sinner as He looks upon Christ. This is the significance of the peace provided in justification. The instrument for receiving this justification is faith. The product of this justification is that we have peace with God. This peace consists of the tranquility of the believer in the presence of God. First, it is the peace of having found a right relationship with God, which is the believing relationship. Second, it is the peace from God's wrath by reconciliation. The believer need not (and ought not) live under the fear of God's judgment. Third, it is peace in view of the judgment seat of Christ. The believer can claim now the vindication that Jewish theology placed at the day of judgment at the end of the age. The issue of the judgment of salvation is settled and the believer may rest in confidence.

If this condition rested on obedience, it would be insecure, because its basis would be in a man and would rest on temporal assurances. Instead of works Paul offers faith. The security of that faith is not its perfection, but the fact that it is in Christ. So Christ becomes the security for faith and for justification. The significance of this is that Christ is the One through whom "we have the right by faith to enter into this grace in which we stand and in which we are rejoicing in the hope of the glory of God" (5:2). Paul uses an interesting mixture of verbs in this statement. The first verb has the force of saying that we have received and still have the right of access to grace (perfect tense). The second verb means that we have been made to stand and are still standing in this grace (perfect tense). The third verb means that we are now rejoicing in the hope of the glory of God (present tense).

These statements introduce a list of the results of the experience of justification in the heart and life of the believer. The first result already given is that we have peace with God. The second is we have a new attitude toward the appearance of the glory of God. The appearance of the glory of God is the prospect of the last day, when Christ (Messiah) himself shall appear. For those who lived under constant fear that they might not have fulfilled all God demanded of them, this is a prospect of terror. Now that the issue of peace and judgment have been resolved in justification, the believer rejoices in the prospect of the glory of God.

The third result is that the believer is given a new interpretation of life. This new interpretation enables the believer to "rejoice in suffering, knowing that suffering produces patient endurance" (5:3). In the framework of the old life suffering tends toward bitterness. Bitterness is the common core of many extremes such as Epicureanism and Stoicism, deism and pantheism, depressive seriousness, and frivolity, calloused endurance and aggressive defensiveness, and many others. These are all worldly attempts to handle suffering. In grace there is no need for such worldly placebos as those mentioned above. Grace does not remove suffering; it transforms the results into the spiritual grace of patience. The fourth result of justification is proven character: "And patience [produces] proven character and proven character [produces] hope" (5:4). This is produced out of patience. Spiritual character which has shown patience in tribulation has demonstrated its genuineness. This in turn produces hope. Hope is used here in the sense of claiming a promise that has not yet been seen in experience (cf. Romans 8:24, 25). The final day of redemption has not yet appeared; so, the believer is enabled to wait patiently for the fulfilling of the promise of God, the fruit of justification. This hope will not be put to shame; that is, it will not come to nothing. Paul will deal with the assurances of this security later (Romans 8); it is sufficient now to make the promise.

The fifth result of the new life is the love of God shed abroad in the heart of the believer: "And hope does not make ashamed because the love of God has been poured out in the heart by the Holy Spirit whom the Father has given to us" (5:5). For Paul, the pouring out of the love of God in the heart has value; "hope does not disappoint" (*NIV*) because the love of God has been poured out in the heart. In natural terms, one cannot prove he has been justified; this is a faith claim before God and is not observable in natural circumstances. One can only profess his hope, but he cannot demonstrate its fulfillment except in the evidences of the love of God (cf.

1 John 3:14). This is evidence of the hope we have, though yet
unseen. The Agent of this hope is the Holy Spirit. He is the
Father's gift to His people in the last days (Joel 2:28-32; Acts
2:17-21; Luke 11:11-13). Believers are living in the age of the
kingdom in their justification and in the gift of the Holy
Spirit.

In 5:6-11, Paul elaborates the security of the believers'
hope. We can be assured of our hope because of the obstacles
that the love of God had to overcome in order for God to
provide salvation for us. This is demonstrated, first of all, in
what Christ did for us: "While we were still helpless, at the
appropriate time[13] Christ died for the ungodly" (5:6). (*Note:
The terms "ungodly" and "helpless" are parallel, and each defines the
other.*) Paul's emphasis is that while we continued in our
impious ways, Christ died on behalf of us. This is contrary to
all human expectations; even the sacrifices of the Old Testament assume that the sacrifice is less valuable than the persons
for whom sacrifice is offered. It was better for a lamb to be
slain than that the firstborn sons be slain; so the Passover was
born (Exodus 12). "Very rarely will someone die for a righteous man; for a good man someone might dare to die" (5:7).
Paul's point is that such a thing might happen in men's value
systems, although it is extremely rare, but Christ died for
unworthy and helpless men.

This love is further demonstrated by what God did for us:
"God demonstrated His own love for us because while we
were still sinners (and were still sinning), Christ died for us"
(5:8). Father and Son concur in the single act of love—the
sacrifice of the life of the Son for the unworthy. Paul wants to
emphasize that God did this while we were still committing
sins, not after we ceased to sin (Luke 5:27-32). Even the death
of God's Son was for our sin (Acts 2:23; Luke 23:34).

The impact of this should be immediately apparent:
"Therefore, much more now that we have been justified in
His blood we shall be saved from wrath through him" (5:9). If
God gave love instead of wrath while we were sinners, it is
even more to be expected that He will give love (demonstrated
in salvation) and not wrath now that we have been justified in
Christ's blood. The salvation of which Paul speaks has three
points of emphasis in this statement. First, it is *justification*;
that is, it is a right relationship with God—a relationship of

peace, as defined earlier. Second, it is *salvation* in Christ's blood. The substitution of Christ's life for our life is essential to the biblical doctrine of atonement. Third, it is *salvation* from *divine wrath*. The believer is rescued from the destruction of divine wrath.

This concept of salvation involves *reconciliation*—the reconciliation of God to man and the reconciliation of man to God. The idea of reconciliation depends upon the fact that God as righteous Judge held our offenses against us. Reconciliation provides a substitute recipient of this judgment; this is the point of substitutionary atonement. An innocent substitute fulfills the sentence of the guilty. Reconciliation also carries the idea that men were angry against God as is demonstrated in their unbelief and disobedience. In 5:10, Paul applies the same reasoning to the issue of reconciliation that he earlier applied to justification: "If we were reconciled to God through the death of his Son, how much more now that we are reconciled shall we be saved in his life" (5:9). The death of God's Son is the event of reconciliation. There God became reconciled to the sinner because His wrath had been fulfilled (Romans 3:25, 26; 2 Corinthians 5:18-21). There, the sinner and his sins were covered from God's judgment. The believer has been removed from judgment and he no longer bears the sense of disapproval from God; he loses his sense of condemnation and hence his own enmity against God. These are the products of the death of God's Son. If His death produces reconciliation, how much more is the fulness of salvation assured in His life?

Now the believer's way of life is the way of rejoicing: "And not only this, but we rejoice in God through out Lord Jesus Christ, through whom we have now received the reconciliation" (5:11). Such is the transformation of a life through justification.

THE TRANSMISSION OF SIN AND RIGHTEOUSNESS

The passage in Romans 5:12-21 is designed to show how grace is transmitted from Christ to believers. In order to show this Paul assumes the corporate solidarity of mankind with Adam, and the corporate solidarity of Christ with believers. It is more than an assumption without evidence; this idea of corporate solidarity is integral to the Old Testament.[14] Paul sees all the children of Abraham as a being in the one Person, Jesus Christ. The high priest, in going into the Holy of

Holies, stood for all the tribes of Israel and made atonement
for all. The writer of the epistle to the Hebrews says, "Levi
also, who received tithes, payed tithes in Abraham" (Hebrews
7:9). This is what we mean by the term "corporate solidarity."
Paul seeks to establish a direct connection between the doctrine of reconciliation (5:1-11) and the doctrine of the transmission of sins. The point is that if man can be reconciled in
the manner Paul has described, there must be established a
personal connection between the justifier and those who are
justified (cf. Hebrews 2:11). Paul's argument is that this kind
of connection is fundamental in all human relations. It was
operative in the transmission of sin from Adam; it is operative
in the transmission of righteousness from Christ. "In verses
12-21 the apostle develops the parallel between Adam and
Christ, Adam as the head of the whole human race, Christ as
the head of the new humanity . . . . There is analogy, but
analogy in respect of what is completely antithetical. We
cannot grasp the truths of worldwide significance set forth in
this passage unless we recognize that two antithetical com-
plexes are contrasted. The first is the complex of sin-
condemnation-death and the second is righteousness-justification-
life. These are invariable *combinations*."[15]

Paul's opening statement is, "On account of this [that is, the
principle of reconciliation—vv. 1-11], just as through one man
sin entered into the world, and through sin, death, so also
death entered into all men because all sinned" (5:12). The one
man who sinned clearly is Adam whom Paul names in verse
14. Paul is not discussing the origination of sin, but the
entrance of sin into the world of mankind. The sin of Adam
(that is, his first sin, not all the sins that he might have
committed throughout life) caused sin to enter his posterity—
all those who were in him in the unity of the human race. Sin
brought with it judicial results, death. Death extends throughout the seed of Adam exactly as sin did. Death passed to all
because[16] all sinned. This does not mean that every man personally and actively sinned the sin of Adam, but that in his
(Adam's) act of sin all sinned. Paul specifically notes there
were those who did not sin after the likeness (similitude) of
Adam's transgression (5:14).

Verses 13 and 14 are a parenthesis in which Paul explains the subject he introduced in verse 12. This subject also demands the explanation of such matters as the definition of sin and the presence or absence of the law. So, Paul takes up these explanations. Paul's first statement in this explanation is that sin was in the world even though the law (here the law of Moses is intended) had not come. This must be established before Paul can go on to his next point, concerning the reigning of death (v. 14). Sin was a fact of this world order before the law of Moses was given. With the law there came the specific definition of sin. With this statement Paul adds, "But sin is not accounted while there is no law." Sin in the terms of the violation of Moses' law was not charged against man. It is clear that sin was in the world by virtue of the fact that death was in the world. The next statement shows this: "But death reigned from Adam to Moses even over the ones who had not sinned in the manner of Adam's transgression, who is the type of the One who is coming (5:14). Verse 13 did not say there was no sin in the world until the law of Moses was given. The fact is, death reigned during this time as it did after the giving of the law. Death is the penalty of sin, and it entered with sin (5:12). Death reigned even over those who did not commit the sin Adam committed. Paul's point is that death reigned and the only way death can reign is for there to have been prior sin. This prior sin is Adam's transgression. Paul means the one sin of Adam that is under discussion—the sin that brought death into the world. Paul is not discussing Adam's life as a pattern of sin, but his first sin. This explains what Paul means in verse 12 when he says, "because all sinned." The law of Moses has nothing to do with this act of sin; this act was Adam's violation of covenant with God (Genesis 2:15-17). It is this act in which Adam's posterity stands in corporate solidarity with him.

The connection the transmission of sin has with the transmission of righteous is that Adam "is the type of One who comes" (5:14b). Now, Paul is ready to develop the comparisons (though antithetic as noted above) between the transmission of sin and the transmission of righteousness.

Paul's broader concern is the entire covenant of grace; justification is the one experience that stands for the entirety of this covenant. Sin and grace enter the world by identical patterns; the heart of those patterns is the principle of corporate representation in one man. For sin it is Adam; for grace it is Christ. There is another concern here, and that is to show how grace abounds over sin. It is by the transgression of one that many died (5:15a). The entire history of mankind is adequate testimony of this. Above that, however, grace entered into the world, which Paul describes here as "the grace of God and the gift in grace" (5:15b). Grace and gift are one and the same; the grace of God is the gift of God, and it is this gift that triumphs over Adam's transgression and its results. This grace entered into the world by the righteousness of one Man Jesus Christ (5:15c). The type which Adam established in sin, Christ fulfills in righteousness. He and His righteousness triumph over Adam and his sin (5:15c).

Verses 16 and 17 explain the areas of the triumph of grace over sin. The first triumph lies in the fact that the offense of Adam brought condemnation when there was no long tradition of obedience and no generations of righteous ancestors. On the other hand, the righteousness of Christ was fulfilled after the descendants of Adam had established a record of sin and its consequences for thousands of generations. So "the gift of divine grace is out of many offenses unto justification" (5:16). The entrance of righteousness is the record of the righteousness of one Man overcoming the offenses of many (all the generations of men from Adam to Christ) for the establishment of justification. The second triumph is the triumph of life over death: "For if by the offense of one man death ruled through one man, how much more shall the ones who are receiving the abundance of grace and the gift of righteousness reign in life through one Man Jesus Christ?" (5:17). In the first part of this analogy, Paul speaks of men being ruled over by death. In the second part, he speaks of men reigning by life. This is triumph because it breaks the bondage of death; in its place grace gives men rulership in life. Death is enslavement; life is liberty. It is translation from bondage to rulership, and translation from death to life. Life and rulership were fulfilled in the righteousness of Christ and transferred to those who are in Him.

The third triumph is the triumph over condemnation: "Consequently then, as through one man's offense [condemnation came] to all men for judgment, thus also through the righteousness of one man [the gift of divine grace came] unto all men for righteousness of life" (5:18). The grace of God in justification triumphs over the record of the sins of the race and the record of the sins of the individual believer. In place of the condemnation, which descended to all of Adam's posterity, grace has placed righteousness and forgiveness above all the record of sinfulness. This thought is completed in 5:19: "For just as through the disobedience of one man many were made to be sinners, so through the obedience of One many were made to be righteous." The positions of sin and grace are not merely positional. By the disobedience (unwillingness to hear and hence, to disobey) of Adam, his posterity became, in actual fact, sinful in nature. They are not simply sinful in nature. They are not simply sinful in position; they became depraved. On the other hand, by the obedience of Christ, his posterity (those who are the children of God in Him) became righteous. Again, they are not simply placed in the position of righteousness. They became righteous because they take on the nature of Jesus Christ. Here the apostle shows that the position in which God places men by His act of judgment agrees with their actual nature. The judgment of sin is accompanied by the condition of sinfulness. The judgment of righteousness (justification) is accompanied by the condition of righteousness (2 Peter 1:4). In this brief statement, Paul opens up the subject of regeneration, though his primary emphasis has been justification.[17]

The entrance of the law serves God's purposes by making sin abound (5:20). Paul does not mean sin increased because the law came; the law is not the origin of sin. The specific nature of the law makes the definition of sin specific, and it defines as sin many things that would not be considered sin. In this sense "the law entered, in order to make sin abound" (5:20a; cf. Romans 4:15; 7:7, 8; Galatians 3:19). As Galatians 3:19 shows, the law serves another purpose, and that is to provide for the coming of the promise; so, here Paul can say "where sin abounded grace flowed without measure" (5:20b). Calvary is the end of the road for sin; there sin abounded when the seed of the first man Adam put to death the last man Adam, Jesus Christ. But there the righteousness of the last man Adam triumphed over the sin of the first. Here the righteous ones from Adam to Christ are gathered with the righteous ones from Calvary to the end of the age.

Paul immediately applies this truth to redemption: "In order that as sin ruled in death, thus also might grace rule through righteousness unto the end of life everlasting through Jesus Christ our Lord" (5:21). In death, sin abounded because death is the reigning instrument of sin, but that is based on the law (1 Corinthians 15:55, 56). But the law serves another purpose and that is to lead us to Christ (Galatians 3:23-25). The reigning instrument of grace is eternal life; so in eternal life righteousness abounds. This is the epitome of the overflow of grace. It triumphs over death by bringing eternal life. It is not simply the reversal of death in the restoration of mortal life. It is triumph over death with eternal life.

It is a mistake to deal with these issues only on the grand scheme of redemptive provision. We must understand that what happens in the provision of salvation is intended to happen in the experience of salvation. If grace abounds over sin at Calvary, God intends for grace to abound over sin in the life and experience of the believer. The promise of grace abounding is an individual promise. Paul will show how this is so in Romans 6-8.

CHAPTER THREE
END NOTES

[1]In addition to its use in this passage, the word *apolutrosis* is used in the New Testament of the day of redemption at the coming of the Lord (Luke 21:28; Ephesians 4:30), of the resurrection of the body (Romans 8:23), of Christ who had been made by God to be our redemption (1 Corinthians 1:30), of Christ in whom we have redemption (Ephesians 1:7; Colossians 1:14), of the redemption of all those who have been sealed by the Holy Spirit (Ephesians 1:14).

[2]Joseph H. Thayer, *Greek-English Lexicon of the New Testament* (Grand Rapids: Zondervan, 1962), p. 65.

[3]It is foolish to make an analogy of this ransom to the criminal's ransom, the kidnapper's ransom, or the slave holder's ransom. Such analogy has the effect of having Christ pay Satan for the release of those whom He redeems. The correct analogy is that man had forfeited his original heritage, which included his holiness and liberty before God. When man sinned, he forfeited the heritage that God had given him; and the heritage returned to God whose it was and who had bestowed it. The ransom that is offered by Christ is offered to God; Christ pays the price necessary to restore man's forfeited heritage.

[4]This word is related to the verb "to be merciful" (Luke 18:13), and to make reconciliation (Hebrews 2:17). It is also related to the noun translated "propitiation" (1 John 2:2; 4:10).

[5]Forgiveness is often confused with a compromising of the standards of judgment. What we sometimes call forgiveness is simply indulgence, and such indulgence does compromise standards. In the perfection of His holiness and justice God cannot simply overlook sins. His acts of forgiveness must have a proper judicial basis, a basis that does not contradict the declaration of the prophet, "The soul that sinneth, it shall die" (Ezekiel 18:4, 20). Every soul that sins must face death, unless the penalty can be removed without compromise of the law of God. By the appeal to the blood, the life of Christ given in sacrifice of atonement, Paul offers the ground for the satisfaction of the law of God and a covering of the sinner and his sins from the wrath of God.

[6]Paul, here, moves away from accepted rabbinical theology, which understood forgiveness to be reserved for the day of judgment. Both judgment and forgiveness were apocalyptic events. Paul does not remove judgment from the realm of the apocalyptic, but he does make forgiveness a present experience, eschatological in nature. As God demonstrates His righteousness in judgment, He also demonstrates His righteousness in forgiveness. These are both kingdom realities.

[7]A destructible law or one of temporal enforcement has no moral value.

[8]*Makarismos:* the word is consistently used in Scripture to describe divine favor. Note Matthew 5:3-12.

[9]The reason Paul uses the ceremony of circumcision is that the Jewish legalists had made it the essence of righteousness, and a requirement of salvation. In this theology, circumcision had come to represent the entirety of the law. So, Paul, by dealing with the one rite of circumcision, was dealing effectively with all aspects of legalism or works-righteousness.

[10]The two words "sign" and "seal" both presuppose the prior validity of the claim or document to which they are attached. A government seal does not make a document valid; it recognizes the validity of the document which has already been demonstrated. It follows, then, that a seal logically comes after validity has been established.

[11]This statement does not exonerate violaters of the moral code even though they do not have the specific law of Moses. Paul has clearly shown that transgression can be defined in the conscience of men and of society (Romans 2:14, 15).

[12]It is a mistake to use Abraham as if he were the perfect model of faith. His faith was not perfect; there were occasions of serious lapses of faith in his religious experiences. An equally important reason this is a mistake is that justification is not based on perfect faith. We must not demand that faith be perfect in order for it to be valid, or in order for it to be the instrument of justification. When we do this, we twist the concept of faith into a new form of legalism. In the name of faith we fall into the same trap we are attempting to avoid.

[13]We have translated the Greek *kata kairon* with the English "at the appropriate time." This seems to be a parallel expression with "the fulness of time" (Galatians 4:4). Paul does not choose to elaborate on this idea in this context, but it was integral to his theology.

[14]There are many biblical illustrations of this sense of the union of many people in one person. The first and most comprehensive example is Adam. Paul sees it in the promise of the Seed of Abraham. In Galatians 3:16, Paul emphasizes the singular in the promise of a seed for Abraham: "The promises were given to Abraham and to his seed. The Scripture does not say 'and to seeds,' meaning many people, but 'and to your seed,' meaning one person, who is Christ" *(NIV)*.

[15]Murray, op. cit. I:178, 179.

[16]The prepositional phrase *eph ho* is best understood here to mean "because," though it could mean "in whom." Cf. Blass, DeBrunner and Funk, 235:5.

[17]Roman Catholic theology criticizes Protestant theology on this point. Perhaps Protes-

tants have carelessly stated the doctrine of justification in such a way as to imply that justification is not accompanied by righteousness of nature and behavior. We should be very clear in pointing out two facts. First, justification and regeneration go hand in hand; it is impossible to speak of being justified without also speaking of regeneration. They are both essential to the saved experience. Second, justification demands holiness of life. God does not justify in order to allow a person to continue in sin. To be justified anticipates the pursuit of holiness or sanctification; this also is essential to the saved experience (Hebrews 12:14).

CHAPTER FOUR

THE NATURE OF SANCTIFICATION

ROMANS 6, 7

Paul's purpose in Romans 6 is to show that the gift of grace calls for holiness of life. The position granted by God's judgment in justification is a right relationship with God. This position—justification by faith—demands that the believer live in accord with that declared position. Romans 6 deals with the believer's responsibility to live a holy life in harmony with God's judgment about him. In this chapter Paul will deal with the redemptive provision for our sanctification and with the manner of appropriating this provision to the believer's life. In Romans 7 Paul will show how this relates to the believer's relationship with the law. Paul has built his argument that justification must be by faith; now he must show how holiness of life must also be by faith. The attempt to achieve holiness of life by obedience to the law, by self-discipline or by spiritual practices is futile and legalistic. This is true even when these attempts and instructions are couched in "gospel terminology."

There is no break in Paul's mind when he moves from chapter 5 to chapter 6. So, the question that opens Romans 6 is in direct response to Romans 5:20, 21. The presumptuous question is "Shall we remain in sin (that is, continue in the practice of sin) in order that grace may abound?" (6:1). This question would be asked by two groups of people, the legalists (Judaizers) and the antinomians. Paul's enemies among the Judaizers—those who wished to maintain bondage to the law—would ask this question in order to ridicule Paul and his doctrine. They want to say that if grace abounds where sin abounds, then we ought to keep on sinning in order to give grace a chance to abound. They would claim that Paul's doctrine logically leads to this conclusion.

Others of Paul's enemies would find an excuse for antinomianism. Antinomianism is the view that attempts to throw off all restraints, claiming the law has nothing to say about salvation and the saved way of life. They say that their continuing in sin while professing justification shows God's grace is greater than their sin because it saves them in their sinful practices. There was apparently such an element in the Corinthian church; notice how they seem to boast of their tolerance for the man involved in incest (1 Corinthians 5:1, 2).

THE CRUCIFIXION OF THE OLD NATURE
6:1-7

Paul recoils at this suggestion from any source; he shouts the prohibition that we translate "God forbid!" He follows with his reasoned answer immediately: "We died to sin, how shall we continue to live in it?" (6:2). This is out of character for the believer. First, it is out of character in the light of our new position in Christ. One must not live a contradiction of what God has given him. Second, it is out of character in the light of the believer's new nature. One cannot continue to live a contradiction of his own character. Being dead to sin we must not continue in its bondage and practice.

The spiritual experience of being baptized into Christ's death is the fundamental consideration in this pursuit of holiness. Verses 3-7 develop this thought in answer to the question raised in verse 2.

It is not possible to speak of being baptized into Christ without also speaking of being baptized into His death. To be in Christ is to be in His death. Paul explains for us the meaning of the phrase "being baptized into Christ" in 1 Corinthians 12:13: "For we were all baptized by one Spirit into one body—whether Jews or Greeks, slave or free—and we are all given the one Spirit to drink." This baptism is by one Spirit, the Holy Spirit. It is baptism into one body, the body of Christ. In this baptism we have been given the one Holy Spirit to drink.

Baptism into Christ's death provides personal identity with Christ in His crucifixion and resurrection: "We have been buried with Him through baptism into death" (6:4a). Here Paul speaks specifically of the believer's identity with Christ's cross. In this identity of death the believer makes Christ's cross his own. The purpose of this identity and baptism into death with Christ is identity with Christ in His resurrection: "in order that just as Christ was raised up through the glory of the Father, so we also might walk in newness of life" (6:4b). Here the instrument of Christ's resurrection is called the "glory of the Father." This expression lays special stress on the work of the Father in the resurrection of Jesus. The particular expression probably emphasizes the fullness of the Father's power and holiness brought to bear on His Son. The Father delivers His Son from death and verifies His good pleasure in His Son. For the disciple, identity with Christ in death and burial also identifies him with Christ in His resurrection. The transformation accomplished by resurrection, in both cases, is radical. For Christ, the resurrection marked His change from mortality to immortality and from answerability to sin to victory over sin. The believer's participation in Christ's resurrection marks for him a radical change. First, the believer is identified with Christ because he (as Christ) is raised up by the glory of the Father. Second, the believer is changed from a walk in sin to a walk in newness of life (cf. 1 John 2:1). In Romans the contrast of the two ways of life is represented by the description of man in Romans 3:10-18, and the description of man in Romans 8 (cf. Ephesians 2:1-9). Paul specifically identifies the departure from the old way with crucifixion ("for if we have been buried with him in the likeness of his death," 6:5a). Just as specifically he identifies the new life with resurrection ("we shall be also in the likeness of his resurrection," 6:5b). By associating the experience of the believer with Christ's death and resurrection, Paul has shown the closest possible connection of redemptive experience with redemptive provision. We are not dealing with the achievement of holiness by behavioral change, but holiness by redemptive experience.

To this point Paul's emphasis has been on the death of the believer to sin. If this is to be a fact of experience, there must also be a provision for the death of sin in relation to the believer. This is Paul's next emphasis: "Knowing this that our old man has been crucified, in order that the body of sin might be destroyed so that we should not serve sin any longer" (6:6). Two phrases in this statement call for particular attention. The first is "our old man." This same expression appears in Ephesians 4:22 and Colossians 3:9. In each case (as here) the phrase refers to the old way of life which is described as corrupted according to deceitful lusts. It also stands in contrast to the new way of life represented by the expression the "new man" in Ephesians and Colossians. The second phrase is the "body of sin." Paul never uses this expression to designate the body of mortality; he does not regard mortality as sinful. The closest parallel with this term is the phrase the "body of carnality" (Colossians 2:11). In this context Paul speaks of the "putting off of the body of carnality (sarx) in the circumcision of Christ." These two expressions mean the same thing, and in each context they are dealt with redemptively. All the expressions we have dealt with refer to the carnal nature. The old man is a figure of speech designating the principle of sin in man. We sometimes refer to it as the Adamic nature. It is not the physical body as such, but it is the physical body as it serves its appetites and brings the inward man into oppression by the desires of the body.[1]

The redemptive provision described here is the crucifixion of the old man. The verb "has been crucified" is a past tense verb (aorist). The redemptive provision for the crucifixion was in the cross of Christ (cf. Colossians 2:9-15). God's purpose is twofold. First, He intends, by the crucifixion of the old man, to destroy the body of sin. Second, God intends to provide the believer victory so that he does not serve sin any longer. This is the biblical and theological ground upon which the believer makes the claim of victory. Without this foundation the claim of victory is entirely empty.

The result of this provision is the believer can die to sin: "The one who has died has been set free from sin" (6:7). By referring to "the one who has died" Paul intends those who have died with Christ as in verses 3-6. He declares of them that they have been set free from sin. The word he uses means *to be justified from sin*; it is the same word that has been used throughout concerning justification. In this context it still refers to justification, but it adds the dimension of being acquitted and relieved from any of the accusations, claims or judicial consequences of sin. "The decisive breach with the reigning power of sin is viewed after the analogy of the kind of dismissal which a judge gives when an arraigned person is justified. Sin has no further claim upon the person who is thus *vindicated*."[2] Note also the deliverance that is referred to in Romans 8:1: "There is, therefore, no condemnation to them that are in Christ Jesus."

HOLINESS AND FAITH
6:8-14

These are provisions of grace; this is central with Paul to all experiences in Christ. The pattern of the doctrine of grace set in Paul's doctrine of justification by faith is consistently followed in all other experiences of the Christian life. The ambition to be holy faces the same issue that justification faces—the issue of works (legalism) and grace. The question is, "Can we achieve holiness by works or by faith?" Paul's answer has already been set in terms of the crucifixion and resurrection of Christ. It has to be by grace. If this is so, how is it to be appropriated in the life of the believer? The answer is that sanctification is also of faith (cf. Acts 26:18). Spiritual life must be perfected in the same medium in which it originates. At various points in one's spiritual life faith is specifically directed in terms of personal need. Here faith lays hold on the provisions and promise of holiness.

Paul describes the claims of faith which relate to the believer's call to holiness. The first claim of faith is to claim the result of having been crucified with Christ; crucifixion has, in the believer, the same result that it had in Christ—resurrection: "If we died with Christ, we believe that we shall also live with Him" (6:8). The believer claims the newness of life that Christ received in resurrection. The resurrection of Christ means that He is immortal and death has no further claim on Him either in body or soul: "Knowing that Christ, having been raised from the dead, dies no longer; death no longer rules Him" (6:9). One might ask, "In what sense did death rule Christ?" Certainly, it did not rule Him in the sense that He abdicated His authority as the Resurrection and the Life (John 11:25, 26). Yet the goal of His mortal life was the crucifixion; for this end He came into the world (1 Peter 1:18-21; Revelation 13:8). Having been raised from the dead, Jesus dies no more. The goal of His existence is not to die, but to reign forever. So, death no longer rules over Him. His death is a once and for all event: "He who has died to sin, has died once and for all" (6:10a; cf., Hebrews 9:26-28; 1 Peter 3:18). Paul again expresses the result of Christ's death: "He who lives, lives to God" (6:10b).

The second step of faith in relation to holiness is to "account yourselves to be dead to sin and alive to God in Christ Jesus" (6:11). The term "account yourselves to be" describes the act of faith. It is the same kind of faith Paul described as being in Abraham when he set aside the deadness of his own body and the deadness of Sarah's womb and believed God (Romans 4:18-25). This faith claim is the instrument of death to sin and aliveness to God. This experience is "in Christ." These conditions show up the futility of holiness through self-discipline or any other ways men attempt to create their own holiness. We do not want to leave the impression that the believer can be passive in relation to the practices of holiness. So, Paul calls for specific actions on the part of the believer in the pursuit of holiness.

The third application of faith is described in 6:12-14. In these applications, the believer receives directions for his faith and practice. The Apostle exhorts, "Do not let sin rule in your mortal body to obey its lusts" (6:12). Though the mortal body is not by nature sinful, it is the agent of sinful experience. Even when sin is not practiced outwardly, the lusts of the flesh still represent the sin itself, as our Lord warned us about murder, lust, and covetousness (Matthew 5:21, 22, 27-30; Mark 7:20-23). The way sin dwells in the mortal body is that the person obeys the lusts of the body. The Greek word *epithumia* is most often used by Paul to refer to sinful desires, though this is not its exclusive use. Here it is used to describe the desires of the body that, if uncontrolled, will dominate spiritual considerations. Paul warns against allowing oneself to live in servitude to the desires of the flesh. Paul's exhortation here has a continuing force; it is an exhortation and a commitment that must be continually renewed.

Paul follows this exhortation with a parallel command: "Do not present the members of your body as instruments of unrighteousness to sin" (6:13a). The verb here also has a continuing force (present active imperative). This is important in both of these exhortations. The conquest of sin originates in the one event of Calvary. Its initial conquest may be correctly identified in the personal experience of sanctification. But this is not a claim that can be made once and left in the past as forever settled. Continuously renewed commitment is essential to holy living. This is called for because the desires of the flesh do not ever cease. Even though they are not sinful in nature, there is always the snare of Satan that would lead the believer to compromise his holiness in servitude to the mortal body.

The fourth direction that Paul gives for our faith here is "present yourselves to God as those who are alive from the dead and your members as instruments of the righteousness of God" (6:13b). There are some important changes in this exhortation. First, this is a positive exhortation designed to complement the negative exhortation immediately preceding. Second, this exhortation calls for the commitment of the whole self, not just the members of the body. The entire nature (material and immaterial) of man is to become the instrument for the fulfilling of the righteousness of God in life. Third, Paul uses a verb that emphasizes once and for all commitment (the aorist active imperative). This commitment to the fulfillment of holiness of life is to be a once and for all commitment: "and do not go on, as you have been doing, putting your members at the service of sin, but put them once and for all at the service of God.[3]

The climax of these applications is, "For sin shall not rule over you, for you are not under law but under grace" (6:14). To be under law is to be under sin (Romans 7:5, 6; Galatians 3:19), and Paul has already shown that this is not the status of the believer. To be under grace is to be free from sin and law (Romans 7:4) and to be free from its condemnation (Romans 8:1). The exhortations that we have just reviewed are intended for believers—those who are in grace. It is a foolish and damning mistake for believers to think of a "finished work" that renders these exhortations unnecessary.

ENSLAVEMENT TO HOLINESS
6:15-23

The last part of Romans 6 (vv. 15-23) provides an illustration for living in Christ. Paul illustrates by describing the pattern of servitude. The principle of servitude is the pattern of slavery, and to continue in sin is to continue in slavery to sin: "Shall we sin because we are not under law but under grace?" (6:15). It is an unreasonable and presumptuous question— the same kind of question as that in 6:1. So, again, Paul's initial response is "God forbid!" The real answer to the question is that if you do sin, you are the slave of sin: "Do you not know that to whom you present yourselves servants unto obedience, you are servants of the one whom you obey, whether of sin unto death or of obedience unto righteousness" (6:16). It is as simple as this; no matter what your excuse is for continuing to sin, if you sin, you are the servant of sin. The outcome is equally simple; the end of sin is death. On the other hand, if you obey righteousness, you are the servant of God. This principle is extended in 1 John 3:4-7: "Dear children, do not let anyone lead you astray. He who does what is right is righteous, just as He is righteous. He who does what is sinful is of the devil, because the devil has been sinning from the beginning" (1 John 3:7, 8; *NIV*).

Each system of slavery has its own end. In each case the end of each system is integral to the way of life represented in the system. The way of life that is enslaved to sin by obedience to sin is a way of death. Its primary characteristic is death; therefore, its climax is death. Sinfulness fulfills its own nature. The way of life that is enslaved to righteousness partakes of life. Its primary characteristic is life; so, its climax is life. There is an unbroken movement from the manner of life to the reward of life.

Paul shouts for joy over the new status of the believer: "Thanks be to God! You were the servants of sin, but you have obeyed from the heart that form of teaching by which you have been delivered" (6:18). It is as if Paul had become depressed with the discussion of enslavement to sin, and suddenly breaks through to victory in the shout, "Thanks be to God." The reason for this shout is that "you were, but you are not now servants of sin." The contrast is not merely mechanical as if the Roman believers had only changed in outward behavior: "you have obeyed from the heart." The Apostle had given them the same kind of commendation in his opening remarks (Romans 1:8). Their obedience is described as to "the form of doctrine by which you were delivered." This is a strong statement. They were given over to the doctrine; they had become servants of the teaching. The teaching was the instrument by which they had been delivered. This may seem to be strange to the contemporary situation where we talk about conversion and then talk about discipleship as if they were two separate processes. But the "form of doctrine" was important in the New Testament church. One of the characteristics of the church following Pentecost was "they devoted themselves to the apostles' teaching" (Acts 2:42, *NIV*). Paul described evil behavior as "contrary to sound doctrine" (1 Timothy 1:10). He urged Timothy, "What you heard from me, keep as the pattern of sound teaching" (2 Timothy 1:13, *NIV*). He warned against the day when men would not endure sound teaching (2 Timothy 4:3).

The result of this deliverance is, "Since you have been set free from sin, you have been enslaved to righteousness" (6:18). The statement "enslaved to righteousness" is parallel with the expression "the form of doctrine into which you were delivered." Perhaps we recoil at the idea of enslavement. In Paul's view, however, there is no other word for the condition of sin. He wishes to show that the believer's new condition in righteousness stands in direct contrast to the old; so, enslavement is his word in each case (6:16).

Believers are called specifically to a slave's commitment. Paul warns that he is using a human analogy: "I speak as a man" (6:19a). There is a hint of rebuke here; he adds, "because of the weakness of your flesh" (6:19b). He wants believers to know that they are called on to commit themselves to righteousness as they were formerly committed to sin. In the old way of life unbelievers give the "members of [their] bodies as servants to uncleanness and lawlessness unto lawlessness" (6:19c). This expression shows an escalation in wickedness and a deepening in sinful enslavement. The new way of life calls for the yielding of the members of the body "as slaves to righteousness unto holiness" (6:19d). The pattern of enslavement in each case is the same. The aim of the latter is holiness—*purity*.[4] This purity is a matter of outward behavior as well as inward condition. It is clear from these exhortations (and those in 6:12-14) that Paul regards the human body and the functions of its members as integral to the issues of sin and righteousness. The activities and uses of one's body have direct bearing on one's spiritual nature. There can be no legitimate profession of holiness where the body is used for uncleanness. Paul carries this thought over into 6:20, 21 when he speaks of the former practices as practices of which the believer is now ashamed.

Though there are parallels in the nature of the two enslavements, these two ways of life are mutually exclusive. Bondage to sin left no room for loyalty or answerability to righteousness: "When you were the slaves of sin, you were free from righteousness" (6:20). You recognized no claim of loyalty from the rulership of righteousness. You expected no commendation from that ruler.[5] You expected your life and its rewards to be fulfilled entirely within loyalty to sin. That old system produced an end appropriate to its manner of life; it produced fruit in things of which you are now ashamed (6:21). The real question is, "What was the fruit of the old life?" Aside from its shameful behavior, it bore the fruit of death: "the end of that way is death" (6:21b). The manner of life and its rewards are entirely compatible.

This is not the believer's present status and loyalty: "But now, having been set free from sin, and having been enslaved to God, you have your fruit unto holiness and the end everlasting life" (6:22). The old loyalty has been broken; you are free from sin. The new loyalty is supreme; you have been made servants of God. So now the believer must not bear the fruit of the old. Your manner of life is to reflect the nature of your new Master; His holiness requires the believer's holiness (1 Peter 1:15, 16; Leviticus 11:44). Again, the end of this way of life is entirely compatible with the way of life. The ultimate reward is everlasting life. The life and the reward are harmonious.

The comparisons noted above are entirely proper. But the two ends described (death and life) are opposite. It is obvious that death and life are opposite, but there is an oppositeness of achieving each end. Death is described as "wages earned." Life is described as "gift given." "The wages of sin is death" (6:23a). This is what has been earned by sinful living. Death is its rightful payoff. In this reasoning there is no undeserved result.

"The gift of God is eternal life in Christ Jesus our "Lord" (6:23b). This differs absolutely from the "wages of sin." This is a gift and not wages earned. This is the terminology of grace. Gifts are always the representation of the nature and graciousness of the giver. They never provide commentary on the worthiness of the receiver. Life is the gift of God; death is the judgment of God. The life that is offered is eternal life, not simply the restoration or perpetuation of mortality. This life is provided in another. He is the Agent by whom life is restored. This restoration occurs when the believer is baptized into Him, His death and resurrection (Romans 6:3-7).

FREEDOM FROM THE LAW
7:1-6

It seems almost impossible to discuss holiness of life without seeming to embrace some aspects of legalism. This is a false fear. First, it misunderstands the character of legalism. Obedience to the law is not in and of itself legalistic. The attempt to justify oneself by obedience to the law, and the hope that we shall be finally saved by our obedience to the law are legalistic applications of the law. Second, it misunderstands the nature of the law of God. The law of God is not evil. Romans 7 discusses the relationship of the law to holiness in Christ, and should clear up these misunderstandings. In this chapter Paul deals with two issues. The first is the principle of release from the law (7:1-6) and the second is his personal relationship with the law, which he uses to apply to spiritual experience in general (7:7-25).

The principle by which one is set free from the law is the same as the principle of release from marriage. In his opening statement on release, the Apostle appeals to the fact that his readers know the law (7:1). The most natural way to understand Paul's use of law here is to refer to the Mosaic law. Both Jewish Christians and gentile Christians qualified for this statement. Certainly any group of Christians capable of understanding the epistle to the Romans would have adequate knowledge of Moses' law to receive the analogy Paul is about to use.

No one who knows the law would argue with Paul's statement that "the law rules the man as long as he lives" (7:1). No Scripture (Old Testament or New Testament) ever suggests that the law was temporarily *given*.[6] The law's rulership over a man is lifelong. This maxim is essential for the analogy that follows.

In developing his analogy, Paul says this lifelong commitment is like the law of marriage: "For the wife is bound by law to her husband as long as he lives, but if he dies, she has been set free from the law of her husband" (7:2). The principle of marriage assumes no dissolution in life (Genesis 2:24; Matthew 19:5, 6). The only dissolution of marriage assumed is the death of one of the marriage partners (in this illustration, the husband). This means that if the wife is married to another man (or is bound to him sexually), she commits adultery (7:3a). If the husband dies, the widow is free to remarry. If she does remarry, she cannot be called an adulteress (7:3b).[7]

In applying this analogy to the believer's relationship to the law, Paul turns his analogy to speak of the death of the believer to the law. If he had made a direct analogy, he would have spoken of the death of the law. He does not speak of the death of the law because this would have been improper. The law is divine Word and is eternal (Matthew 5:17, 18; 1 Peter 1:23). The law of the Lord is glorious even if its glory is superseded by the promise (2 Corinthians 3:7-11). In order to carry out the analogy of death, Paul speaks of the death of the believer to the law. This death dissolves the union between man and law.

This death is experienced through Christ's death and resurrection, and its purpose is that we can be married to another. A rebellious attitude that simply assumes that the law can be disobeyed ignores the principle of release through death. Such an attitude is spiritual adultery. This was the cry of the prophets against backsliding Israel (7:41). In the same way, a Jew could not have converted to Christianity simply by saying Christianity offered a better law. Until there is a spiritual death to the law, default from it is spiritual adultery. When this death occurs, the believer is free from the law "to be married to another." The death to be experienced is provided through Christ's body which has been raised from the dead (7:4b). In this way Paul attaches the experience of death to the law to Christ's redemptive work. Paul had earlier set the pattern for this application in Romans 6:3, 7. Death, however, is not a sufficient experience. In order for there to be redemptive purpose in death there must be resurrection; so, identification with Christ in His death must involve identification with Him in His resurrection. Death to the law does have purpose, and this purpose is manifested in life.

The purpose of this experience is that we bear fruit to God (7:4c). The former life produced fruit unto death (7:5). This life was lived in the flesh; this is carnality. This was life fulfilled in the passion of sin, and this is what made it carnal (7:5). This carnality became active through the law (7:5b). This does not mean that the law is sinful or has sinful purposes (cf. 7:7). This carnality was fulfilled through the members of the body by yielding them to bear fruit unto death (7:5c; cf. 6:12-14).

The believer has been released from the law, not by rebellion but by having died to it (7:6a). Release from the law does not destroy the law of God. The law of God cannot be destroyed; this is the reason Paul had to change his analogy earlier. He does not wish to speak of the death of the law, but he does want to show release through death. So, Paul notes here that release is based on spiritual death: "having died to that in which we were held" (7:6b). The result of such a deliverance is that we "serve in the newness of the Spirit and not in the oldness of the letter" (7:6b). The Agent of obedience is the Holy Spirit. Under this form of obedience, the law is not repudiated, and the meaning of the law is not "watered down" to a humanly achievable level. This is only another form of legalism. This newness of the Spirit is the subject of Romans 8; its particulars will be noted there. The "oldness of the letter" is Paul's way of describing the attempt to use the law as a means of fulfilling righteousness.

THE LAW AND MORAL ACCOUNTABILITY
7:7-13

Romans 7:1-6 has dealt with the general principle of our relationship to the law. Now Paul takes up the matter of our personal experience with the law. He does this in an autobiographical way. His purpose is to show how the law works in any life. What Paul says here is universally applicable.

If Paul speaks of the necessity of being released from the law in order to bear fruit to God, one might well ask (as Paul imagines here), "What shall we say, is the law sin?" (7:7a). This is unthinkable, for if the law is sin, there is no standard of morality. So the law is not sin, and it is not evil. The law does define sin and brings out its evil nature as the example of covetousness shows: "I had not known sin except through the law, for I had not known lust unless the law had kept on saying, 'Thou shalt not covet' " (7:7; cf. Exodus 20:17; Deuteronomy 21). The word translated in KJV as "lust" and "covet" means simply *desire*. Here it is used of *wrong desire*, hence the interpretative translations of *lust* and *covet*. It means, in this context, the desire for what is morally forbidden. The law defines and exposes this sinful act and condition.

In the light of this exposure sin became active in all areas of moral corruption: "But when it had taken an opportunity the commandment worked in me all kinds of lust" (7:8). Sin took the occasion of the coming of the law for an occasion to rebel—to lust for the forbidden. Prohibition is not what made sin desirable. Prohibition made sin definable as sin, and showed up the depth of its corruption. This coming of the law renders the sinner without excuse (Romans 3:19). Paul acknowledges that "without the law sin was dead" (7:8b; cf. Romans 5:13). In this statement Paul does not deny the presence of sin. He says that in himself it was not active; it was dead. Verse 9 amplifies this idea.

Of his own moral condition Paul says, "I was alive without the law at one time; but when the commandment came, sin sprang into life" (7:9). When he was not morally aware of the law, he was alive; that is, he did not stand under the condemnation of a violated law. Under these circumstances there was no spiritual death. It seems that Paul has in mind his coming to the age of moral accountability.[8] The commandment came and brought moral awareness. In the context, the commandment referred to is the one under discussion for illustration: "Thou shalt not covet." When Paul (and by application all men) really heard this commandment, "sin sprang into life," or "came back to life." Paul does not say sin originated at this point. The sin that was already there (Romans 5:12-21) sprang into life. It was at this point that Paul said, "I died." By this experience he came to know the nature of divine judgment. He was aware that he was not acceptable to God. The paradox Paul sees here is that the law, which is called "the commandment which is unto life," brought death (7:10). The character of the law is life because it is the law of God, but even the law of God cannot give life (Galatians 3:21). The law can and does define the terms and character of life; so, this description of the law is appropriate.

The paradox is that such a law brings death. It brings death because it exposes the sin that was present when the law came. The law, however, is not the source of death; sin is the source of death: "For sin, when it had taken the opportunity through the commandment and through it deceived me, and through it I died" (7:11). Sin used the coming of the law as the occasion to provoke sinful rejection. Its method was deception. Sin used this encounter with the law to slay Paul.

Paul's assessment of the law is, "The law is holy, and the commandment holy, just [righteous] and good" (7:12). The first statement that the law is holy refers to the law of God in general. The second statement which describes the commandment refers to the particular commandment introduced for illustration. It partakes of the excellence of the entire law. The law is holy as God is holy; God's holiness is the ground of all law. Even the so-called ceremonial laws were designed to enforce God's holiness. The other characteristics of the law (as related to this commandment) are also drawn from divine nature. These are all revelations of God's moral excellence. This is the characteristic of the law that gives it authority.

Sin is the opposite of everything that can be said of the law; so, sin must be shown up for its evil, corrupt and defiling nature. The rhetorical question puts aside the quibble, "Has that which is good become death to me? God forbid" (7:13a). It is impossible to defend any concept of morality if this is true. Sin must be shown to be sinful in a moral sense (as distinct from a *pragmatic sense*)[9]: "But sin, in order that it might be shown up as sin, through that which is good [i.e., the law] worked death in me" (7:13b). In this way sin is shown up to be evil. If it is the occasion of death (the judgment of God and the opposite of all God intended for man), it is very evil. The ultimate aim is to demonstrate "the exceeding sinfulness of sin." Herein is the victory of the law over sin; in this encounter between the commandment and sin, it is sin that is shown up as the culprit. The commandment of God exposes sin in all its offensiveness.

PERSONAL STRUGGLE WITH SIN
7:14-25

Paul confesses that there is a clash between the law of God and his own nature: "For we know that the law is spiritual, but I am carnal sold as a slave to sin" (7:14). When he describes the law as spiritual, he associates the law with its origin in the Holy Spirit (2 Timothy 3:16; it was written by the "finger of God"—Exodus 31:18). It is spiritual in the attributes ascribed to it (holy, just, and good, 7:12). It is spiritual because it is unto life (7:10). Paul's condition is described in terms of its carnality and its bondage. Carnality has been defined by Paul as giving one's members to the desires of the flesh and specifically allowing these appetites to damage the spiritual nature (Romans 6:12-14). To this condition Paul confesses he has been sold as a slave by sin.

To this point in Romans 7 Paul has discussed the principle of release from the law. He has discussed his first awareness of the law and with that his experience of death in condemnation. He has just described his carnality and bondage as a man under condemnation and in his unregenerate state. Beginning with 7:15 there is a change of emphasis. Paul no longer speaks of domination by his carnal nature. The language in the rest of this chapter reflects a renewed nature.

In his renewed conscience Paul is aware of a clash between desire and behavior: "For what I am doing I do not know; for I do not do what I wish, but that which I hate that I do" (7:15). Paul uses the strongest terms to describe his antipathy for sin: "That which I hate I do" (7:15b). There is here a disapproval of sin as sin, not just a despisal of its consequences. The hatred of sin is not a quality of the unregenerate spirit. This is a condition of renewal not a condition of a depraved and unregenerate nature (cf. Romans 3:9-18). Verses 16-20 continue this emphasis on renewal as distinct from depravity. It is especially manifested in Paul's compatible attitude toward the law of God: "If that which I do not wish I do, I agree with the law that it is good" (7:16). The word translated "agree" means to say the same thing. Paul's wish to obey the law is his way of saying the same thing the law said. There is a harmony of consent, but not a harmony of behavior. In this, Paul says about his behavior and the law the same thing the law itself says.

Paul's failures here are not as they were before his conversion to Christ. He does not speak of himself as totally depraved. In that condition sin was dominant over his nature. Here sin does not dominate, but it is in him: "As it is, it is no longer I, myself, who does it, but sin living in me" (7:17). The

"I" and the "sin" are not co-extensive as in the case of unregenerate persons. Sin dwells within, but it is not the totality of his nature. This is not a case of Paul's attempting to blame his sin on a source other than himself. It is a recognition that, though he has been spiritually renewed, there is a remnant of the old nature which troubles the new.

This condition comes from the presence of two natures in Paul. He acknowledges that his flesh cannot produce goodness: "For I know that in me, that is in my flesh, there is no good" (7:18a). There is, however, in Paul's nature a will to do good; but there is not a commensurate ability to do good or knowledge to perform: "To will is present with me, but to do good is not" (7:18b). He confesses he is unable to do the good that he wishes and unable to avoid the behavior that he despises (7:19). If this is the case, the basis of the action is not the renewed nature but the old nature. So Paul can say, "If that which I wish not I do, it is no longer I that does it" (7:20a). In this description of behavior Paul identifies his basic nature as the renewed nature. His renewed nature and his "I" are his true personal nature. He describes the sin which contradicts and oppresses this renewed nature as dwelling in him: "It is no longer I that does it, but sin that dwells in me" (7:20b). Sin does not extend to his whole nature, but dwells in a part of his nature.

Paul conceives of this condition as being a condition in which he has two natures, and he describes these two natures. He describes his dilemma in these words: "I find then the law, that, to me who would do good, evil is present" (7:21 ASV, 1901). The presence of evil exists alongside the will to obey God. Paul says of his will to do good, "I delight in the law of God according to the inward man" (7:22). The phrase "inward man"-(esoanthropon) appears only here and in Ephesians 3:16 where it clearly refers to the renewed inner nature. A similar phrase (ho eso anthropos) appears in 2 Corinthians 4:16 when Paul speaks of the renewing of the inner man. The phrase, though infrequently used in the New Testament, is a description of the renewed inward nature of man. It is not simply a description of the immaterial nature of man. Paul has already shown that the unrenewed spirit of man is evil. The phrase "inward man" stands in contrast to "another law in my members." It is the renewed inward man that delights in the law of God. This is a quality of the spiritual person. The depth of this spirituality for Paul (even under terms of struggle) is shown by his statement "I rejoice together with the law of God." There is a harmony of personal nature with the divine nature as it is revealed in divine law. Where this condition exists, there is obedience to the law without the bondage of legalism.

Paul is still conscious of a contrary law, which he describes as "another law in my members" (7:23a). In the last clause of this verse he defines this law as "the law of sin which is in my members" (7:23c). Paul has throughout Romans 6 and 7 dealt with sin as being operative in the physical body. These appetites (whether existing only in lust or in outward actions) are the instruments of sin. This law wars against the inward man, that is the spiritual nature. It is here called "the law in my mind" (7:23b). The mind is the spiritual center for willing and for obeying. Paul confesses that the law in his members holds him captive: "And I see another law in my members warring against the law of my mind and bringing me into captivity to the law of sin which is in my members" (7:23). This is not a confession that Paul obeys entirely this law or that he does not obey the law of his mind. He is captive in the sense that he is held back from the freedom of obedience that he wishes. This is the struggle described in verses 18-20.

The turmoil of this situation provokes the cry and prayer of 7:24: "O miserable man that I am! Who shall deliver me from the body of this death?" The question and prayer are the prelude to the answer in verse 25. The phrase "the body of this death" (not *"this dead body"*)[10] is to be understood as a reference to the carnal nature which hinders the obedience that Paul desires. It is described in this way because it is the body which in the law of its members brings about death.

The answer to Paul's prayer is expressed in his own shout: "Thanks be to God through our Lord Jesus Christ" (7:25a). This shout is the note of victory carried over into Romans 8. Paul closes this development in his reasoning with a reaffirmation of his dilemma: "With the mind I myself [emphatic] serve the law of God, but in the flesh the law of sin" (7:25b). Paul triumphs in a renewed mind to serve God's law. He still confesses to the troublesomeness of the law in his members. Too much has been made of various arguments over whether this chapter describes the believer at specific points of experience. It seems clear from the exposition above that this is a description of a believers's experience rather than an unbeliever's. No believer should ever assume that because of particular religious experiences (such as sanctification or the baptism of the Holy Spirit) he has passed this struggle up, never to have it return. It is the clear evidence of Romans 8 that God's will is for believers to live in the Spirit. The believer need not and ought not to continue to live in such a dilemma.

CHAPTER FOUR
END NOTES

[1]There are amplifying expressions in Romans 7 and 8 that aid our understanding. These terms are the "motions [affections] of sin" (7:5), the "law of sin" (7:23, 25), the "body of this death" (7:24), the "law of sin and death" (8:2), and the "deeds of the body" (8:13). These are all terms used to define the term "our old man" and "body of sin." R. Hollis Gause, *Living in the Spirit: the Way of Salvation* (Cleveland, TN: Pathway Press, 1980), p. 43.

[2]Murray, op. cit., 1:222.

[3]James Denny, *The Expositor's Greek New Testament: St. Paul's Epistle to the Romans*, W. Robertson Nicoll, ed. (Grand Rapids: Eerdmans, 1961), p. 634.

[4]The basic use of the word "holiness" and its derivatives *(hagiasmos, hagiadzo, and so forth)* is purity, and not separation. *Separation* is indeed associated with the idea of a holy life, but separation is secondary in the consideration of holiness. The primary understanding of that term is cleanness. As such it is applied to both material and immaterial things. In the case of the believer it is applied both to body and spirit.

[5]The Scriptures never allow that sinful man is out from under bondage to God. God makes a claim over Israel's evil and non-covenant neighbors. Though they are enemies of Israel and of God, they are answerable to God for their sins. Notice Amos' accusations of Damascus, Gaza, Tyre, Edom, Ammon and Moab (Amos 1:3-2:3). This is repeated many times among the prophets of Israel and Judah. Paul has shown that gentiles are held accountable to God even if they do not have the law of Moses (Romans 1:18-20; 2:12-16). This is a part of Paul's human analogy. The way men see it, when you are the slave of one man, you have no responsibility to or expectations from another slave holder.

[6]There is no dispensation of law as distinct from the dispensation of grace. In Galatians, Paul makes it clear that the law serves in all ages to bring men to Christ (Galatians 3:19-4:7). In God's order of working, men come to the promise through the agency of the law in the conviction of sin. This need prevails as long as sin is in the world.

[7]It is not Paul's purpose here to discuss the full issue of divorce and remarriage. His purpose is to give an illustration. As an illustration the statement cannot deal with all the regulations that govern adultery, fornication, and remarriage. What is said here is certainly pertinent to the question, but it does not give the complete picture. It is not the purpose of this exposition to deal with this issue; our purpose is to apply the illustration to the question at hand.

[8]It is a mistake to try to establish an "age of accountability" as if in a given year children become answerable for their sins. It is also important to understand that accountability deals with moral awareness and not simply with cognitive awareness of what the law says. An individual may be aware that certain things are commanded, but have no understanding of these commandments as they relate to the individual's relationship to God. It is moral awareness that Paul describes here.

[9]Sin is not evil because it has bad results; to define sin in this way is pragmatic and not moral. Pragmatically defined sin has nothing to do with moral value. It is strictly social. Such a definition does not deal with divine authority. It places authority in the very society where "sin" is being practiced. Such definitions are always variable and situational. The biblical view is that sin is evil because it violates God's nature and his will for the creature. This is the reason for warning that sin must be shown to be evil in the moral sense.

[10]This phrase ("the body of this death") should not be translated "this dead body." It is clear from Paul's description of hindrance that Paul does not consider the carnal nature dead. He does consider it a death-dealing instrument if it is not conquered.

CHAPTER FIVE

THE HOLY SPIRIT AND HOLINESS

ROMANS 8

In developing his theology of the order of salvation, the Apostle Paul has discussed the doctrine of justification. In that provision, God has established the judicial basis on which He deals with sinful man. As we have noted, justification by God requires the believer to live in harmony with God's declaration of him. Justification by faith anticipates holiness of life. It was appropriate that Paul should then discuss the doctrine of sanctification. In Romans 6 Paul discusses the redemptive provision for sanctification and the manner in which the believer appropriates this provision to himself. Romans 7 discusses the believer's relationship to the law and applies that relationship to the achievement of holiness. Chapter 7 impresses us with the dilemma of one who wishes to do good but finds himself torn between two natures: the "law of my members" and the "law of my mind." The chapter closes on a shout of victory as Paul anticipates what he is about to say in Romans 8.

God has made provision for man to be holy. He has made that experience available to him by faith. Any attempt to achieve holiness on any other ground is a violation of the doctrine of grace. As justification is by faith, so is sanctification. The Agent for the fulfillment of holiness in the life of the believer is the Holy Spirit. It is by living in the Holy Spirit—in His power and in His spiritual graces—that holiness is fulfilled in the believer.

In Romans 8 the dilemma expressed in Romans 7:13-25 has been resolved. It is resolved by three principles of life: the freedom from condemnation, the law of the Spirit of life in Christ Jesus, and the spiritual mind.

FREEDOM FROM CONDEMNATION
8:1

On the first of these principles Paul shouts, "There is therefore now no condemnation to them that are in Christ Jesus" (Romans 8:1).[1] The word "condemnation" is a legal term, and it expresses the judgment of God. God's answer to condemnation is justification. In justification, condemnation has been resolved. Paul's observation is that there is no condemnation to them that are in Christ. This is the status of life for those who are in Christ. To be in Christ is to be in Him redemptively. It is to be in the state of redemption (reconciliation). To be in Christ is the estate of commitment to Him so that His estate is our destiny. What God has done for Him, He is doing for those who are in Him. This estate of life is no longer primarily of this world order (with its temporal limits and destiny), but is of the heavenly order (the kingdom of God with its eternal nature and destiny). The judgment which this world order anticipates as occurring at the end of the age has for the person in Christ already occurred. That judgment has been resolved in the forgiveness of sins; so, there is no condemnation.

There is no reason to live under a sense of condemnation because that does not represent our true status. Many believers continue to berate themselves for past sins and for the consequences of those sins. If they do, they do to themselves what God does not do; they condemn themselves when God does not. Other believers condemn themselves for the struggle they have in temptation or for the struggle Paul describes in Romans 7. Again, they are condemning themselves when God does not. Condemnation is not the status of the believer before God. Their status is justification. This provides those who are in Christ with the establishment of peace with God (Romans 5:1). God has provided reconciliation between Himself and the sinner. God did this for us while we were still enemies. Now that we have come to faith in Christ, the assurance is even more profound: "For if, when we were enemies, we were reconciled to God by the death of his Son, much more, being reconciled, we shall be saved by his life" (Romans 5:10).

THE LAW OF THE SPIRIT OF LIFE
8:2-4

The second principle of life is government by the law of the Spirit of life in Christ Jesus (8:2). The term "law" is not used here in the sense of a legal code (whether the law of Moses or the law of one's conscience). This law is the principle of life. It is not a circumscription of behavior but it is the life force of being in Christ Jesus. The life force of being in Christ is the Holy Spirit, who is the Agent of life or Source of life. This is life by the Spirit of Christ and not life in the flesh.

The Holy Spirit is also the Agent of our freedom from the law of sin and death: "For the law of the Spirit of life in Christ Jesus has made me free from the law of sin and death" (8:2). Paul has earlier demonstrated what he means by "freedom." When we were in sin, we were free from righteousness (Romans 6:20). The woman whose husband has died is free from the law of her husband (7:3). In other places, Paul speaks of freedom as opposed to slavery (1 Corinthians 7:21, 22; 12:13). In this case, freedom is established from the law of sin and death. The law of sin and death is the same as the "old man" (6:6), "the body of sin" (6:6), the "motions of sin which were by the law" (7:5), the "sin that dwelleth in me" (7:17, 20), the "law of my members" (7:23), the "law of sin which is in my members" (7:23), the "body of this death" (7:24), and the "law of sin" (7:25). The sum of all of these descriptions is that the law of sin and death is carnality. Paul says that the Holy Spirit has made him free from carnality.[2]

The law was powerless to bring about this freedom (8:3). Nothing could have demonstrated this more graphically than Romans 7. The reason the law could not do this is that it was "weak through the flesh." The instruments for the fulfilling of the law under these terms are the members of the body, which are also the instruments of carnality. If freedom is to come, it must come through a provision not limited by the weaknesses of the flesh. The provision must be divine in origin and application. God's answer to the weakness of the law through the flesh was that "when He had sent His own Son in the likeness of sinful flesh and for sin, to condemn sin in the flesh" (8:3). The main thrust of this statement is to show that God did provide redemptive deliverance through

Jesus Christ His Son. Two subordinate themes of extreme importance are also mentioned. On the first, Christ came in the "likeness of sinful flesh." Christ's manhood was complete; his body was the body of a man. His immaterial nature (soul and spirit) was fully human. The incarnation was real, not simply apparent. The flesh of the incarnation was not sinful; sin is not natural to the human body or to any aspect of human nature. Sin is a foreign element that robs man of the fulness of his humanness. Christ could not have provided redemption from sin if He had come in sinful nature.

On the second theme, Christ came for sin; that is, the reason for His coming was the sin that brought man into bondage. In these points Christ dealt with sin in atonement work. In this coming, Christ judged (condemned) sin in the flesh. His life and death brought the whole life of bondage to the law under condemnation. God condemned the presence of sin in the flesh. God's judgment and Christ's death show God's disapproval of the carnal life.

The application of this redemption is that "the righteousness of the law might be fulfilled in us who walk not according to the flesh but according to the Spirit" (8:4). It is God's will that His law should be fulfilled because it is the revelation of His own holiness. Freedom from the law cannot allow for sin. So God has provided for its fulfillment, but not through the instrumentality of the flesh. He has provided for fulfillment by life in the Holy Spirit. In this way of life the nature of man has been made to conform to the nature of the law by the grace of regeneration (cf. 2 Peter 1:4). The flesh of man has been cleansed from all unrighteousness (1 John 1:7-9). The believer walks in the Spirit. To be filled with the Holy Spirit is to walk in harmony with the nature of the Spirit (Galatians 5:18, 22-25). To walk in the Spirit is to walk in a life indwelt by and which dwells in the Spirit of Christ. It is the character of life that obeys the law by inner harmony of nature and not by circumscription: "I say, in the Spirit be thou walking and the lusts of the flesh you will not fulfill" (Galatians 5:16). To be filled with the Author of the law, the Holy Spirit, is the route of fulfillment without bondage. It is freedom in a yoke and ease under a burden (Matthew 11:28).

THE SPIRITUAL MIND *Leeroy messer* ✓
8:5-11

The third principle of government for the spiritual person is the spiritual mind. Paul begins the statement of this principle by a series of contrasts between the carnal mind and the spiritual mind. The first contrast is, "The one whose being is according to the flesh thinks on [savors] the things of the flesh, and the one whose being is according to the Spirit thinks on the things of the Spirit" (8:5). In Romans 6:16, Paul defined slavery (whether to sin or righteousness) in terms of whom one obeys. Here he defines carnality and spirituality in terms of what one thinks about. We have suggested that the word "think" may be understood in the sense of "to savor." Or it may be understood in terms of being minded toward a goal or a commitment of mind. The second contrast is the outcome or the goal of each of these mindsets: "For the carnal mind is death, but the spiritual mind is life and peace" (8:6). Each has a consummation that fulfills its own nature. The mind of the flesh is death. Death represents the doom awaiting the carnal life and is inherent in the carnal life. The mind that feeds itself on this world order partakes of its condemnation. Such a mind feeds on selfishness, lusts, pride, haughtiness, strife, hatred, covetousness, murder, drunkenness—in all the works of the flesh. The mind that feeds on these things is feeding on death. To set one's mind on worldly things—the things of this world order—is to be damned with the world. The other side of this contrast is the spiritual mind. The mind that feeds on the nature of Christ—love, joy, peace, long-suffering, gentleness, goodness, faith, meekness, temperance—partakes of life. Such a mind partakes of the order and nature of the kingdom of God, and rises above this world order in which it must operate. Its value structure and ambitions of achievement are not of this world order; they are of the eternal order of the kingdom of God. Probably no better description of spiritual thinking appears in Scripture than Philippians 4:8: "Finally, brethren, whatsoever things are true, whatsoever things are honest, whatsoever things are just, whatsoever things are pure, whatsoever things are lovely, whatsoever things are of good report; if there be any virtue, and if there be any praise, think on these things" (*KJV*).

The reason for the respective outcomes of these two minds

is their relationship to the nature of God; Paul concentrates on the relationship of the carnal mind: "Because the carnal mind is hostility toward God, for to the law of God it is not subjected, for neither is it able to be" (8:7). It is not that the carnal mind holds or simply possesses enmity toward God. By its very nature and in its totality it is the essence of hostility toward God. As a result—the inevitable result—it does not come under the law of God. In fact it is not even able to be submissive. Paul has shown this impossibility in Romans 7. Herein lies the radicality of Christian experience. It requires the presence of a new nature as in the new birth (John 3:3-7), and it requires the uprooting of the carnal nature (Hebrews 12:14, 15).[3] The conclusion of Paul is, "those who are in the flesh are not able to please God" (8:8). They are not able to conform to His ways.

The antithesis of being in the flesh is to be in the Spirit: "But you are not in the flesh, but in the Spirit if it is true that the Spirit of God dwells in you; and if anyone does not have the Spirit of Christ, this one is not his" (8:9). Living in the flesh is not the status of believers in Christ. The term "living in the flesh" describes the unregenerate condition. Those who struggle between the two natures of Romans 7:13-25 are not living in the flesh. Some may be so infantile in Christ as to be called "carnal" (1 Corinthians 3:1-3), but they are not given over to disobedience. They do not live in the flesh. The status of believers is that the Spirit of God dwells in them.

In this one sentence (8:9) the Holy Spirit is referred to by three designations: the "Spirit," the "Spirit of God," and the "Spirit of Christ." The indwelling of the Spirit is the promise of our Lord (John 14:15-17, 25-26; 15:26; 16:7-16; Acts 1:4-8). The believing body (the church) is indwelt by the Spirit corporately (1 Corinthians 3:16, 17), and individuals are indwelt by the Holy Spirit (1 Corinthians 6:19, 20). The assurance that we are not in the flesh is that the Spirit of God dwells in us. We are born of the Spirit (John 3:5, 6); we bear the fruit of the Spirit (Galatians 5:22, 23). Sanctification occurs through the agency of the Holy Spirit (Romans 8:2; 2 Thessalonians 2:13; 1 Peter 1:2). The necessity of the presence of the Holy Spirit in us is shown by the statement, "If anyone does not have the Spirit of Christ, this one is not His" (8:9b).[4]

To have the Spirit of Christ is also to be in Christ. The order of Paul's language shows this up: "And if Christ is in you, the body is dead on account of sin and the Spirit is life on account of righteousness" (8:10). The phrase "Christ in you" is the spiritual equivalent of the "Spirit of God dwells in you" (8:9a). The phrase "in Christ" is especially significant in Paul's writings. The Epistle to the Ephesians develops this concept. To be in Christ is to be with Him in heavenly places (Ephesians 1:3); it is to be chosen in Him (Ephesians 1:4); it is to be accepted in Him as the Beloved of God (Ephesians 1:6); it is to be redeemed through His blood (Ephesians 1:7, 8); it is to share His inheritance (Ephesians 1:9-12); it is to be sealed with the Holy Spirit of promise (Ephesians 1:13, 14); it is to be where He is in triumph over all enemies (Ephesians 1:19-23). In the passage before us Paul emphasizes that though the body is dead because of sin (cf. Romans 5:12; 6:23), the Spirit is life because of righteousness. This passage is not dealing with the spiritual principle of the crucifixion of the old nature, but with the fact that the indwelling of the Holy Spirit reverses the results of sin. The death resulting from sin is not only the mortality of the physical body; it is the entire judgment of God which includes the mortality of the body. This passage refers to the death of the body. This is confirmed by the fact that the Holy Spirit is life.

Life in the Holy Spirit produces the resurrection life in the believer: "And if the Spirit of the One who raised Jesus from the dead, dwells in you, the One who raised Christ from the dead shall also quicken your mortal bodies through His Spirit who dwells in you" (8:11). The Holy Spirit has provided life in the full reversal of sin; this includes spiritual life. The emphasis here contrasts with the death of the body; so Paul assures the believer of the resurrection of the body. The assurance is based on redemption through Christ. First, it is based on the resurrection of Christ; He is the firstfruits of them that slept (1 Corinthians 15:20-23). Second, God raised His Son from the dead through the agency of the Holy Spirit (Romans 1:4; Acts 13:33-35). Third, if the personal Spirit whom God used to raise Christ from the dead dwells in us, He will raise us as He did Christ. The presence of the Holy Spirit is the believer's assurance of his own bodily resurrection (cf. 2 Corinthians 5:1-5).

THE SPIRIT OF HOLINESS
8:12-14

By the provision of the gift of the Holy Spirit, God wishes His people to live unique lives. Walking in the Holy Spirit provides two groups of blessings for the believer. The first group of blessings is the Holy Spirit enables and obligates the believer to put to death the deeds of the flesh: "Therefore, brethren, we are not obligated to the flesh to live according to the flesh" (8:12). Redemptively, we have been set free from all such connections to the old way of life; there is no legitimate claim of loyalty to the flesh. To live according to the flesh is to live under the sentence of death: "For, if according to the flesh you live, you are about to die" (8:13a). As Paul has shown earlier, death is inherent to the way of the flesh. Here he speaks of that death as imminent in the way of life. On the other hand, living according to Spirit provides the route for putting to death the deeds of the flesh: "But if in the Spirit you put to death the deeds of the body, you shall live" (8:13b). The expression "deeds of the body" is parallel with Paul's description of carnal living under other terms that we have seen already. Putting to death the deeds of the body occurs by the power of the Holy Spirit. This is the route of being made free from the law of sin and death (8:2). The Holy Spirit is the redemptive Agent for the crucifixion of the old man. To attempt to mortify the deeds of the body by self-will is legalism; it is also a work of the flesh itself. It is futile as well. Though it is not in our power to crucify the old man, it is in our power to commit him to the cross by faith. There Christ will crucify him as He has already done at Calvary (Romans 6:3-7). This connection with atonement requires the application of the atonement by the Holy Spirit. So, it is in the Holy Spirit that the righteousness of the law is fulfilled (8:4). The Spirit forbids our living according to the flesh and joins us to Christ in life. This lifts the plane of living from the earthly to the heavenly. It is appropriate that believers should live on the level to which they have been exalted by grace. It is a logical step for Paul to move from this exhortation to a description of the believer's status as the child of God. Those who are the children of God cannot live by the "spirit that now works in the children of disobedience" (Ephesians 2:1, 2).

The second provision the Holy Spirit offers the believer is assurance that they are the children of God. This assurance comes first in the leadership of the Holy Spirit: "For as many as are led by the Spirit of God, they are the sons of God" (8:14). The spirit of disobedience leads the children of disobedience. The Spirit of God leads the children of God. This evidence of being a child of God rises above the tests so often used by believers: emotional liberty, success or failure, wealth or poverty, illness or health, and a host of other man-made assurances. Neither is this leading an indescribable mystical experience that simply serves as emotional release. One should not even use the experience of speaking in tongues (or other such outward expressions) as evidence of being a child of God. Such experiences as these standing isolated in a disobedient and fruitless life tend simply to confirm existing spiritual conditions even though they may be wrong. This wrong use of these experiences tends to sanction in our minds spiritual shortcomings. It helps us avoid scriptural and spiritual soul search by convincing us that we are acceptable despite our carnality. This provides a slave to the conscience, and we dodge the rebukes and corrections of the word of God.

What, then, is the guidance of the Holy Spirit that assures us that we are the children of God? The Holy Spirit moves us to confess that Jesus is Lord (1 Corinthians 12:3). The Spirit of God is, by name and nature, holy. Therefore, He leads the believer to holiness of life. "The title 'holy,' applied to the Spirit of God, does not only denote that he is Holy in his own nature, but that he makes us so; that he is the great fountain of holiness to his Church; the Spirit from whence flows all the grace and virtue, by which the stains of guilt are cleansed, and we are renewed in all holy dispositions, and again bear the image of our Creator."[5] There is no acceptable definition of holiness except that which is in the Scripture. This definition calls for love and unity both toward God and toward our brethren.

We are to love because God is love (1 John 4:7, 8). As God loved us, we are called to love one another (1 John 4:9-11). If we love one another, God dwells in us and we in Him, because He has given us His Holy Spirit (1 John 4:12, 13). He that dwells in love dwells in God (1 John 4:16). This love

fulfilled casts out fear (1 John 4:18). This is the love of
God that we keep His commandments (1 John 5:2, 3). It
is guidance toward these fulfillments that assures us we are
the children of God. By the nature of our being the children
of God we are led by the Spirit through the chastening of
God which proves our sonship (Hebrews 12:7, 8). He leads us
to partake of His purity (Hebrews 12:10) and yields the
peaceable fruit of righteousness (Hebrews 12:11). If there is
any point at which we are aware of the Spirit's leadership, we
know that we are the children of God. If there is in our heart
a hunger for holiness for life, this it the Spirit's witness that
we are God's child.

THE SPIRIT OF ADOPTION
8:15, 16

The status of which the Spirit witnesses is not one of
servitude, but of sonship: "For you have not received the
spirit of bondage again to fear, but you have received the
Spirit of adoption" (8:15). The spirit that now works in the
children of disobedience is the spirit of bondage (slavery) and
fear, but "God has not given us the spirit of fear, but of
power, and of love, and of a sound mind" (2 Timothy 1:7).
The Spirit is called here the "Spirit of adoption." This term
"adoption" (*wheothesias:* the legal status of being a son contrary
to birth) recognizes that we were not, by nature, children of
God. It is the Holy Spirit who ministers to us this grace. It is
in the Holy Spirit that we cry "Abba, Father" (8:15).[6] The
Spirit invites us, who are children contrary to nature and by
adoption, to come to the Father in the same intimacy in which
His only begotten Son came. It is also significant that the Son
used this address (at least so far as biblical record shows) in
the deepest agony of His prayer life and in the most intimate
of prayers recorded from His lips. These circumstances indicate the height of privilege that the Holy Spirit affords us.

Our adoption is further confirmed by mutual testimony
between our spirit and God's Spirit: "The Spirit himself bears
witness with our spirit that we are the children of God" (8:16).
The Spirit of God knows the deep things of God as the spirit
that is in man knows the heart of man (1 Corinthians 2:10,
11). In a spiritual sense "deep calleth unto deep" (Psalm 42:7)

to give this witness. From out of the deepest recesses of the heart of God to the deepest recesses of the heart of man there comes a call of assurance and a harmony of witness that we are the children of God.

HEIRS OF GOD
8:17-22

Eveline

Jesus is Heir & we are Joint H.

The fulness of the status of our sonship is shown by the fact that we become the heirs of God: "And if we are children, we are also heirs: heirs of God and joint-heirs with Christ, if we suffer together [with Him] in order that we may also be glorified together [with Him]" (8:17). The most intimate inheritance that a child receives—especially an adopted child—is to receive the name of the family. This is especially true in our adoptive relationship with the Father: "Behold what manner of love the Father has given us that we should be called the children of God. And we are!" (1 John 3:1). If God has called us children, then we are children. To bear the name of God is an intimate present identity with what we shall be when Christ returns (1 John 3:2). The bearing of the name of God places us in the inheritance of God. This inheritance is received through Jesus Christ. By virtue of His being the only begotten Son and by virtue of His perfect life, He is sole heir to the Father. But the meaning of His redemption is that He shares His heritage with those who are His brothers and sisters in adoption—those who had no right, either by descendancy or by obedience, to the inheritance. This is the meaning of our being joint-heir with Christ; what was His solely, He shares with us in the kingdom.

This heritage involves the entire redemptive provision: death and glory. In this heritage, there is no glory without suffering. This is the way it was in the provision of redemption; this is the way it is in the inheritance of redemption (Philippians 2:1-11; Philippians 3:9-11). It is unfortunate that believers sometimes treat the suffering as a negative experience only to be endured (and barely tolerated) because it is necessary for the receiving of glory. Christ's cross was His exaltation (John 8:28, 29; 12:32, 33). The Philippian believers looked on their sufferings and glory to be gifts of God's grace (Philippians 1:29). The Apostle Paul was told from the point of his conversion to Christ that he must suffer for Christ's sake:

"But the Lord said to Ananias, 'Go! This man is my chosen instrument to carry my name before the Gentiles and their kings and before the people of Israel. I will show him how much he must suffer for my name.' " (Acts 9:15, 16). Note the extent to which this calling was fulfilled in Paul's life: five times beaten with 39 stripes, three times beaten with rods, stoned, three times shipwrecked, a night and a day in the deep, in perils of waters, robbers, countrymen, heathen, wilderness, the sea, false brothers, in weariness, painfulness, hunger, thirst, fastings, cold, nakedness and the care of the churches (2 Corinthians 11:23-28).

No one should think that suffering is pleasant, but it can be glorious if it goes through the cross on the way to the resurrection. So, the believer learns to rejoice in sufferings (Romans 5:3). Paul understood the burden of suffering and asked God three times to remove his thorn in the flesh. But when Christ said to him, "My grace is sufficient for you, for my power is made perfect in weakness," he could respond with his own words, "Therefore I will boast all the more gladly about my weaknesses, so that Christ's power may rest on me. That is why, for Christ's sake, I delight in weaknesses, in insults, in hardships, in persecutions, in difficulties. For when I am weak, then I am strong" (2 Corinthians 12:8-10, NIV). The real triumph of suffering is that God so masters them that He causes our afflictions to contribute to our glory: "For our light affliction, which is but for a moment, worketh for us a far more exceeding and eternal weight of glory" (2 Corinthians 4:17). Both suffering and glory represent our participation with Christ in the kingdom of God.

The kingdom of God is at hand (Mark 1:15); it is present among us (Luke 17:21: "Behold, the kingdom of God is among you"). The events of the last days are occurring, especially in the outpouring of the Holy Spirit upon all flesh (Joel 2:28-32; Acts 2:14-21). The believer, though still in this world order, is a participant in the kingdom of God. The fulness of the kingdom has not yet come; the believer stands in an anticipatory relationship to the consummation of the kingdom. The Holy Spirit enables the believer to stand in both relationships of the kingdom so that the foretaste becomes participation in the kingdom and guarantee of its fulfillment. Paul applies these relationships to the kingdom to our suffering and glory.

Paul describes the sufferings as taking place "in the present time." This is a technical reference in Paul to describe this present age, this world order. This expression stands in contrast to the age that is to come. It is in this world order that sufferings occur because of the cross. Those who have gone to the cross and have suffered there with Christ suffer the same antipathy from the present time that Christ Himself suffered. This present time is the time of the rejection of Christ and the persecution of those who are His. Suffering for Christ's sake is a part of the kingdom's contradiction and condemnation of the present age. Paul assures us these sufferings are not at all comparable to the glory which the sufferings provide by Christ's grace and the power of the Holy Spirit: "For I account it that the sufferings of this present age are not worthy to be compared to the glory which is about to be recealed to us" (8:18). This is the interpretation which faith places on sufferings ("I reckon that;" "I account it to be;" "I consider that," *NIV*). Notice that faith does not deny that sufferings exist; it does not set as its primary goal the escape from sufferings; it does not imply that sufferings are a result of sin or the weakness of faith. Regardless of how severe sufferings may be, they cannot compare with the glory about to be revealed. The sufferings contribute to the glory (2 Corinthians 4:16-18). The glorification is "about to be revealed." This is the language of imminence and it is the language of the return of Christ and the fulfillment of the kingdom of God.

HEIRS OF THE KINGDOM OF GOD
8:17-22

The presence of the Holy Spirit now, however, means that the glory is already being realized in part. First, the Holy Spirit teaches us through the Word that the whole creation is partner with believers in anticipating the coming of the kingdom of God. The expectation of the creation waits for the manifestation of the sons of God: "For the earnest expectation of the creation waits expectantly for the revelation of the sons of God" (8:19). The term "earnest expectation" offers a word picture of someone waiting with head erect or outstretched.[7] It carries the implication of suspense and anxiety. This expectancy is personified as the attitude of all of creation. The creation intended is defined in verse 20 as that part of creation which had been involuntarily subjected to sin. Fallen men and angels are not intended because their subjection to sin was voluntary. Paul refers to the nonrational creation—earth, heavens, heavenly bodies, beasts, and so forth. All these realms of creation were affected by the fall of man. There is a kind of frustration in their existence in that they have not fulfilled the full purpose God had for them in original creation. The realization of this purpose was tied to man and his holiness, because God placed all under him (Psalm 8; Genesis 1:26, 28-30; 2:19, 20). So, the fall of man had cosmic results, bringing a curse upon all that was subject to man (Genesis 3:14-19). The expectation of the creation is attached to the "revelation of the sons of God." The hope of creation can be fulfilled only when redemption is complete and the sons of God are declared by God. The single event fulfilling this hope is the manifestation of Christ and those who appear with Him in glory (Colossians 3:3, 4; Philippians 3:20, 21; 1 John 3:1-3). The goal of creation and redemption are the same—the revelation of the sons of God. Paul sees redemption as fulfilling the aim of original creation. In these general terms Paul has announced the expectation of creation. He turns now to the "frustration" of creation.

Creation did not realize its full end before the fall, nor did the "sons of God." As a result of the fall they are both in a position of bondage and expectation. In relation to the fall, Paul says the creation was subjected to vanity: "For the creation was subjected to vanity, not willingly, but on account of the One who subjected it in hope" (8:20). The passive voice verb (*was subjected*) shows that the agent of the subjection was not the creature itself. Such a verb was frequently used in Hebrew (and Rabbinic) language to refer to the agency of God. This is Paul's intention here. This is confirmed by the fact that the agent of the subjection of the creation is also the One who subjects it in hope. Even if we attribute the subjection of the universe to the rebellion of Satan or the fall of man, we cannot say that it is in their power to provide the hope that is anticipated in this subjection. The One who subjected the universe to vanity is the One who can provide and fulfill its hope. God has, in fact, placed an element of hope in the curse. The biblical concept of judgment for sin is that God himself is active in the imposition of the curse. If

God is active in the curse, the curse serves His purpose and not the purposes of any creature, not even the rebel. In this order, the curse runs the course that God set for it and has the results which God ordained for it. When God imposed His curse upon mankind and His universe, He did so with a view toward redemption. This is the meaning of the statement that He subjected the creature to vanity in hope. In the curse and in the accursed He placed anticipation of and longing for the lifting of the curse. This interpretation regards the act of God as both a judicial act and a redemptive act. As judicial act the curse represents the sentence of judgment upon man and his environment. As redemptive act it identifies the agent of redemption with the agent of judgment. Since the curse is identified with the fall of man and God's judgment of him, restoration is identified with God's redemption of man and His revelation of His sons in glory and liberty.[8] Paul describes the creation as if it exists under frustration. The word for "vanity" carries the import of "void of truth" or "void of appropriateness." By this description, Paul shows that the cursed condition is not inherent in creation, whether material or immaterial. The present condition is not God's intention for the creation, and it does not show the potential that it has for glory.

The cosmic nature of redemption is promised in Paul's words, "Because the creation itself shall be set free from the bondage of corruption into the liberty of the glory of the children of God" (8:21). The condition of the universe is one of bondage to corruption; that is, it is enslaved to decay, turmoil and violence. Neither man nor his environment is abandoned to this bondage, nor are they destroyed. They are redeemed. "If words means anything, these words of Paul denote not the annihilation of the present material universe on the day of revelation, to be replaced by a universe completely new, but the transformation of the present universe so that it will fulfill the purpose for which God created it."[9] The first aspect of this redemption is to be delivered from the bondage which corruption has brought on: the decay and frustration of purpose. The second aspect of this redemption is to be set free into the freedom of the glory of the children of God. The liberty of redeemed men is the liberty of the whole creation. The glory of God descends upon redeemed man. Man's environment—the creation—shares in this glory and liberty. This is not simply liberty from the bondage of sin; it is the liberty of bearing the glory of God, which is God's purpose for all that He has made.

The effects of the fall of man affect both man and his environment; the Fall is cosmic in its effect. Redemption also affects man and his environment; so, the redemptive plan of God is also cosmic. Both man and the rest of creation join in anticipation of redemption. The sign of this anticipation is in their common groaning under the curse: "For we know that the whole creation groans together and agonizes as in child-birth together until now" (8:22). Both verbs, here, carry two particular ideas. First, there is in the present condition real agony; verses 20 and 21 have described it in terms of frustration. Second, there is a union of this agony throughout the creation. This is a condition of *the present,* that is, the present world order, which is under judgment. These two verbs, the second in particular, also carry the idea of pains of birth. In nature the reality of birth pains is not to be questioned, but there is a higher reality and that is the reward of the birth of a child (John 16:21). Another word picture here is "the winter's cold—the groaning earth gives birth in travail to what has been formed within her."[10] All of creation is together in this agony and in the anticipation of the age to come. The untamedness and viciousness of the beasts, and the fact that one lives off the life of another are witness to the coming mountain of God in which the lion, the bear, and the calf will lie down together, eat straw together like the ox and be led by a little child (Isaiah 11). The present turmoil witnesses to a new heaven and a new earth. The clap of thunder testifies to a clear sky. The earthquake testifies to a stable earth. The raging storm testifies to a world at peace. The raging and destroying flood testifies to the river of life.

THE SPIRIT'S WITNESS OF THE KINGDOM
8:23-27

Man joins this chorus of agony and witness "And not only [they], but we ourselves who have the firstfruit of the Spirit, we—even we—groan within ourselves while we wait expec-tantly [for] for the adoption which is the redemption of the body" (8:23). Redeemed men are already partakers of the age to come because they have the firstfruit of the Spirit. The

Spirit Himself is the firstfruit of the kingdom (2 Corinthians 1:22; 5:2-5; Ephesians 1:13, 14). The Holy Spirit is the Father's gift of the kingdom (Luke 11:13; cf. Matthew 7:11) and our foretaste of its glory.[11] God has implanted in the believer, who still lives in this age with its agony, the very character of the kingdom that is to come.

The receiving of the foretaste of the kingdom to come does not remove the believer from this world order; neither does it remove the agony of corruption from him. In fact, the believer has to live in two world orders: this present age of corruption and decay, and the age to come which is eternal life. This disparity is one aspect of his agony. But this agony is the agony of hope. The Spirit's presence and His message tell us what we are waiting for—the redemption of the body. In this ministry, the Spirit assures us that our present suffering and mortality are witnesses to freedom from suffering and to immortality. Paul uses the evidences of suffering to show that the glory has already been appointed and is already working. It is not necessary for him to appeal to any other evidences of glory for his assurance. Paul is not using the coming glory as "compensation for the suffering; it actually grows out of the suffering. There is an organic relation between the two for the believer as surely as there was for his Lord"[12]

What we earlier called a "frustration" between the two ages, in which the believer lives, is in fact a harmony. The believer's mortality and the firstfruits of the Spirit are a twofold witness of the redemption of the body. It is the witness of the body crying for redemption; it is the witness of the Holy Spirit as the foretaste of redemption. The anticipated glory is represented by two terms in this passage: *adoption* and *redemption*. The first term is used of the Holy Spirit as the "Spirit of adoption" (8:15; cf. Galatians 4:5; Ephesians 1:5). Adoption is also used to describe the believer's relationship with God as His child (8:14-17). Adoption is the present condition, and it looks forward to the "revelation of the sons of God" (8:19) and to the "liberty of the glory of the children of God" (8:21). This inward experience is for the believer the assurance of the resurrection of the body, here called the "redemption of the body."

Suffering and anticipated glory occur in the same body. The body in which travail takes place and in which the firstfruits of the Spirit are placed is the body that is to be raised from the dead. This is the meaning of redemption of the body. The whole person must be redeemed if redemption is to be complete; so, the resurrection of the body is essential to the biblical doctrine of salvation.

Here is evidence of resurrection and redemption that the world cannot understand. Present deterioration testifies to the building up of the inward man and the body of glory (2 Corinthians 4:16-18). Corruption testifies to incorruption. Death is our witness to immortality. God placed all these things upon the earth and its inhabitants in an act of judgment. His continuing judgment testifies to redemption. If He can judge, He can give relief in redemption. As long as the evidences of His judgment are present, they are testimony of His mercy and power to redeem.

We have no way of knowing these things about redemption and the witness to redemption except by the witness of the Holy Spirit. Death in and of itself does not testify to resurrection. So, Paul tells us that "we have been saved by hope" (8:24a). He uses the term "by [in] hope" to describe the manner of life in salvation. We do not live by sight; we do not yet see the new heavens and the new earth; we do not see, nor have we yet experienced the resurrection of the body. We have not even seen the interruption of the process of dying (Psalm 90:9, 10; Hebrews 9:27). God has given believers inward, invisible, and spiritual experiences of salvation: justification, regeneration, adoption, sanctification, the indwelling of the Holy Spirit. These are accomplished facts as shown by the past tense verb used by Paul here: "we have been saved." All these anticipate the fullness of redemption in resurrection. However, there are no proofs of the reality of redemption other than the evidences Paul gives here. There is no sight to confirm the coming of the new heavens and new earth and the attendant liberty of the children of God. The believer is left with a life in hope that has as its evidence for the resurrection the groanings of this present state. This is salvation by hope. Paul explains, "hope that is seen is not hope; for that which a man sees why does he hope?" (8:24b). If this goal of ultimate salvation could be seen, it would not be hope. At the same time, Paul considers that which is seen as temporal and that which is unseen as eternal (2 Corinthians 4:18). It is this hope in the invisible that keeps the believer living in expectancy: "But if we hope for that which we do not yet have, we wait for it patiently" (8:25, *NIV*).

In verse 26 Paul moves to a new level of evidence of the coming freedom of the children of God. This is a continuation of the idea introduced in verse 23, that the Spirit is the firstfruits of the kingdom. An important way in which the Spirit fulfills this function in us is by His work of intercession: "In the same way the Spirit comes to help our infirmity, for we do not know what we should pray as we ought, but the Spirit Himself intercedes for us with unutterable groanings" (8:26).[13] The infirmities of the believer are not simply physical; they are also spiritual. We do not know how we ought to pray; even when we understand the direction in which we should pray, our attempts at prayer are weak and faulty. Paul does not make this observation for rebuke, but as further evidence that in our infirmities we are moving toward the fulfillment of redemption. The role of the Holy Spirit is to come to our side and help us with this infirmity. The word we have translated *comes to help* means to come to the side of someone and lay hold of an obstacle with him. In this way He points us to fulfillment. The way He helps us to pray is a foretaste of our perfect communion with God in the day of the revelation of the sons of God.

The intercession of the Holy Spirit is experienced in *unutterable groanings*. Paul uses essentially the same word for "groanings" here that he used in verse 22 of the groaning of the physical universe, and the same word he used of our groaning for the redemption of the body in verse 23. As the body and the soul are joined in infirmity, they are also joined in the groanings which anticipate full redemption. The groanings in spirit do not originate in the creature, but in the Holy Spirit. God the Holy Spirit is within us providing intercession that takes up where our infirmity leaves us in imperfect prayer. It is appropriate to connect this description of the ministry of the Holy Spirit with Paul's expression of "praying in the Spirit" (1 Corinthians 14:15). Though the origin of this praying is the Holy Spirit, it is experienced in inarticulate utterances on the part of the believer. The description of these prayers as unutterable groanings must be applied to the manner in which they are expressed in the believer's praying. When he cannot say what he wishes or what he ought in prayer, the Holy Spirit helps him in praying by moving him to pray "in the Spirit." Unutterable groanings cannot be the form of communion which God the Holy Spirit has with God the Father and God the Son; His communion with them is perfect and perfectly expressed. So this passage is not dealing with how the Holy Spirit speaks to the Father and the Son. It is dealing with how He moves the believer to speak when his own mind cannot articulate the prayer. He speaks in groanings which cannot be expressed by human language. In such a prayer the believer speaks mysteries in the Spirit and only God understands him (1 Corinthians 14:2); God does understand the believer in this prayer even though the believer's understanding is unfruitful (1 Corinthians 14:14, 15). Even those utterances in tongues that are not interpreted by divine gift are valid as utterances to oneself and to God (1 Corinthians 14:28).[14]

The perfection of the Spirit's intercession is described in verse 27: "The One who searches the heart knows the mind of the Spirit, because He makes intercession for the saints according to the will of God." The Searcher of the heart of man is God (Psalm 139:1, 2; 1 Corinthians 4:5). The Father is especially in view in this statement. As He searches the heart of man (man's deepest nature—1 Corinthians 2:11), He knows the burdens and He hears the groanings, even if these groanings are not audible. They may be the bleeding of a crushed heart, or the ache of a bruised spirit, or the confusion of a bewildered mind. He also knows the mind of the Holy Spirit. There is divine union between the mind of God and the Spirit of God, so that each knows the will and thoughts of the other (1 Corinthians 2:10, 11). So God moves by His Spirit to give intercession; in His intercession for the saints, the Holy Spirit is fulfilling the will of God (John 16:12-15). The Holy Spirit offers intercession for believers (the saints) according to the searching of God. When we do not know our own mind, or the circumstances in which we pray, when we do not know the mind of God (and many times we do not), when we do not know the future (and always, we do not), there is for us an Intercessor who knows all these things because the Spirit knows the mind of God. He makes intercession which is in perfect balance with all the circumstances of our needs. It is not even necessary that we understand what our groanings mean; it is only necessary that God understands them, and He does.

GOD'S PROVISIONS FOR THE BELIEVER
8:28-39

It is a natural transition for Paul to move from an interpretation of our infirmities and the ministry of the Holy Spirit to a listing of God's provisions for us. Paul applies all of these provisions against the background of our infirmities and our life in this world order. The believer is an alien in this world order, and the pattern of life in this world order is inimical to the believer's purpose of existence and prospect for victory. So, the assurances of the believer must come from beyond this world order.

The first assurance Paul gives us is "And we know that God is working all things for good to the ones who love God—to the ones who are the called according to [His] purpose" (8:28).[15] The personal Agent for the fulfilling of this promise is God himself. God is actively involved in the directions and events of this world order. He is governing these things with the intention of providing for the well-being of those who love Him. This is an absolute promise; all things are controlled with this view in mind, and by God. There is a universalism of time in this promise by the use of the present tense: "God is working . . . for good." There is no point in time and there is no extension of time where this promise is not real.

The persons to whom this promise is made are "the ones who love God—the ones called [ordained] by God. These are not two groups, but two ways of describing the believers. They are the ones who groan under their infirmities of body, who do not know how to pray as they ought, and the ones for whom the Holy Spirit makes intercession according to the will of God. The ones who love God are the ones who are joined to Him and are born of Him (1 John 4:16-18). They have been called of God to fulfill His purpose. His purpose is that they be conformed to the image of God's Son (8:29). So the promise is made to those who have not yet achieved their goal of existence, and it is made to them while they are in a world alien to their nature and purpose.

It is important to understand that this promise is not made

on the basis of merit or perfection in any area. The terms of this promise are the grace of God. They are not conditions of merit. The terms of this promise are expressed in the two designations above (the ones who love God—the ones who are called according to His purpose); these are terms of grace. They originate in God. The fulfillment of this promise is an exercise of the sovereignty of God. God exercises authority over evil things as well as good things, and He makes them all the servants of His will. In this way He makes them servants of the saints.

The good that God desires for the believer is that he be conformed to the image of His Son (8:29). In this way Paul establishes the necessity of Christ's redemptive work with the accomplishment of the purposes of grace. Verses 29 and 30 are often the subject of debate because of the Reformation doctrine of predestination. We need not think a creedal use of the word "predestination" is confirmed simply because this same word appears in Scripture. Our understanding of this word must be based on Scripture and not on the form that has been given to the words by creeds and dogmaticians. The Greek noun equivalent to "predestination" does not occur in the New Testament. The verb we translate as "to predestinate" appears in Acts 4:28; Romans 8:29-30; 1 Corinthians 2:7; and Ephesians 1:5, 11. It means to decide before hand (Thayer, p. 541). All of these passages deal with the counsel of God as being eternal, which is consistent with God's nature as infinite and eternal. Acts 4:28 and 1 Corinthians 2:7 deal specifically with God's plan of redemption and kingdom, and do not make even implied applications to individual salvation. Romans 8:29, 30 and Ephesians 1:5, 11 relate God's eternal purpose to the experience of salvation. We should not conclude (as is almost axiomatic in Calvinistic theology) that these statements support a doctrine of salvation by decree. Salvation by decree violates the doctrine of grace in the same way as salvation by works. Salvation by decree is arbitrary; salvation by grace is not. The primary thrust of all these passages is the goal of salvation. The passage before us applies predestination to the goal of our conformity to God's Son. Ephesians 1:5 applies it to our adoption, which is consistent with this passage. Ephesians 1:11 applies it to the fulfillment of God's purpose and the counsel of His will. God established this aim for redemption and the redeemed before the foundation of the world. So

God's goal for our redemption reaches from eternity to eternity. He knew us before the foundation of the world. He established the goal of our existence in His foreknowledge. This is God's will for the nature of man, but it is an especially set goal for the redeemed. The expression "being known by God" is a covenant designation (1 Corinthians 8:3; Galatians 4:9). "When God takes knowledge of people in this special way, He sets His choice upon them. Cf. Amos 3:2; Hosea 13:5."[16] From our temporal perspective this is "foreknowledge," and it cannot be separated from the omniscience of God. In His foreknowledge He appointed the goal of existence in Christ. His appointed goal for the redeemed is for them to be brought to the image of Christ. God has shown us the image of His holiness in the face of Jesus, and it is His will that we come to the "knowledge of the Son of God, unto a perfect man, unto the measure of the stature of the fulness of Christ" (Ephesians 4:13; Colossians 1:28). To represent this aim, Paul refers to Christ as the "firstborn among many brethren." Christ is the only begotten Son, and has the rights of the firstborn. In redemption, God has set the pattern in which He receives many other children as the brothers of the Firstborn. This shows us the intimacy of adoption with its accompanying experiences in grace. Our relationship with God includes adoption, but it also includes the grace by which believers are transformed in the image of Jesus from glory unto glory (2 Corinthians 3:18).

God accomplishes this goal through the experiences of salvation: "The ones whom He foreordained these He also called; and the ones whom He called these He also justified and these, He also glorified" (8:30). The sweep of God's plan of salvation reached from eternity to eternity, beginning in the counsels of God before the foundation of the world and reaching fulfillment in the purposes of God in the fullness of His kingdom and the revelation of the sons of God. So foreordination effects calling; calling effects justification; justification effects glorification. Paul uses past tense verbs in each of these statements, and treats them as accomplished. Some refer to this as the "prophetic past" in the pattern of the Hebrew prophets. The plan of salvation cannot be correctly understood if it is divided into steps, each distinct from the other. Glorification is the aim of justification.[17]

The next assurance Paul offers us is the love of God. He presents this assurance in a series of rhetorical questions. He bases these questions on what he has already established in verses 28-30: "What shall we say, therefore, to these things?" (8:31a). The first question is, "If God be for us, who can be against us?" (8:31b). If God is sovereign from eternity to eternity, and if He has invested in us His foreknowledge and foreordination from eternity past, justification now through His Son, and eternal conformity to His Son, the only question is, "What creature can be against us?" The question has the force of saying, "Who would dare be against us?" The enemy of the child of God challenges the eternal and sovereign God.

The second question deals with the extent to which God has shown His love: "He who did not keep back His own Son, but gave Him on behalf of us all, how will He not also with Him give us all things?" (8:32). This question is similar to Paul's reasoning in Romans 5:10 in which Paul reminds us that even while we were enemies God provided reconciliation. If God would do this for us while we were enemies, what will He do for us now that we are reconciled? The question here advances beyond that. Why would God give the greatest treasure of His heart, which is His own Son (the language is emphatic), and then withhold from those who accept Him any of the lesser treasures of His heart? Compared to God's only begotten Son, streets of gold, gates of pearl, and ivory palaces are mere trinkets. The ministry of angels has no value when compared with the love-value of His Son. The word that describes what God has given us is the word for *grace*. The point of the language is to show that what God has given us is given to us in Christ. God cannot give more than His Son, and in giving Him, God has given everything of temporal or eternal value.

The third question is, "Who will bring charges against God's elected one? God is the justifier" (8:33). God is the One who has established our election and in that our justification; it is rooted in eternity. God is the Judge who has heard the charges against us; when He heard the charges, He forgave them. Who will challenge the Judge of all the earth?

The fourth question is a logical follow up of the third: "Who is he that condemns?" (8:34a). The term "condemns" is the language of the court, and carries the idea of bringing charges that are convicting before the court. The third question anticipates a challenge of our justification from creatures who have no authority before the court. Though they have no right to challenge the judgment of God, they do attempt such challenges. This question anticipates an accusation that has validity in the court. So Paul answers that it is Christ who can offer such an accusation, but He hastens to add qualifiers that show Christ as Intercessor and not as accuser: "[It is] Christ Jesus who died, but rather who has been raised, who is also at the right hand of God, who also makes intercession for us" (8:34b). All of these qualifiers refer to Christ as Redeemer and not as accuser. He dies for us to provide the blood of redemption (cf. Romans 3, 4). Though He died, He has been raised for our justification (Romans 4:25). He is at God's right hand, which shows His acceptance in the presence of the Father. There, He is making intercession and not accusation. If He does not condemn, if He died for us, and if He rose and makes intercession for us, who has the authority to accuse us? Our position is secured by the justifying act of the Father and the interceding work of the Son.

The fifth question is, "Who shall separate us from the love of God?" (8:35a). In filling out the full significance of this question, Paul lists the things that attack the believer and try his faith: "tribulation, calamity, persecution, famine, nakedness, danger or sword" (8:35b). Shall these things separate us from God's love? The answer is "No." He will intensify the list of attackers in verses 38 and 39, and the answer is still "No."

Paul cites Psalm 44:22 to show that these things will come upon us: "For your sake we are being killed the whole day; we have been accounted as sheep destined to be slaughtered" (8:36). In the context of this passage in the psalm, the calamity has come upon the people of God even though they had not forgotten God's name and had not lifted up their hands to foreign gods (Psalm 44:20). So, our being in Christ gives us no immunity to suffering. In fact, it is for the sake of Christ that these things come to believers: "For we who are alive are always being given over to death for Jesus' sake, so that his life may be revealed in our mortal body" (2 Corinthians 4:11). Paul even refers to such suffering as "treasures in earthen vessels" (2 Corinthians 4:7). Our being in Christ is a guarantee of difficulties (2 Timothy 3:12).

Paul's assurance is that victory lies in the midst of these very things that are designed by the enemy to destroy us: "But in all these things we are victorious more than enough through the One who loved us" (8:37). Even after the conquest, there is more than enough strength to conquer again. It would be presumptuous and very dangerous for anyone to think that this strength is in himself (1 Corinthians 10:12). The victory is a victory, not of our determination of stamina, but of God's grace; for we conquer through the One who loved us. Paul's conclusion is, "I am persuaded that . . . [no] creature shall be able to separate us from the love of God which is in Christ" (8:38, 39a). This is a strongly worded assurance. Paul says, "I stand persuaded;" meaning the persuasion comes to him from another (passive voice verb) and it is a present persuasion based on a past event. Then he lists every temporal enemy and every potential enemy: death, life, angels, principalities (the word is used predominantly of evil forces in high places), the things that now exist, the things that are (or may) exist hereafter, strongholds (cf., 2 Corinthians 10:5, "every high thing that exalts itself against God"), depths or any other creature. There are two things these enemies have in common. First, they are creatures. Second, they are temporal. In these same two things the victory of the believers is superior. The love of God is not a creature. It is an attribute of God, the essence of the divine Being ("God is love," 1 John 4:8). The love of God is as God is eternal. After listing all the categories of enemies in verses 38 and 39, Paul concludes with the phrase "nor any other creature." No instrument of time and no creature can separate us from eternal love. The love of God is eternal in His nature. It is eternal as to its origin; this is involved in Paul's words in verses 29-30. It is eternal in the Person through whom it is supremely manifested and given to us—Jesus Christ.

CHAPTER FIVE
END NOTES

[1]The Greek text from which the KJV was translated has the clause "who walk not after the flesh but after the Spirit." The best textual evidence indicates that Romans 8:1 should stop at the point quoted in the text. Virtually all modern translations of this passage treat it this way. So, our comments are based on the short reading given in the copy.

[2]The Wesleyan doctrine of sanctification has correctly identified sanctification as cleansing "from all the pollution of the flesh and spirit" (John Wesley, *Sermons*, "A Call to Backsliders" quoted in *A Compend of Wesley's Theology*, Burtner and Chiles [New York & Nashville: Abingdon Press, 1954], p. 186). The Wesleyans are correct in attributing this experience to the Holy Spirit. It is not correct, however, to confuse the act of sanctification with the baptism of the Holy Spirit. Sanctification is the cleansing and preparation of the heart. The baptism of the Holy Spirit is the filling and anointing of the heart.

[3]Reformation is not radical. It assumes that the first goal of change is the change of behavior. Some even postulate that change of behavior can change character, but it cannot. Reformation still works from the standpoint of the carnal mind. In the assumption of reformation, ethical behavior is a pragmatic judgment. Reformation turns from a socially unacceptable (or nonproductive) form of behavior to a socially acceptable (or productive) form of behavior. Man cannot do anything to give himself a new nature or to take out the root (hence, radical) of bitterness. An act of atonement (redemption) is called for and it must be appropriated by faith.

[4]Pentecostals are often attacked on this passage. Non-Pentecostals understand Pentecostals to say that a believer does not have the Holy Spirit until the experience of speaking in tongues, or the baptism of the Holy Spirit. Though there are isolated instances in which Pentecostal believers have said this, this has never been the statement of Pentecostal doctrine. For clarification we note the following: Romans 8:9 does not refer to the experience that Pentecostals refer to as the baptism of the Holy Spirit. He is the divine Agent of their spiritual experience—their union with Christ. We have been baptized by one Spirit into one body (1 Corinthians 12:13). The baptism of the Holy Spirit (becoming filled with the Spirit) was promised by our Lord to His disciples who accompanied Him to the mountain of Ascension. This promise was initially fulfilled on the Day of Pentecost (Acts 2). Subsequent occurrences of the outpouring of the Holy Spirit recorded in the Book of Acts distinguish between initial faith in Christ and the outpouring of the Holy Spirit. In every instance in which seekers were filled with the Spirit they were identified as believers in Christ prior to the outpouring of the Spirit. For a detailed discussion of this distinction and scriptural evidence see *Living in the Spirit*, R. Hollis Gause (Cleveland, TN: Pathway Press, 1980), pp. 79-87.

[5]Burtner and Chiles, op. cit. p. 92: John Wesley's sermon, "On Grieving the Holy Spirit."

[6]This address of God appears in only three places in Scripture: the prayer of Jesus in Gethsemane (Mark 14:36), in Galatians 4:6 and here. The word "Abba" is an intimate and informal Aramaic word normally used by children in the home. Jesus broke tradition when he used the term in addressing God in prayer. Such intimacy would have been interpreted as sacrilegious in traditional Judaism. The Christian believers in using this prayer-address of the Father are certainly following the precedent set by Jesus Christ, the only begotten Son of the Father.

[7]Thayer, p. 62.

[8]Certain philosophic idea (humanism and materialistic evolution particularly) deal with curse as a product of either society or the organisms that struggle with limitation and violence. The idea of a curse placed by God for moral evil has no real place in this view. The language of sin and curse may be used, but only in a mythological or didactic sense. The moral order in this view is strictly pragmatic, either socially or mechanically. Such a moral order can offer no hope. It can speculate about hope and can offer certain trajectories (some real and some imaginary). It can offer no hope because the source of the "curse" is also the source of the problem. No redemption can be anticipated under these circumstances.

[9]Bruce, op. cit., p. 170.

[10]William F. Arndt and F. Wilbur Gingrich, *A Greek-English Lexicon of the New Testament* (Chicago: University of Chicago Press, 1952), p. 801.

[11]The word "firstfruits" is used of the firstfruits of harvest, which is a token and pledge

of the full harvest. In the Old Testament this word (or its Hebrew equivalent) is applied to the first portion of dough from which the sacred loaves were baked (Numbers 15:19-21). In the New Testament it is applied to Christ as the Firstfruits of the resurrection (1 Corinthians 15:20, 23). Paul speaks of the household of Stephanas as the firstfruits of his labor in Achaia (1 Corinthians 16:15). The one-hundred and forty-four thousand of Israel are referred to as firstfruits (Revelation 14:4; cf. Romans 11:16). The word in sue becomes the equivalent of the word "earnest" as a sampling and pledge of future fulfillment (2 Corinthians 1:22).

[12]Bruce, op. cit., p. 169.

[13]The intercessory work of the Holy Spirit should not be confused with the intercessory work of Christ. Christ's role as Intercessor is that of a priest, the high Priest. His work of intercession is an intervention against the judgment which has been satisfied by the offering that He has made. He stands in place of the sinner who does not have personal access to God and offers gifts and sacrifices on his behalf. The site of His intercession is heaven. The role of the Holy Spirit as Intercessor is that of a helper in prayer. He prays with and in the believer, helping him in his praying. The site of His praying is the heart of the believer.

[14]There is a view (sometimes heard even in Pentecostal circles) that such a use of speaking in tongues or unutterable groanings is an evidence of immaturity. Nothing in the Scriptures supports this view; it certainly has no place in this context and in 1 Corinthians 14. The restrictions that Paul places on speaking in tongues (1 Corinthians 14) are for the sake of order. The disorder of the Corinthians was the product of their immaturity. These regulations are in place because of this disorder, not because the experience is an exercise in immaturity. In this context prayer in the Holy Spirit is an evidence of infirmity, but it is the infirmity that belongs to this age. It is also infirmity that testifies to the age to come.

[15]The text as translated above has greater ancient textual support than the KJV "we know that all things work together for good . . ." The promise is not an impersonal thing that implies that circumstances are themselves good. This is a promise of personal government by God over all the circumstances of our lives.

[16]Bruce, op. cit., p. 177.

[17]Distinctions of definition and order of experience are made in Scripture, but these distinctions must not be allowed to fragment the plan and application of redemption. "Justification anticipates and requires holiness of life. Regeneration by the Spirit anticipates living in the Spirit, who is the Begetter of the new life. Adoption anticipates the life of a son of God in the Spirit of adoption who is both witness of sonship and intercessor for God's children.

"As the pinnacle of the mountain is distinct from the path leading to it, the baptism of the Holy Spirit is distinct from those experiences which anticipate it. On the other hand as the pinnacle and the mountain are integral to each other, all the prior experiences are bound up in the life in the Holy Spirit." Gause, op. cit., "Introduction."

CHAPTER SIX

ISRAEL AND GRACE

ROMANS 9-11

Chapters 9-11 are designed to show that the principles of grace set forth in Romans 1-8 are not only applicable to individual salvation, but also to the entire covenant relationship. It is not possible to separate individual salvation from covenant provisions. Neither is it possible to imagine that God provides New Testament salvation in a way different from Old Testament salvation. Salvation is one in all ages, and for all races. God deals with Israel as He does with gentiles. This is not something new; this has always been God's role in relation to Israel and redemption.

PAUL'S COMPASSION FOR ISRAEL
9:1-3

At the beginning of this section Paul expresses his own intense burden for Israel. The intensity of his zeal for his own nation presses him to words that are virtually like an oath: "I am speaking the truth in Christ. I am not lying, my conscience bearing me witness in the Holy Spirit" (9:1). He calls to witness His relationship to Christ, for it is a person in Christ by faith and redemptively that He speaks. Christ's relationship to truth (the incarnation of truth) is an appropriate witness of one's speech. The second witness is His own conscience: his moral sensitivity in his inner nature. Certainly one ought not to speak on any issue (especially concerning his burden in Christ) except in such clarity of conscience. The third witness is the Holy Spirit, who is the guard of his conscience. The Spirit as the Spirit of truth is also an appropriate witness of Paul's words.

The burden of Paul is stated in the most intense of terms: "I have great sorrow and endless pain in my heart" (9:2).

Paul, as befits his Hebrew upbringing, speaks of his entire inner nature when he speaks of his heart. His entire immaterial nature (soul and spirit) is the seat of mind, emotions and will. Paul expressed the depths of his sorrow by an impossible wish. He knew that it was impossible, but he could say honestly, "I could wish that I myself could be damned from Christ for the sake of my brethren, my kinsmen according to the flesh" (9:3).[1] The closest biblical parallel with this prayer is Moses' plea, "But now please forgive their sins—but if not, then blot me out of the book which you have written" (Exodus 32:32, *NIV*). The Apostle takes pain to show that this wish is on behalf of ethnic Israel by the expression "my kinsmen according to the flesh." He does not imagine fleshly descent from Abraham saves or has any merit (9:6). However, it is drawn to his own nation by such deep love that he would lay down his live and salvation for their salvation (cf. 1 John 4:11). There is no need for Paul to defend himself against the charge that he loved Israel more than he did the nations to whom he had been sent as an apostle. One cannot read 2 Corinthians 11:16-33, Philippians 1:12-26, and 1 Thessalonians 2:1-12 without realizing how deeply Paul loved the Gentiles.

This expression of desire for Israel provided Paul a springboard to give a list of benefits which had come to Israel as the ones to whom God revealed Himself. We should observe that the order of revelation and salvation established in Romans 1:16 is to the Jew first, and then to the gentile. This is also the order of judgment (Romans 2:9, 10). Since Paul has already established these principles, he shows us two things. First, there is no respect of persons (or nations) with God. Second, these blessings are not intended to terminate on Israel.

Paul had raised the question of advantage in 3:1. There he responded to his own question by giving only the advantage of having received the oracles of God (3:2). Here he extends the list to show the great spiritual benefits that accrued to Israel as the covenant people. The fact that he lists here only spiritual benefits shows that he does not consider being an Israelite according to the flesh, to be a substitute for grace.[2] We will look at the advantages in the order of their listing. The first is *the adoption* (Romans 8:15, 23). Israel is called God's son (Exodus 4:22). The nation is corporately joined to the King-Messiah who is also called God's Son (Psalm 2:6, 7;

Isaiah 9:6, 7). The second advantage is *the glory.* The glory of the Lord is the manifestation of His holiness upon His people; this shows them to be His people (Deuteronomy 7:6; 14:1, 2). This was visibly represented by the Shekinah.

The third advantage is *the covenants.* The plural here recognizes the several covenant renewals that had occurred in Israel's history (Abraham, Isaac, Jacob, Moses, David, and others). He thinks specifically of the fulfillment of covenant in Jesus Christ (Galatians 3:14-29).

The fourth advantage is the *giving of the law,* which Paul explained in Romans 3:1-4. It is more fully explained in Galatians 3:15-4:6. The fifth advantage is *the service.* The term is used in the sense of the service of God, as in worship. It is doing the work of God. The same word is used in John 16:2, Romans 12:1, and Hebrews 9:1, 6.

The sixth advantage is *the promises.* The promises are the content of the gospel, which began to be spoken in the Old Testament and was preached before to Abraham (Galatians 3:8, 16-18). Note also the divine power of the "exceeding great and precious promises" by which we are made "partakers of the godly nature" (2 Peter 1:4). The seventh advantage is *the fathers*: the patriarchs. The heritage of the fathers (especially Abraham, Isaac, and Jacob) provided not only the content of the gospel, but the personages of the promises for Israel's heritage.

The climax of this list of advantages for Israel is the greatest advantage and the highest privilege that the covenant people could have: "and out of whom is Christ according to the flesh, who is God over all blessed forever, Amen" (9:5).[3] It is a fundamental point of New Testament theology that Christ be in the flesh because He must be produced of human lineage. He is the Seed of Abraham (Galatians 3:16). Israel is the fleshly line of ancestry (Romans 1:3; note also the gospel genealogies Matthew 1:1-16 and Luke 3:23-38). This One who came in the flesh is also "God of all, eternally blessed." As God over all, He is Creator and Sovereign (John 1:1, 14 and 18; Colossians 1:16; 2:9; Philippians 2:5-11 and Hebrews 1:1-3). Christ is not only called God in this verse, He is also worshiped as God. The doxology is a reflection of Psalm 41:13 (cf. Romans 1:25).

Paul moves directly into a discussion of the nature of Israel according to promise. He has shown the advantages that belonged to Israel in her ethnic history. Now, he moves to show that the real issue of being "Israel" is spiritual and not physical. The Israel of grace cannot be identified according to the fleshly descendants of Abraham (9:5, 6). This does not mean the word of God has failed. The strength of 9:6a is an exclamation: "But it is not possible that the word of God has failed."[4] This exclamation seems to reflect Paul's statement in Romans 3:2, 3 where he notes that though Israel received the oracles of God, some did not believe. The word of God has not failed if some do not believe.

The fact is "all of those who are out of Israel are not Israel" (9:6b; cf. 9:7; 2:28). The identity of Israel is according to promise. Paul strengthens this emphasis with the statement, "Nor because they are his descendants are they all Abraham's children" (9:7a, *NIV*). Paul's appeal for authority is to the promise made to Abraham and Sarah in Genesis 21:12, "In Isaac shall thy seed be called" (9:7b). The word for "shall be called" is the ground of Paul's doctrine of election. The seed of Abraham is the seed of promise according to God's call and appointment. In Galatians 3:16, Paul interprets this seed to be Jesus. Other inheritors are in the promise because they are in Him. To enforce the spirituality of the identity of seed, Paul explains, "The children of the flesh: these are not the children of promise" (9:8). In God's providence Isaac eliminates Ishmael because Ishmael was not born of promise, but of a default of faith (Genesis 16; Genesis 21:12 is a specific rejection of Ishmael). Ishmael was born out of a vain plan of Abraham and Sarah to help God fulfill His promise. Isaac also eliminated Esau. As the prophet of God and as the patriarch, Isaac placed the blessing on Jacob (Genesis 27:27-29). He refused to withdraw this blessing, even when he realized he had been deceived about the identity of Jacob. The reason is he was aware that he had spoken the oracle of God. The speech itself bestowed the blessing, and Isaac could not withdraw it (Genesis 27:33-37). In this utterance he confirmed what God had said earlier to Rebecca (Genesis 25:23; 9:12, 13). One should also compare Galatians 4:22-31.

The promise of God produces the seed; they are, therefore, called the "children of the promise" (9:8). The one who makes children the seed of promise is not the human begetter of the children, but the divine Author of the promise: "For this is the word of promise, 'According to this time, I will come to you and Sarah shall have a son.' " (9:9; Genesis 18:9-14). In the Genesis setting, the Speaker is the Angel of Jehovah, who is the Lord himself. He is the One who comes and fulfills the promise (cf. Romans 4:16-25). This promise was given to Abraham and Sarah at a point in life when they had no natural prospect for a child.

The same relationship of word of God and heirs of promise was carried down to Isaac and Rebecca. Paul explains that when Rebecca had conceived, the promise was placed on Jacob. The conception was natural by Isaac, but the child was the seed of Abraham by promise. The promise was placed upon Jacob (the younger) by divine oracle before the birth of the children (9:11-13). The promise was also placed before the children had done either good or evil. The purpose of this order is "that God's purpose for election might stand" (9:11). This is the positive side of the promise; it places the determination of the mercy of God in God and His sovereignty. This order is a rejection of all the devices of the flesh: "that it should not be of works" (9:11b). For Paul, the term "works" includes any devices originating in man, whether works of the law or the "merit" of ethnic birth. The promise and its fulfillment is "of Him that calls" (9:11b). The God who gives the promise of sonship is also the One who accounts descendants to be children of the promise. In describing the descent of the promise through the patriarch, Paul is showing that there is (and must be) a rejection of merit in covenant, as there is in individual salvation. Conversely, there is a necessity of grace in covenant as there is in individual salvation.[5]

The oracle of election is here quoted from Genesis 25:23: "It was said unto her, 'The greater [elder] shall serve the lesser [younger]' " (9:12). The one who speaks is the One who gave the promise. He is the One who calls and shows mercy. Clearly, Paul takes this to be divine Word. This prophecy was fulfilled in Jacob's receiving the blessing, which was intended to be the passage of the birthright to him (cf. Genesis 27:28, 29). Though there is no biblical record of Esau's having been Jacob's servant, the prediction was fulfilled in the histories of the two peoples (2 Samuel 8:14; 1 Kings 22:47; and 2 Kings 14:7). In this turning of the blessing to the younger, God is setting aside another man-made custom. Men had set the custom of favoring the eldest son, but God would not bind the transfer of covenant by human traditions. In a figure, God set the "law" aside before the giving of the law.

GOD'S PROMISE AND GOD'S SOVEREIGNTY
9:13-21

Paul enforces this prediction by a quotation from Malachi 1:2, 3: "Just as it is written, Jacob have I loved, but Esau have I hated" (9:13). Any interpretation of this passage must be guarded by certain important considerations. First, Paul does not say that God said this before Jacob and Esau were born. There is no record of this statement in Genesis. Second, this is a prophetic (oracular—Malachi 1:1) utterance concerning Esau and Jacob after their nations had demonstrated their character. These are judicial statements and are based on the persons being judged as having done good or evil. The judgment of God is to love the faithful, and to judge the unfaithful (cf. Malachi 1:3-5 for God's judgments upon Edom). The statement is an application of the oracle of election. " 'Love' here means 'prefer'; 'hate' means 'reject' or 'love less' " (9:14-21).[6] The first question is, "What shall we say, 'Is not God unjust?' God forbid!" (9:14). Paul's answer is an appeal to what is morally right and wrong. If there is unrighteousness with God, there is no basis for moral judgment. There is no such thing as wrong. Paul appeals to another quotation from Scripture: "For he says to Moses, 'I will have mercy on whom I will have mercy, and I will have compassion on whom I will have compassion' " (9:15; Exodus 33:19). The statement was originally given in the context of Moses' request to see the Lord. God declared His sovereignty over the revelation of His face and applied the same sovereignty over the gift of His mercy. The knowing of God and being known of God are both acts of grace. So none can earn either. A benefit earned cannot be a work of grace, and it cannot be called a gift. The statement is in the form of a Hebrew parallelism; so, we should not go to extremes to distinguish between mercy and compassion. They are two ways of saying the same thing.[7] The reason for this is that the mercy of God remains an act of grace and is not a product of merit; "therefore, it is not of him who wills, neither of him who runs, but of God who shows mercy" (9:16; cf. John 1:12, 13; and Ephesians 2:8).

God's relationship with evil men and nations is always one of sovereignty and justice. Pharaoh is an example: "For the Scripture says to Pharaoh that for this very purpose I raised you up so that I might show in you my power and so that my name might be announced in all the earth" (9:17).[8] From this statement, it is clear that evil men arise under terms of the sovereignty of God, and they serve His purpose. In them God demonstrates His power, and His name is glorified in the course of their lives and the fulfillment of their judgment. In raising up evil men, God does not stop them from doing evil and being evil. He controls their evil in such a way as to cause the wrath of man to praise him (Psalm 76:10). When God triumphs over evil and demonstrates that evil men serve Him, His name is glorified. There is no man who is not a servant of God. Some men are reconciled servants of God. They serve Him under terms of redemption. Others (as Pharaoh) are unreconciled servants of God. They serve him under terms of judgment. God's name is proclaimed in glory throughout the earth when this is demonstrated. In the fulfillment of these purposes God remains the Author of both mercy and judgment: "Therefore, whom He wills He has mercy upon; whom He wills He hardens" (9:18).

This statement and the reasoning that preceded it, provoke the second question: "You will say to me, 'Why, therefore, am I still being blamed, for who has withstood His will?' " (9:19). This question attempts to make God the author of the sins of those who glorify Him even in their evil deeds. It reasons that if none can resist God's will, they cannot be accused of sin as if their sin is what God willed. The difficulty here is that it destroys the basis of its own argument. If God works the way this question presupposes, there is no good or evil. The antagonist destroys the bases of his own argument.

Paul answers the question in verses 20 and 21. The first step in the answer is to say the question is presumptuous: "On the contrary, Oh man, who are you—the one that contradicts God?" (9:20a). The contrast is between "man" (creature) and "God" (Creator). Can the creature "talk back to" the Creator? Paul continues the question: "Can the molded [as a clay pot] say to the molder [as a potter], 'Why have you made me this way?' Or does not the potter have power over the clay to make one vessel for honor and another vessel for dishonor?"

(9:20b, 21). Paul asks this question in such a way as to prompt a positive answer, "Of course he does!" The terms "honor" and "dishonor" are practical use terms to serve the illustration. It is a false application of this statement to say God creates some men for redemption and others for damnation.

VESSELS OF WRATH AND VESSELS OF GLORY
9:22-29

Paul applies these lessons to God's purpose in making His mercy known to those who are chosen according to grace (9:22-29). God uses the "vessels of wrath" to show His wrath, to make His power known, and to show the riches of His glory. Judgment is a demonstration of the wrath of God. It is a false notion that looks upon wrath as it is in God as beneath the dignity of God and as destructive of His love.[9]

God's judgments also make His power known. Few events in history more dramatically displayed God's power than the events in Egypt. These judgments upon the Egyptians show how divine power is perceived among the obstinate only when God intervenes against the disobedient and all the things they consider powerful. It is significant that the plagues in Egypt attacked the very things the Egyptians worshiped as their gods. Such obstinate men will not see the power of God in His dealings with those who comply with His will; the evil men will despise their submissiveness. But when God conquers the rebel and shows the bankruptcy of all of his power structures, none can doubt His power.

In this same demonstration, God also chose to show His mercy even upon the vessels of wrath; He "bore with much longsuffering the vessels of wrath" (9:22). As a case in point, who among men had such dramatic demonstrations of power as Pharaoh and the Egyptians? Whoever has as many reprieves from judgment upon the promise of compliance as did Pharaoh, and who has as sorry a record of default on his "repentance" as Pharaoh? Pharaoh is a demonstration of God's patience and mercy. God's attitude toward evil men and nations is not immediate and merciless destruction, but patience. If one doubts that let him ask why the world was not torn apart and hell filled up the day men murdered Jesus, the Son of God? The forbearance of God in relation to the vessels of wrath also demonstrates the power of God. Such men are called "vessels of wrath fitted for destruction" (9:22). Here Paul is making the term "vessels of wrath" parallel with his illustrative use of "vessels of dishonor" (9:21). They were prepared (perfect passive participle) for their destiny by their rebellion under terms of God's mercy and judgment. The judgment to which they moved in life was being built up by the sinfulness of their ways (Romans 6:21-23; cf. Romans 2:5 which speaks of storing up wrath to the day of wrath). The predominate use of the word "destruction" (*apoleian*) in the New Testament is of final judgment or perdition. These people are by the pattern of their lives being prepared for hell.

In contrast, God shows the riches of His glory in the vessels of glory. His glory is the manifestation of His nature upon those who trust Him; it is further manifested in the destiny for which He prepares them. Everything that God does shows His glory; judgment, long-suffering, mercy, mighty acts, and so forth. The emphasis here is that the vessels of glory are those in whom the nature of God is being manifested. It is also appropriate that they should be called "vessels of mercy," because they have their position in the mercy of God. They also stand in parallel with Paul's illustration as "vessels unto honor" (9:21). The glory now being manifested in the vessels of mercy is the glory to which they move and for which they are being prepared; they are called "vessels of mercy which He [God] has prepared beforehand unto glory" (9:23). God has prepared them for this destiny, so their lives are an anticipation of the final glory to which they move in the grace of God.[10] He makes them vessels of glory in order that they might be inheritors of everlasting glory.

God's calling of the vessels of glory is according to grace and not merit or race. Here they stand in contrast to the vessels of destruction, who earn their destiny. Their destiny is described as the wages of their lives (Romans 6:23). In verse 24 Paul turns to the use of the first personal pronoun "us" to describe those who are called: "Even us whom He [God] called not only out of the Jews but also out of the Gentiles" (9:24). This is actually the climax of the question Paul began in verse 22. Paul is here describing the whole company of those who are called of God to be vessels of glory, who also show up the power and glory of God in contrast with the vessels of wrath. The purpose of the extension of this description is to show that the remnant (vessels of mercy) is drawn from among both Jews and gentiles. This is confirmed in the prophecy of Hosea 1:10 and 2:23. Paul applies this prophecy especially to the gentiles and their salvation. The promise is, "I will call the one who is not my people my people" (9:25a). Those who by God are called His people are His people. God's call does not depend on fleshly descendancy. Covenant relationship is established and carried out by the call of God. The promise continues to affirm the personal relationship established by God in His call: "I will call the one who is not beloved, beloved" (9:25b). In Hebrew literature the terms "beloved" and "chosen" (elected) run together; they become virtually interchangeable.[11] The term "beloved" is used in this passage as in interpretation of calling or election. It is also used to bring in the personal quality of the love of God for the elected. We are not dealing with cold decree, but with the extension of the heart of God.

The promise of God has the effect of transforming those who are not God's children into His children: "And it shall be that in the place where it was said to them, 'You are not my people,' there they shall be called the sons of the living God" (9:26; Hosea 1:10). This prophecy was originally addressed to Israel and Judah. Israel in particular is being confronted with her sins (1:6, 7). So, this prophecy is addressed to them when they were alienated from God—so much alienated as to be called foreign. They are likened to the children of Gomer ("children of unfaithfulness," 1:2), who bore children of her adulteries while married to Hosea, the prophet of God. One of those sons was named "Lo-Ammi," which means "not my people" (1:8, 9). This represents the rejection of Israel with the drastic result that they can no longer claim to be God's people. In the same place where they were rejected, however, they will be received again and God will say to them, "You are the sons of the living God" (1:10). God's decree of judgment had made them "Lo-Ammi,"—not my people. His decree of mercy will make them "Ammi,"—my people. This decree is effective for Jew and gentile.

From Isaiah, Paul makes an application of prophecy to Israel's redemption on the basis of remnant identity, not merely national identity: "And Isaiah cries on behalf of Israel,

'If the number of the sons of Israel be as the sand of the sea, the remnant shall be saved' " (9:27; Isaiah 10:22). To have such a numerous seed was promised to Abraham (Genesis 22:17; 32:12). Abraham's children became presumptuous on the physical number and identity; they assumed that their population was the fulfillment of divine promise. But God said, "the remnant shall be saved." The definite article indicates a specific identity of the group that is to be called "the remnant." By this principle of the remnant, God separates between the Israel of flesh and the Israel of faith. God has always worked by the principle of the remnant (Isaiah 6:8-13). This is God's rejection of the human value systems which identify divine blessings with man-made standards of merit. By applying Isaiah 10:23 as he does, Paul brings this fulfillment into an eschatological realm: "For the Lord will carry out his sentence on earth with speed and finality" (9:28, *NIV*). The term translated "sentence" is the Greek word *logos*. God's judgment is His word. Here it is referred to as being brought to its completion swiftly; these are the terms of the last days. The salvation of the remnant is God's judgment on the non-remnant. The background of Isaiah's prophecy is that a part of Israel will go into captivity and a remnant will return. This is divine judgment, and it stands as a type of the great day of God's judgment.

The salvation of the remnant is God's mercy to Israel by which He preserves the people: "Unless the Lord of Sabaoth had left us a seed, we would have become like Sodom and we would have been like Gomorrah" (9:29; Isaiah 1:9). The divine title "Lord Sabaoth" (Lord of hosts) appears only here and in James 5:4 in the New Testament. It has its background in many Old Testament passages (translated in the KJV with "Lord of hosts"). The Lord is regarded as leader of the armies of heaven (cf. 1 Chronicles 17:24; Psalm 24:10; 46:7, 8 and many other passages). In Paul's quote, it is virtually a transliteration of the Hebrew. Paul interprets the preservation of the remnant as an act of divine mercy. The remnant is saved by the Lord's defense of His people. The remnant is a product of divine intervention. If it had not been for this intervention the fate of Israel would have been the same as the fate of Sodom and Gomorrah. The cities of Sodom and Gomorrah are used as examples in evil and as examples in total destruction (Genesis 18:16—19:29).

Israel's failure is related to the issue of faith and works. The paradox presented in this failure is that gentiles entered into righteousness instead of Israel: "What shall we say, then? The gentiles—the ones who were not seeking righteousness—have received righteousness: The righteousness of faith" (9:30). What Paul is expressing here is the conclusion of his reasoning in 9:1-29. Clearly Paul means here the gentiles, as racially distinct from Jews. They were not seekers after righteousness. Paul has shown that they are no better than the Jews (Romans 1:18—2:16; 3:9). Salvation comes to those who are known by God (Galatians 4:9). We love God because He first loved us (1 John 4:19). Paul makes a specific application of this truth in Romans 10:20 (cf. Isaiah 65:1). They received righteousness, but it was not the righteousness of human effort or the law; it was the righteousness of faith. The righteousness of faith is the subject of Romans 3:19—5:11 (note especially 3:21, 22; 4:11, 13). This is the essential righteousness of justification.

The other side of the paradox is that the Jews did not receive righteousness: "But Israel, seeking a righteousness of law, did not attain to the law" (9:31). The assumption of any seeking after righteousness is that it is humanly achievable (cf. Mark 10:17-22). The charge Paul brings against Israel is that they attempted to establish their own righteousness—the righteousness of their own achievements guided by the law (Romans 10:3; 2:17—3:9). The reason for the failure is that they did not seek out of faith, but out of works (9:32). They sought works and not a gift. The difference between the expectancy of faith and the expectancy of works is that faith acknowledges the bankruptcy of man. In faith, man is a supplicant and a believer. In works man is a bargainer attempting to trade value for value. Israel misunderstood three essential issues. First, they did not perceive their own inability in relation to obedience. Second, they did not take into account the necessity of absolute perfection as the standard of the law (Galatians 3:10). Third, they did not understand the purpose and limits of the law—that it could not and was not intended to give life (Galatians 2:16; 3:21-25).

With these misunderstandings, the Savior himself was a stumbling stone for Israel: "They stumbled at the stone of offense, just as it is written, 'Behold, I place in Zion a Stone of offense, and a rock of stumbling, and the one who believes on

Him shall not be disappointed in his hope' " (9:32b, 33; Isaiah 8:14). The New Testament writers consistently use this Old Testament passage and this figure of speech of Jesus Christ (cf. 1 Peter 2:6-8, which also appeals to Psalm 118:22; Luke 20:17, 18. Cf. also Daniel 2:34, 44, 45). In this statement, Paul comes to Israel's encounter with, and rejection of Christ. The prophecy of Isaiah recognizes that the Lord is the sanctuary of believing Israel (Isaiah 8:13, 14), but for unbelieving Israel He is the snare. Paul adds to this quotation another designed to interpret his statement (Isaiah 28:16).

This stone is placed by the act of God. It is set in Zion, for it is the city of salvation and judgment (Romans 11:26, 27; cf. Isaiah 59:20, 21). The Lord sets this stone as a snare; this is the significance of the word "offense." There are many aspects of Christ's appearance and redemption that were snares to Israel (1 Corinthians 1:18-31; 1 Corinthians 2:6-16). Paul speaks here on one aspect of the snare; it is the issue of faith. The very thing Israel rejected, Paul assures them and all that it will not fail: "The one who believes on Him will not be disappointed in his hope" (9:33b). The stumbling stone is also a saving stone. Faith in Him will not come to nothing.

In 10:1 and 2, Paul expresses again his desire for Israel (cf. Romans 9:1-3). Here his expression deals more with Paul's sense of pleasure in the prospect of the salvation of Israel. He speaks of the "good pleasure of his heart" (10:1). His entire inner nature, in fact his whole being, yearns for this pleasure. It is the provocation of his prayer that Israel be saved. Paul's role as an intercessor for those who do not know the Lord is alluded to. The specific petition of this prayer is for Israel according to the flesh, and for their salvation. The assumption of the prayer is that those who do not believe are lost.

The pity of their lostness is that these people have a "zeal of God, but not according to knowledge" (10:2). Paul himself could bear witness to this kind of zeal. He had seen it among his associates prior to his conversion. More importantly, he had seen it in himself more than in others (Galatians 1:13, 14; Philippians 3:4-6). His assessment of this condition was that he was the "chief" of sinners (1 Timothy 1:15). The flaw in this kind of zeal is that it is not according to knowledge. The fact that it is well-intentioned zeal does not make it saving, and it does not keep the zeal from becoming corrupt and evil all in the name of a good purpose. The word Paul uses for knowledge is consistently used to refer to knowledge revealed by God.[12] It is this special knowledge in which they were lacking. The result is that they were ignorant of the righteousness of God (10:3a). For Paul the "righteousness of God" is the same as the "righteousness of faith." In the absence of this saving knowledge, the Jews substituted their own wisdom and attempted to establish their own righteousness (10:3b). This is morally damnable: "and seeking to establish their own righteousness, they have not submitted themselves to the righteousness of God" (10:3). In this statement we are to understand that "their own righteousness" is the same as the "righteousness of the law." Their righteousness became a substitute for the righteousness of God. As long as they had this sense of self-sufficiency, they stubbornly resisted the righteousness of God. The word which stands behind "have not submitted themselves to" is an accurate description of Jewish haughtiness. They would not subject themselves to God's offer of salvation by gift.

The righteousness of God is provided in the fact that "the end of the law is Christ for righteousness to everyone who believes" (10:4). The Greek term for "end" may be used to mean perfection, fulfillment (goal), or termination. The meaning of the term in this statement would seem to be fulfillment. Christ said of His mission that He had come to fulfill the law and the prophets (Matthew 5:17). Christ has fulfilled the law in His righteous life and in His obedient death in which He met the judgment of God. This explanation combines both the idea of perfection and fulfillment.[13] The reason for His work in the fulfillment of law is to provide righteousness for those who believe in Him. The very law in which men have miserably failed, and will continue to fail, is the standard of righteousness. In this point of failure Christ offers righteousness, which matches the perfection of the law, but which is not based on man's works. The result is that the "righteousness of the law might be fulfilled in us who walk not after the flesh but after the Spirit" (Romans 8:3; cf. 2 Corinthians 3:7-18).[14] This is the issue involved in the acceptance of Christ. It is either the attempt to establish your own righteousness or it is submission to the righteousness of Christ, which is a complete demonstration of the righteousness of God (Romans 3:21-26; 1 Corinthians 1:30). The instrument of receiving this righteousness is faith, which is where Paul began in Romans 1:16, 17.

THE RIGHTEOUSNESS OF THE LAW AND THE RIGHTEOUSNESS OF FAITH
10:5-13

In order to introduce the character of faith and the word of faith, Paul appeals to Moses: "Moses describes in this way the righteousness that is by the law: 'The man who does these things will live by them' " (10:5; Leviticus 18:5). In the original setting of this statement, Moses describes the way of life prescribed for Israel. This way of life distinguished Israel from Egypt (from which they had been delivered) and from the neighboring tribes in Canaan. The way of the law is the way of life. Paul's application of this principle shows up the necessity of perfect obedience under terms of the law. Righteousness which is according to the law can allow no interruption of obedience; it can allow no flaw in obedience.[15] The failure of Israel is that they divorced this concept of obedience from the provisions of grace. They assumed what the Old Testament never did—that a man can achieve life by his own discipline and perfect obedience to the law (cf. also Galatians 3:11, 12). It should be clear that holiness of life is not legalistic. Legalism is the assumption that one can achieve salvation by personal acquire; the person who does this demands of himself perfect and perpetual obedience to every jot and tittle of the law.

Over against this system of life, Paul offers and describes the word of faith. Paul personifies the righteousness of faith and ascribes the words of Deuteronomy 30:12-14 to faith. It is not strange that Paul should treat the Old Testament passage in this way. In biblical understanding the word of God and the person of God are inseparable. The Word is described as the Person of God, as having the attributes of God, as doing the works of God and as being worshiped (Psalm 56:4, 10; 105:19; 107:20; 119:50, 140; 138:2; 147:15-19; 148:8). Moses' purpose in the original setting was to assure Israel that the Word of the Lord was present with them. Paul is making the same application to the presence of the word of faith. Paul makes a specific New Testament application of this passage by relating this passage to the incarnation and resurrection of

Christ. As Moses could say to Israel, Paul can now say, "Do not say in your heart, 'Who shall ascend into heaven?' that is to bring Christ down, or, 'Who shall descend into the abyss?' that is to bring Christ up out of the dead" (10:6, 7; Deuteronomy 30:12-14).[16] Then as now, faith does not become involved in quibbles about the presence of the Lord simply because He is not visibly among us. In the question, "Who shall ascend?" Paul is responding to those who raise questions about the coming of Christ in the flesh. The question is in essence a denial of the incarnation; they are still asking the question, "Who will bring Christ down from heaven to us?" John identifies this question as being the essence of antichrist (1 John 4:3). The second question was a question about the resurrection: "Who shall descend into the grave?"[17] This is the unbelieving question that denies the resurrection of Christ. It treats the physical absence of Christ as proof that he did not rise from the dead. If this be the case, the word of faith is a farce (1 Corinthians 15:12-18). Both of these questions represent the antagonistic questions of skeptics. They raise questions that strike at the essence of the Christian faith.

Paul's answer to these unbelievers is Moses' answer to the skeptics in his day: "The word is near you, in your mouth and in your heart" (10:8). Paul's answer is the same because the questions are essentially the same. Moses deals with the essential spirituality of the word of the Lord; its presence in Israel was not primarily the presence of the stone tablets. The Word was spiritually upon the mouths and in the hearts of the faithful; this is consistent with other Old Testament concepts of the presence of the Word (Psalm 19:7-14; 119:11). Paul is ascribing the same intimate presence of the word of faith. By the parallelism between "mouth" and "heart" Paul (and Moses) embrace the entirety of man. Paul is also preparing for the necessity of belief in the heart and confession of the mouth in verses 9-13. We must caution, however, that Paul does not intend to fragment man as if word and heart could be disparate. There is assumption of unity of inward commitment and outward speech. We should note that Paul uses the word *rhema* in this quotation and in verses 17 and 18 for the term "word." This term emphasizes the word as "that which is or has been uttered by living voice."[18] The term fits this context because of the personification of the word of faith as a speaking entity in the ears and hearts of believers.

Paul calls this message of Christ's coming in the flesh and His being raised from the dead the "word of faith which we preach that if you confess in your mouth Jesus is Lord, and believe in your heart that God raised Him from the dead, you shall be saved"(10:8b, 9). The word of faith and the word of proclamation are one and the same.[19] As Paul notes later in this passage the "word of proclamation" is saving word. The word which is proclaimed is the word that is to be confessed and believed. The Greek word for confess means "to say the same thing as another."[20] It is a responsive word; the confession responds to the proclamation with "Amen." Confession, as Paul speaks of it here, is a reflection of an ancient creed of the church: "Jesus is Lord" (cf. 1 Corinthians 12:3; Philippians 2:11). In this confession, the earthly name of Jesus is combined with the divine title of Lord. Paul intends to identify the Object of faith by the name of the Redeemer in His historical appearance and in His title of deity. In this way he drives faith and proclamation back to the historical Jesus. Jesus did not become Lord in the resurrection; in his pre-crucifixion and pre-resurrection history He was Lord and is still so identified. This is the confession. It is also important to know that the confession is not merely creedal. The Object of faith is a Person, the Lord Jesus. Saving faith is a personal relationship, not simply an intellectual persuasion.

This personal relationship is shown up by the nature of belief in the heart. The heart is not used here to refer to emotions alone; it stands for all of man's spiritual awareness: mind, emotions, and will. This is the area in which saving faith occurs. James is careful to show the ineffectual nature of intellectual commitment standing alone (James 2:19). The belief of the heart is in exact agreement with the confession of the mouth: "that God raised Him from the dead." Though Jesus is Lord prior to the resurrection, the resurrection is treated as God's vindication of His Son, and as the great enthronement act for the Son (Acts 13:39; Romans 1:4; Psalm 2:7; 1 Corinthians 15:20-28). To believe God has raised Jesus from the dead is to believe He is Lord. In this way heart and tongue agree; confession and faith are identical.

In this order proclamation, confession, and faith in the heart are one. The Christ who has come in the flesh and has been raised from the dead is the Christ of the gospel. Faith in

Him as He is so presented is saving faith. So, Paul assures the believer that whoever believes shall be saved (10:9). In verse 10, Paul summarizes this formula: "For in the heart one believes unto righteousness and with the mouth confession is made unto salvation." Paul does not intend to set up a two-step order of religious experience. Heart and mouth affirm one confession, and this confession is saving. Faith is the persuasion of the inward nature of man. Confession is faith made verbal. The product of this faith is the "righteousness of faith." As Paul has developed his various designations of righteousness, the righteousness of faith is the righteousness of God (Romans 4:13) and the righteousness of the law fulfilled in those who walk not after the flesh but after the Spirit (Romans 8:4). Paul appeals to Scripture again: "For the Scripture says, 'Everyone who believes on him shall not be put to shame'" (10:11; Isaiah 28:16; Romans 9:33).

In this appeal to Scripture, Paul emphasizes the universalism of this provision; it is for everyone who believes.[21] Paul extends this universal provision to another application: "For there is no difference between Jew and Greek, for He is Lord of all, rich unto all that call upon Him." (10:12). Paul has earlier pressed the point that there is no difference between Jews and Greeks (Romans 3:22). In this context, he pressed the point that as there is no difference in their being sinners, there is no difference in the offer of salvation. In this context he makes the point that there is no difference, because the Lord whom we confess is Lord of all. The antecedent of "He" in verse 12 is the "Lord Jesus" ("Jesus is Lord") in verse 9. The Lord whom we confess is now designated as Lord of Jews and Greeks (cf. Romans 9:5). The thrust of Romans 9 is that unreconciled men and nations (or noncovenant) and reconciled men and nations (or covenant) are servants of God. The lost are servants even in their lostness. The result of this universal lordship emphasized here is that as Lord of all, Jesus is rich to all who call on Him. The universality of His mercy depends on the universality of His authority. The riches of Christ are proportional to the scope of His sovereignty. He is rich enough in mercy to provide salvation to all those who call on Him (Ephesians 1:7). There is no depth of unworthiness that His mercy cannot reach.

In the clause "unto all those who call on Him," Paul moves

into an eschatological reference. In confirmation of his claim and as a signal of the eschatological reference, the Apostle appeals to Joel 2:32: "For everyone who calls on the name of the Lord shall be saved" (10:13). The understanding that they were living in the last days had been with the disciples of the Lord since the days of John the Baptist (Matthew 3:1-3); Jesus emphasized the presence of the kingdom (Matthew 4:12-17; Luke 17:21—"The kingdom of God is among you"). Peter used the Joel passage to interpret the outpouring of the Holy Spirit as an event of the last days (Acts 2:16-21). The climax of Peter's quotation is the verse from Joel that Paul cites here. The context in Joel shows that the promise is to be saved from the "great and terrible day of the Lord" which will be marked by wonders in heaven and earth, the sun turned into darkness and the moon into blood (Joel 2:31, 32). Paul spoke of being justified in the present time (literally the "now time" which is an eschatological reference, Romans 3:26). He spoke of other benefits in this same reference to the last days (Romans 8:18; 11:5). To be saved is to be saved now from the wrath of God which is to come in the last days. In the scheme of God the New Testament believers are living on the threshold of the great and terrible day of the Lord. But the threshold for the believer is also the threshold of salvation (Romans 13:11). The confidence offered here is that the danger of the Lord's wrath is absolved in faith. This is the confidence in which the believer lives. He lives as one delivered from the day of the Lord's wrath. His faith will prevail when the believer stands before the judgment seat of Christ, and we all shall (Romans 14:10; 2 Corinthians 5:10; Hebrews 9:27). This statement also shows that the pattern of faith in the earthly life is the pattern of faith in the day of judgment. The day of judgment is the supreme moment of calling on the Name of the Lord. Let none approach this day as if he merited that Name or its salvation (Matthew 7:21-23), or as if he did not need that Name (Acts 4:12). The Name on whom the believer calls is the name which has been confessed: "Jesus is Lord" (10:9). The Name of the Lord which has prevailed in mortal life is the deliverance in the Day of Judgment.

THE WORD OF FAITH
10:14-21

Paul has shown the relationship between proclamation, faith, and confession. With verse 14, he turns to the vital question of the hearing of the Word. In this section, he shows that the word of proclamation is not designed out of human brilliance, that the authority to proclaim it does not rest in man's authority, and that the power of this word does not rest in man (cf. also 1 Corinthians 2:1-5). He does this by a series of questions all strung together in verses 14 and 15.[22] The first question is, "How shall they call upon one whom they have not believed?" (10:14a). This is an important commentary on what Paul means by calling on the name of the Lord. "The original Hebrew [of Joel 2:32] means, not simply 'make appeal to Yahweh,' 'invoke Yahweh,' but implies that the Israelite, in so doing, places himself on Yahweh's side, professes allegiance to Yahweh, and so for Paul, the words mean 'to profess oneself a Christian. ' "[23] To call on the name of the Lord is a confessional statement. Such requires believing. This raises the second question: "And how shall they believe One of whom they have not heard?" (10:14b). Paul has shown this faith has a specific content (Christ has come and He has been raised from the dead, 10:5-10). Paul's question here shows that men must know Christ as revealed in Scripture if saving faith is to be born. The third question logically follows: "How shall they hear without one who proclaims?" (10:14c). We have noted earlier the sense of authority in the word *kerusso* (to proclaim; to preach; cf. 10:8). Paul intends this question to raise the question of authority of message and messenger. His next question raises these issues: "And how shall they preach unless they have been commissioned?" (10:15a). The word which we have translated "commissioned" is related to the word "apostle." The New Testament uses these words to refer to the bestowal of authority to carry a message. The message carried has the authority of the commissioner (not the commissioned). Note Christ's commissioning of the apostles (John 20:21, 22) and the Holy Spirit's commissioning of Barnabas and Saul (Acts 13:2, 3).

These questions climax in the citation of Isaiah 52:7: "Even as it is written, 'How beautiful are the feet of those who preach good things!'" (10:15a; cf. Nahum 1:15 and Ephesians

6:15). The setting in the original Isaiah passage is a description of the one who comes bearing the good news of restoration from Babylonian captivity (Isaiah 52:1-12). There the proclaimer proclaims peace, good tidings, and salvation. The promise transcends the promise of deliverance and restoration after Babylonian captivity, and looks to the restoration of all things in the appearance of the Messiah. The messenger of such news is pictured as running swiftly, and as having taken on the beauty of his message; his feet are thus characterized as beautiful because of his mission. Paul sees this prophecy as being fulfilled in Christ's coming. So he describes the preacher of Jesus Christ as God's messenger for the last days (cf. 1 Corinthians 4:9). Paul does not cite the Isaiah passage exactly, but adapts it to his own application. He also sees the messenger transformed into the same beauty of the message that he brings. His word for beauty emphasizes the grace of movement. The message of preaching is described by two important elements in this statement. First, he uses the word *euangelidzomai* which may be translated "I announce good news." By the time of the writing of Romans this word had become a special word in New Testament literature and in the preching of the early Christian community. It was the equivalent of the gospel of Christ. So, Paul is speaking about the proclamation of the gospel. The second element here is the term "good things." This term (*ta agatha*) means the good things of the messianic age. Mary sang, "He has filled the hungry with good things" (Luke 1:53). Jesus said that the Father knows how to give good things to His children (Matthew 7:11). In Luke 11:13, these good things include the gift of the Holy Spirit, who is God's gift for the last days. Christ is the High Priest of the good things to come (Hebrews 9:11) and the law is a shadow of the good things to come (Hebrews 10:1).[24] In the light of this evidence we may say that Paul says the proclaimer is preaching the message of the last days and the good things of the kingdom which have been and are being given. This is the kingdom promised through the prophets of Israel.

What has been said above is very important for the point Paul is about to make: "But all have not obeyed the gospel" (10:16a). Paul states this in sharp contrast with what he has just said. It seems a strange twist of words to talk about obeying the gospel, but the offer of faith (and the righteousness of faith) does represent a moral obligation. Calling on the name of the Lord (10:13) is the moral obligation of every man. The record of Israel in Paul's day was a repeat of Israel's record in Isaiah's day: "For Isaiah asks, 'Lord, who has believed our report?' " (10:16b; Isaiah 53:1). John placed the same assessment on the response of the multitudes to Jesus' ministry (John 12:37, 38). The setting in Isaiah is his prophetic description of the Messiah (the suffering Servant). The disbelief is the historical precipitation of His suffering.

The statement of Israel's rejection prompts Paul to define again the origin of faith: "Consequently, faith comes from hearing and hearing is through the word of Christ" (10:17). Faith has a specific cognitive content. Paul has defined that earlier (10:9). Saving faith cannot be defined as the intellectual ability to believe; neither can it be defined as a nebulous belief in a "higher power," or the "power of prayer." Saving faith arises out of the message of Christ; faith comes through the word of Christ. Paul continues to use the word *rhema* as the utterance of Christ. That which is proclaimed in the gospel is Christ's act of speech in and through the church. Murray offers a comment that is appropriate here (though he is speaking of verses 14 and 15): "A striking feature of this clause is that Christ is represented as being heard in the gospel when proclaimed by the sent messengers. The implication is that Christ speaks in the gospel proclamation."[25] This is the only word that has in it the power to create faith in Christ. As the word of command is the word of enablement, the word of Christ is the word of faith. The proclamation produces the faith.

Israel's disbelief raises the question whether they have heard: "But I say, 'Have they not heard?' Indeed!" (10:18a). Throughout this discussion Paul is talking about the situation of Israel's hearing. He is not discussing the revelation of God to the gentiles. So the answer he gives from Psalm 19:4 applies this Old Testament passage to Israel. The entire series of quotations are applied to Israel and her disbelief.[26] The answer to the question whether Israel has heard is that the revelation has gone into all the world: "Into all the earth their word has gone out, and into the boundaries of the world" (10:18b). Under these circumstances, it is clear that Israel has heard. Their sin is inexcusable, though it is pardonable in grace.

Paul sees in this situation in Israel a reflection of her history all the way back to Moses. His conclusion from his citation of Psalm 19:4 is that Israel did know: "But I say, 'Did Israel not know?' " (10:19a). His intention by the question is to say Israel did know. He enforces this conclusion with his quotation of Deuteronomy 32:21: "I will provoke you to jealousy by those who are not a people (in other words, not a covenant people; cf. Romans 9:25, 26; Hosea 2:23; 1:10); by a people without understanding, I will anger you" (10:19b). In his address in Deuteronomy, the setting is similar to this. Israel had provoked God with idolatry: "They made me jealous by what is no god and angered me with their worthless idols" (Deuteronomy 32:21a, *NIV*). God promised to punish this sin with a similar provocation of Israel—the covenant nation provoked by non-covenant people. Now in relation to the word of Christ, Israel has done the same thing, and God is punishing it with the same kind of provocation of Israel. In this, Paul is anticipating what he will say in deatil in Romans 11. Isaiah's ministry met with the same kind of unbelief: "And in boldness Isaiah says, 'I was found by those who were not seeking me, and I became visible to those who were not asking for me" (10:20; Isaiah 65:1). Isaiah is representing God as speaking in the first person, and these words represent His judgment of Judah. It is His description of Israel's refusal to hear and see. The nation that prided itself in knowing and approving the will of God is a non-hearing, non-seeing and non-obeying people. On the other hand, the response of gentile nations to the revelation of God is to hear and see. They are considered to be non-seeking and non-seeing peoples. This is a commentary on Paul's use of Deuteronomy 32:21. When Israel sees the blessings of the covenant inherited by people whom they consider to be non-covenant, they will realize their forfeiture.

Paul continued his quotation of Isaiah to show how deep this provocation of God was: "And He says to Israel, 'All day long I have reached out my hands to disobeying and rebelling people' " (10:21; Isaiah 65:2). God is still speaking in the first person. This utterance graphically describes the constancy of God's mercy; extended even during long periods of disobedience. By this selection of passages from the Old Testament, Paul shows such rejection of divine revelation had been a pattern in Israel. Their rejection of Christ is consistent with their history (Cf. Acts 7 where Stephen describes Israel's history in the same way).

THE REMNANT OF ISRAEL
11:1-10

Romans 10 closes on a dismal note. Israel is described as a nation who has continually rejected the outstretched hand of divine mercy. Over against this picture, Paul now offers the comfort that God will fulfill His purpose. He also assures us that God's purpose involves Israel according to the flesh.

In his familiar style, the Apostle asks, "Has God driven His people away? God forbid!" (11:1). Paul asks the question in such a way as to show that it requires a negative answer; so his "God forbid" is given for emphasis. It is the strongest way that he could say, "No!" Paul has constantly assured us that this is not the case (Romans 3:4, 6, 31; 6:2, 15; 7:7, 13; 9:14).[27] This also reflects Old Testament assurances. Though Samuel rebuked the people for their sins (especially their desire for a king and accompanying sins), he assured them that God had not and would not cast off His people (1 Samuel 12:22). This promise is inherent in the promise to David that God would preserve his throne and his descendants forever (2 Samuel 7:11-16).

In proof of this statement, Paul offers himself: "For I myself am an Israelite, of the seed of Abraham, of the tribe of Benjamin: (11:1b). The term *Israelite* is used consistently to refer to Israel according to the flesh. Paul is emphatic in his statement, especially as he refers to himself. He calls attention to the aristocracy of his lineage—of the tribe of Benjamin (Philippians 3:5). Paul's primary interest is to show that he is proof that God has not rejected Israel; he is an example of the remnant concept he introduced in Romans 9:27. Paul can say with the psalmist, "God has not driven away his people whom He foreknew" (11:2; Psalm 94:14; Paul does not quote this passage, but he translates the promise to a fulfillment statement). The clause "whom He foreknew" appeals to the covenant God established and placed upon Isaac when he existed only in divine promise (9:6-9), and which He passed on to Jacob while he was still in the womb (9:10-13).

Even in the times of greatest discouragement for the faithful, God has preserved a remnant according to grace. The example Paul cites from the Old Testament was the seven thousand who had not bowed the knee to Baal in Elijah's day. The Scripture (and not Elijah, the discouraged prophet) is the authority of appeal: "Or do you not know what the Scripture says in Elijah?" (11:2). "In Elijah" has the effect of saying "in the case of Elijah."[28] This is characteristic of rabbinic expression. The reference is to 1 Kings 19:10-18. The prophet's prayer is a complaint against Israel: "Lord, they have killed your prophets and they have demolished your altars; and I alone am left, and they are seeking my life" (11:3). The full prayer in 1 Kings 19:10, 14 charges Israel with rejecting the covenant, breaking down the altars and killing the prophets. Elijah assumed he was the only one left who had not compromised with Jezebel, Ahab, and the worshipers of Baal. The mistake he made was to assume that all others had compromised simply because they had not opposed Baalism in the same way he had. The implication in Elijah's complaint is that if the Lord lets the enemies get by with this plan, this is the end of the line for the covenant.

God was quick to rebuke this presumption: "But the oracle of God says to him, 'I have reserved for myself seven thousand men; these have not bowed the knee to Baal'" (11:4; 1 Kings 19:18). Paul personifies the "oracle of God" here. This term is used in the New Testament only here. It is a word designed to refer to divine speech. The verb form of this word is used in most occurrences in the New Testament to refer to revelation by God (Matthew 2:12, 22; Luke 2:26; Acts 10:22; Hebrews 8:5; 11:7; 12:25). This statement serves Paul's argument perfectly. The speech of God is treated as the very presence of God, which is true to the biblical concept of God's voice. The oracle is pictured as speaking in the first person: "I have reserved to myself . . ." Those who had not bowed the knee to Baal had been kept by God's grace to them. They could not boast in their standing.

Paul applies this lesson to the present time: "Even at this present time, there is a remnant chosen according to grace" (11:5). The term "this present time" (literally, "the now time") places this fulfillment among the events of the last days. The preservation of the remnant is God's eschatological work. This work of God culminates in the salvation of the remnant represented by the 144,000 in Revelation 7:1-8 and 14:1-5. This period is marked by division in Israel (Luke 12:49-53; John 7:40-44). In the period of the New Testament, some embraced Christ publicly; others as Nicodemus and Joseph of Arimithea kept their discipleship quiet, while remaining faithful to the tenets and patterns of spiritual practice under the old covenant.

The term "remnant" is a term of grace because it represents

a disavowal of the peril of fleshly descendancy from Abraham. Paul is quick to point out that the remnant is according to grace and this excludes any appeal to merit: "and if by grace, [it is] no longer by works; otherwise grace is no longer grace" (11:6). Paul has shown that works and grace are mutually exclusive; there can be no mixture without destroying the character of grace. This is the principle Paul expressed in Romans 4:1-5 and 9:10-13. The fulfillment of God's purpose must be His and His alone. This reasoning also forbids any Israelite from claiming an inheritance among the remnant on the basis of blood-line (John 1:13).

This calls on Paul to explain the position of non-remnant Israelites. In the eyes of the Scripture unbelieving Israelites are non-covenant Israelites: "What then? That which Israel sought diligently, this she did not attain; but the elect (according to grace) has attained, and the rest were hardened" (11:7). Paul has shown that Israel's zeal for the law and its righteousness was intense (Romans 10:2). He has also shown that they sought their goal wrongly; so they failed to receive the promise. Those who did receive the promise received it as promise and gift; they did not seek it by works or lineage (Romans 10:20). The rest were hardened. Paul's use of the passive voice verb is designed to indicate that God is the Agent of their being hardened. This is a judicial hardening in which God uses the sinful determination of men to bring judgment on them. The same thing was observed in God's judgment of the gentiles (Romans 1:21-32). Now unbelieving Israel is being judged in the same manner as the gentiles. This judgment is confirmed in Scripture: "Just as it is written, 'God gave them a spirit of stupor, eyes that they should not see, and ears that they should not hear even until this very day'" (11:8). The Apostle has taken portions of Deuteronomy 29:3, 4 and Isaiah 29:10 and woven them into a single interpretive statement.[29] Under divine judgment their obstinacy in refusing to see and hear produced insensitive minds, dull eyes, and deaf ears. In the Isaiah passage the prophets themselves are the instruments of their not seeing and hearing. Paul climaxes his indictment with a citation from David: "And David says, 'Let their table become a snare and a trap and a stumbling stone and a retribution to them. Their eyes have been darkened that they should not see, and their back always bowed down'" (11:10; Psalm 69:22, 23; 35:8). The incongruity of all the judgments cited here is that the very instruments of seeing, hearing, and understanding are the instruments of blindness, deafness, and ignorance. The constancy of this judgment is especially reflected in the last statement—"their back always bowed down."

God's purpose in the call of Abraham was that in him all the nations of the earth would be blessed (Genesis 12:3; Galatians 3:8). Throughout Old Testament history, God brought the non-covenant peoples into saving contact with Himself through the ministry of Israel. A mixed multitude left Egypt with Israel; though they were the origin of many of Israel's spiritual problems, they were ultimately absorbed into the nation (Exodus 12:38). Rahab and her family were taken into the nation of Israel (Joshua 6:17-25), and she included in the people of faith (Hebrews 11:31; James 2:25). Ruth the Moabitess became ancestress of David and the Messiah (Ruth 4:16-22; Matthew 1:5). Jonah took God's message of repentance to Nineveh (Jonah 3). The period of the 70 years in captivity offers many examples of Israel's ministry to her captors; note particularly Daniel, Ezra, and Nehemiah. On the occasion of the birth of our Lord, God extends the revelation of His birth to men of the Far East (Matthew 2:1-12). God intended to bless the nations by His covenant with Abraham. The covenant was not a covenant of exclusion of the gentiles; it was a covenant of inclusion.

THE BLESSING OF THE NATIONS
11:11-16

Even though Paul had begun this section of Romans with assurance of salvation of the remnant, he also showed that Israel had sinned and had been judged by God. Now, he faces the question that some may raise; whether Israel has been utterly rejected: "I say, therefore, 'Did they stumble in order that they might fall?'" (11:11). He responds with his usual "God forbid!" Paul's framing of the sentence is designed to show the arbitrariness of the question. Israel was not judged arbitrarily; it was a necessary outcome of her sins. Yet the judgment was not eternal; it falls in the pattern of chastisement, which is designed to restore (Psalm 103:9-14).

God does use this occasion of judgment to further His purposes. His purposes are twofold. First, He provides occasion to offer salvation to the gentiles (Acts 13:46). Second, He provides provocation to the Jews to return to the Lord. These two purposes dominate Paul's consideration through verse 32. In relation to the first of these purposes Paul says, "But through their transgression, salvation [has come] to the gentiles" (11:11). Paul has shown this already in 9:24-26 and 10:19, 20. He and Barnabas demonstrated this pattern in turning to the gentiles when they had been rejected by the Jews (Acts 13:46). He will illustrate this with the symbol of grafting later in this chapter.

This purpose of God serves His other purpose: to save Israel "in order to make them jealous." The hope is that Israel will see demonstrated in the gentiles the provisions of the covenant borne through them. They will, in this way, be provoked to return to the benefits they have forefeited. Paul sees in this outcome even greater blessings for the world than those already received: "And if their transgression is the riches of the world, and their failure the riches of the gentiles, how much more their fulness!" (11:12). The first part of this verse is stated in parallels. The transgression of Israel is their failure. "The world" means the gentiles. So, in this parallelism Paul has emphasized the sin of Israel. More importantly, he has emphasized that God has governed this failure in such a way that its judgment is a blessing. It is the blessing of the gentiles in that they become the special objects of the gospel, especially in the ministry of Paul. Paul, under the direction of God, set the direction of evangelism in the church. This direction has dominated the spread of the gospel from that day to the present. The other aspect of this blessing has Israel in mind. If in their jealousy, Israel is provoked to repentance, she will be restored. Paul leaves no doubt this will be the case. It did not please God to judge Israel, but His sovereign grace triumphs over the results of judgment to provide restoration. This restoration is represented in the words "their fulness." "No word could serve to convey the thought of the thoroughness and completeness of this contrast better than the term 'fulness.' For if 'fulness' conveys any idea it is that of completeness. Hence nothing less than a restoration of Israel as a people to faith, privilege, and blessing can satisfy the terms of this passage."[30]

For these reasons Paul can take pleasure in his role as the

Apostle to the gentiles: "And I say to you, the gentiles, 'Because I am, therefore, the apostle to the gentiles, I magnify my ministry'" (11:13). This function of Paul's ministry was attested from the first of his calling, and it was accepted by the church (Acts 9:15, 16; 15:3, 22-29; Galatians 2:1, 2, 7-10). The zeal Paul had for the fulfillment of his ministry is ample evidence of his magnifying his office. Paul can also take comfort in the fact that his function as apostle to the Gentiles contributes to the salvation of his kinsmen according to the flesh: "If in some way, I may provoke to jealousy my flesh, and that I might save some of them" (10:14). As we have noted earlier the term "jealousy" is used in the best use of the term jealousy. Here it means to awaken in the hearts and minds of Israel a desire for their heritage which they had lost. It does not express a desire to deprive the gentiles of the blessings of Christ. In appropriate modesty, Paul does not propose that his ministry will provide for the salvation of all Israel; he hopes to affect some for salvation (1 Corinthians 9:19-23).

In verse 12 Paul had spoken generally of the blessing that would come from the restoration of Israel; in verses 15 and 16 he becomes more specific. He first deals with the question of the blessing that came from the rejection of Israel: "If the rejection of them was the reconciliation, what will the receiving of them be, but life from the dead?" (11:15). Paul does not suggest that the gentiles could not have been reconciled unless Israel had been rejected. He does show that the extension of gentile evangelism had been precipitated by Israel's hardness of heart toward Jesus Christ (Acts 13:44-48). To show this contrast of judgment and blessing, Paul uses two words totally opposite each other: rejection and reconciliation. One is the product of judgment; the other is the product of atonement. The benefit God provided through Israel has now become the covenant blessing of the gentiles. They live in the spiritual tradition of Israel (Cf. Romans 4:18-25; 9:6-9; Galatians 3:15-18; 4:21-31). The question is, "If an act of judgment brought blessing, how much greater will the blessing be when God fulfills His mercy upon Israel?" The Apostle suggests that the blessing would be analogous to resurrection from the dead. The word "receive" stands in direct opposition to the earlier word "reject." So, it is clear Paul expects a restoration (a receiving again) of the people who had been judged and rejected. At no point does Paul ever suggest an irrevocable rejection of Israel. The word "receive" by contrast stands for reconciliation of Israel as the gentiles now enjoy reconciliation. The expression "resurrection from the dead" is taken by some scholars to refer to the resurrection of the dead on the occasion of Christ's return.[31] It is significant that the sealing of the 144,000 is directly related to the consummation of God's will in the world and the consummation of the kingdom of God (Revelation 7). "Whatever this result may be it must denote a blessing far surpassing in its proportions anything previously obtained in the unfolding of God's counsel."[32] We should also observe that the rejecting and receiving are both represented as God's act. This is another commentary on the grace of God; the statement of Romans 5:20b, "Where sin abounded, grace did much more abound," is especially appropriate at this point. Paul describes the nature of this blessing in the symbolic language of verse 16: "For if the firstfruit is holy, the whole lump is holy; and if the root is holy the branch is holy." The first symbolism is drawn from Numbers 15:17-21. The teaching is that by the sanctification of a portion of the first bread made from the first harvest in Canaan, the whole harvest was also made holy. Nehemiah observed this practice in the restoration after the 70 years captivity (Nehemiah 10:37; cf. also Ezekiel 44:30). Paul's assurance of the sanctification of the whole lump is that the patriarchs were indeed sanctified by the Lord (11:28). Paul uses a similar analogy from the concept of the holiness of the root and by this the holiness of the branches growing from the root. In the analogy the patriarchs stand in the pattern of the root. Paul probably also intends this analogy to provide an easy transition to the lesson to follow—the grafting of the gentiles into the olive tree.

The important thing set forth here is the grace of God. Israel and the gentiles are themselves secondary; they are not God's plan. God's plan is the setting forth of His mercy upon the fallen. Israel and gentiles are God's instruments for setting forth this plan. God can and will do this through either Israel or gentiles.

THE OLIVE TREE
11:17-25

The analogy of the olive tree is designed to demonstrate the power and the grace of God. The use of the olive tree figure was an appropriate choice by Paul. He had precedent for this analogy in the Old Testament (Jeremiah 11:16, 17; Hosea 14:6). Similar parables had been used by the illustration of the grape vine to show God's relation to Israel (Isaiah 5:1-7; Hosea 14:6, 7). Jesus had used the analogy of the vine with Himself as the Source of life for the branches (John 15:1-8). The analogy Paul uses is the breaking of the natural olive branches out of the tree. Paul does not speak of the complete stripping of the natural olive tree: "And if some of the branches were broken off" (11:17a). He has shown all along that not all Israelites rejected Christ; hence not all Israelites were broken out of the olive tree (11:1). This is fundamental in the idea of the remnant. The use of the passive voice verb reflects the action of God; their expulsion was an act of divine judgment. The next step in this analogy shows how God included the gentiles: "And you, being a wild olive, were grafted among them, you have become partakers of the richness of the root of the olive tree" (11:17b). The injury created by the breaking of the natural branch provides the occasion for the grafting of the wild olive branch into the natural. There are occasions in which horticulturists might graft a wild branch into a domestic stock, but this is not the usual pattern of grafting. This is important in this analogy; God, by this act, demonstrates the character of His grace.[33] Israel was prepared to accept the idea that some Israelites were unworthy of the covenant (for instance, the publicans); they were not prepared to think gentiles would be brought in to become partaker of the root and life of the tree where an Israelite had been broken out. The unnaturalness of this procedure enhances the concept of divine intervention. Paul again uses the passive voice verb to indicate divine agency in this act. As the natural branch had been broken off by God's act of judgment, the wild had been grafted in by God's act of mercy. Paul uses several pointers in this sentence to show the completeness of this union with Israel. The gentiles are grafted in among the remaining olive branches. They are made partakers together with the rest of the olive branches, that is, with the Jews. They partake of the same root (life source) with the other branches, and they bear the same fruit. The gentiles grafted in are indistinguishable from the Israelites who have remained in the olive tree.

This entire word picture is designed to show that the gentiles have no more claim of merit than the Jews; therefore, their being grafted in among the natural olive branches calls for humility on their part: "Do not boast against the branches, and if you boast [you should know that][34] you do not bear the root, but the root you" (11:18). It is possible for gentiles to assume a superiority identical with Israel's haughtiness—to consider Jews less worthy than themselves for the kingdom of God.[35] We should observe that Paul's warning is that the gentile Christians should not take a superior attitude toward the branches who have been broken off. Even those who have been judged by God are not to be looked on as inferior and more unworthy than the gentile branches who have been grafted in. To enforce this point, Paul reminds the gentile believers they are partakers of the root; they do not bear the root. It is Israel, according to the flesh, who had the advantages of grace listed in Romans 9:1-5. They under God produced the offer of salvation to the gentiles. The gentiles did not produce the offer of salvation to the Jews.

Paul imagines a rejoinder from some gentile believers: "You will say, therefore, 'Branches were broken out in order that I might be grafted in' " (11:19). The presumption of this statement is that God excluded some Israelites in order to include gentiles. Paul answers, "That is granted" (11:20a). This is only part of Paul's answer, and what it means is "that it is true that you were grafted in where natural branches were broken out." It does not mean gentiles can take a superior attitude toward Israel. Paul completes his answer in these words: "They have been broken out by unbelief, and you stand by faith. Do not be arrogant, but be fearful" (11:20b). The reason for Israel's rejection was her sin of unbelief; there was nothing arbitrary about the breaking out of the natural branches. So the gentile believers stand where they do, in God's covenant by faith. The term "by faith" means here as it does in other places "in grace." Therefore, gentile believers are no more meritorious than those in Israel who have been rejected. Paul's warning is sharp; he warns the gentile believers against arrogance. This is the weight of this word. Over against arrogance he exhorts them to fear.

The reason they ought to fear is that they may be stripped out of the tree into which they have been grafted: "For if God did not spare the natural branches, neither will He spare you" (11:21). God had demonstrated his longsuffering with Israel, but He had also shown the seed of Abraham can provoke Him to severe judgment. God will certainly not allow in gentiles what He would not allow in Israel. God's action in relation to Israel and gentiles demonstrates both His graciousness and His severity: "Behold the goodness and the severity of God—upon those who have fallen severity, but unto you the goodness of God, if you remain in goodness otherwise you will be cut off" (11:22). The term "goodness" is related to the word "grace" and carries the connotation of unmerited favor. Paul is reminding the gentile believers they must remain in their relationship of grace (believing, obedient, and humble: all the spiritual virtues of grace are included). The warning is clear: "if you do not you will be cut off." The words "cut off" have the same meaning for the gentiles that was applied to Israel.

Paul opens up a subject which he will develop later: the possibility of restoring the natural olive branches. The Jews can be grafted in again just as the gentiles were and on the same basis: "And those, if they remain not in unbelief will be grafted in again just as the gentiles were on the same basis: "And those, if they remain not in unbelief will be grafted in; for God is able to graft them in again" (11:23). They were excluded by divine judgment; they must be reincluded by divine act. Paul continues to use the term "graft" to show that there is no natural return. They have no right to return; their return will be by the goodness and the sovereign act of God. On the other hand, the gentile believers ought to know that the Jews can be grafted in again much more naturally than the gentiles were grafted in: "For if you being a wild olive tree by nature were broken out and grafted into a good olive tree contrary to nature, how much more shall these by nature be grafted into their own olive tree" (11:24).

In verse 25 the Apostle turns to the climax of his teaching concerning Israel. He sees a fulfillment of God's purpose, not only in relation to Israel, but also in relation to gentiles. In His dealings with each, God is moving toward the fulfillment of His kingdom. Paul does not want the gentiles to think they are the "last step" in God's plan. God still is working toward the salvation of Israel: "For I do not want you to be ignorant, brethren, of this mystery, that you should not be arrogant, because hardness has happened to part of Israel until the fulness of the gentiles has come in" (11:25). Paul uses the term "mystery"[36] to designate knowledge known only by divine revelation. In this context, he uses the word to describe God's plan for Israel and gentiles. It is God's will as graphically represented in the analogy of the olive tree. The mysteries of the New Testament were not given to an inner and superior circle of believers to be held from the rest of the body; the mysteries were given for the purpose of sharing with all the body. So Paul here enlightens the gentile believers in their proper relationship with Israel. These believers must not be arrogant in relation to Israel, not even the Israelites who have been excluded for their unbelief. Paul uses the term "hardness" to describe the condition of the Israelites who have not accepted Christ. This is the damnable spiritual condition that God must and does judge. He had done so with Israel.

There are four things Paul wants the gentile believers to know about this hardness. First, it is a hardness that has come on only some of Israel. Second, it is a hardness that will be removed. Third, this hardness does not bar Israelites from the opportunity of salvation, and it must not discourage evangelization among the Israelites. Fourth, its removal will serve God's purpose in the fulfillment of His will in relation to the gentiles. The specific limits of this hardness are represented by the clause "until the fulness of the gentiles has come in." The term "fulness" describes the fulfillment of a purpose, or a time, or a number, or a plan. In this context it refers to the fulfillment of God's purpose to provoke the Jews to jealousy by the inclusion of the gentiles. This does not mean God must reject the gentiles in order to include the Jews. It does mean God will accomplish His purpose in Israel by the extension of the gospel to the gentiles. God's grace to the nations will produce repentance in Israel. God will then remove the hardness from Israel.

THE FULFILLMENT OF GOD'S PURPOSE
11:26-32

God will not remove this hardness arbitrarily, but He will remove it redemptively; so Paul declares, "And thus all Israel shall be saved" ((11:26a). There are certain safeguards which we should call attention to. First, this is not a promise that every Israelite will be saved. Second, this is not a promise that men will be saved because they are the physical seed of Abraham. Third, this is not salvation by decree; it is still salvation by grace. So the question is: what does the term "all Israel" mean? We cannot interpret the term *Israel* in this verse any differently from the way we have interpreted it throughout this section of Romans. So, Paul does envision and predict a return of the mercies of God to Israel. It is the grafting in again of the natural olive branch. This return of Israel to the word of God (the word of the promise) is provoked by God's work among the gentile peoples; the coming in of the fulness of the gentiles occasioned this result.

Paul cites as his reasons for the assurance of the salvation of Israel a series of Old Testament quotations: "The Redeemer shall come out of Zion; He shall turn ungodliness from Jacob, and this is my covenant with them when I take away their sins" (11:26b, 27; Isaiah 59:20, 21; Psalm 14:7; Isaiah 27:9; Jeremiah 31:33, 34). Paul not only appeals to these Scripture statements for authority, but he also shows the eschatological perspective in which they will be fulfilled. The Old Testament passages expect fulfillment of this covenant in the last days. It seems clear that Paul expects the same pattern of fulfillment. Zion stands for all Israel, the nation who had produced the physical ancestry of the Redeemer (Romans 1:3, 4; 9:5). Zion also stands for all the covenant relationships between the Redeemer and the object of His redemptive work. The arising of the Redeemer out of Zion is God's covenant. The emphasis of these passages is the Atonement. He will take away the impiety and ungodliness for which Israel has been judged. God calls this provision the essence of the covenant He made with Jacob (Israel). This covenant is fulfilled when He takes away their sins. The Old Testament passages extend the predictions to describe the character of the eternal kingdom. Isaiah 59:21 promises the coming of the Holy Spirit, the work of the Holy Spirit to place the word of the Lord in the mouths of Israel, and the abiding of this promise forever.

The gospel had become the dividing issue between Israel and the gentiles: "With reference to the gospel, they are enemies on your account; with reference to the election, they are beloved on account of the patriarchs" (11:28). Romans 9 and 10 were taken up with the offense which Israel took to the gospel message. Chapter 11 has described the inclusion of the gentiles. The gentiles offended the Jews by claiming that what they had received from God is what the covenant had promised; so they did become enemies on the issue of the gospel. Note the animosity Paul describes in Galatians 4:21-31. The term "beloved" designates the relationship of electedness; this belovedness comes to Israel because of God's faithfulness to the patriarchs and the promises which He made to them (Genesis 12:1-3). God's promises are not made for failure: "For the gifts and election of God are irrevocable" (11:29). By "gifts and election" ("gifts and calling", KJV) Paul has in mind the covenant provisions for the seed of Abraham. It is a remnant according to grace (Romans 11:5, 6) who will represent the fulfillment of this promise and will demonstrate the irrevocable nature of God's call (Cf. Revelation 6:1-8). As a remnant according to grace the inheritance is in Christ (Galatians 3:16).

In our comments on Romans 3, we used the terms "universal exclusion" and "universal inclusion," and we noted there that the *universal inclusion* in redemption was based on a *universal exclusion* because of sin. Paul now applies this principle to the relationship of Israel and gentiles in the fulfillment of God's mercy on each. Here, however, he adds the dimension of God's use of each nation in providing the salvation of the other. The mission of the redeemed is always the salvation of those still disobedient. This was Israel's mission to the nations; this is now the mission of the gentiles to Israel: "Just as you who were at one time disobedient to God have now received mercy as a result of their disobedience, so they too have now become disobedient in order that they too may receive mercy as a result of God's mercy to you" (11:30, 31; *NIV*). This is a summary of the lesson of the olive tree, but it is also a clear statement of mission. The mission of Israel was the salvation of the nations. They ought to have served this function in obedience and in faith. Instead, they disobeyed and disbelieved. God judged them and rejected them, and in their rejection they served the mission of the salvation of the gentiles. Now God turns the mission to the gentiles; their mission is to provide a route of the mercy of God to Israel. Disobedience by Israel was not necessary nor desirable for Israel to provide the route of salvation for the gentiles. The extension of the promise and blessing was provided on the assumption of faith in the part of Abraham and his descendants. However, God used their failure for the blessing of the nations. The return of these blessings to Israel does not require the disobedience of the gentiles. Neither does it require or seek the rejection of the gentiles. So the return of the blessings to Israel does not involve the withdrawal of blessings from the gentiles. God's promise is that with the return of the blessing to Israel, the nations will be even more blessed than before; it will be the holiness of root and branch (11:15, 16). This is a product of God's mercy to the gentiles. The mission of mercy is always the extension of mercy.

God applies salvation through the process of conviction of sin: "For God had made all prisoners in disobedience in order that He might have mercy upon all" (11:32). In summary this is the principle of *universal exclusion* and *universal inclusion*. The respite of mercy can come only when the conviction of sin is inescapable. The law was given to serve the purposes of the promise—to bring men to the promise. It serves this function by the conviction of sin (Galatians 3:22).

THE DOXOLOGY
11:33-36

Paul introduced this explanation of the restoration of Israel by using the term "mystery." He has not proposed to remove the mystery; neither has he proposed to explain the depths of this mystery. A completely explicated mystery is no longer mystery. Paul's awareness of the presence of the mystery of God provokes the doxology concluding this section of Romans. His doxology is composed of several Old Testament references and probably represents a doxology used in the worship of the early Christians. The praise of God is the ultimate resolution of all the mystery of God.

Verse 33 is an exclamation reflecting on the mystery that Paul has just taught: "O the depth of the riches and wisdom and knowledge of God; how unsearchable are His judgments, and His ways beyond tracing." This statement shows God's dealings in judgment and mercy are beyond comprehension; they are also worship inspiring.

The incomprehensibility of God's ways is represented by a series of questions drawn from Old Testament passages: "For who has known the mind of the Lord? Who has become His counselor? Or who has given to Him and it shall not be given to him again?" (11:34, 35). These questions reflect the Hebrew parallelism of their Old Testament source. They also anticipate and require the answer, "None!" The mind of the Lord is infinitely deep. Only the Son knows the Father and the Father the Son (Matthew 11:27). The Spirit searches the deep things of God (1 Corinthians 2:10, 11). The first questions are drawn from Isaiah 40:13 where they are applied to the mind of the Holy Spirit (1 Corinthians 2:16). Verse 35 seems to reflect the question God asked Job (41:11). Paul varies the question, taking it from the first person and asking it now in the third person. The question deals with the riches of God; none can give to Him whose riches are infinite. These questions seem to reflect back on the three qualities of God's depth mentioned in verse 33. His riches are immeasurable; so none can give to Him. That which men receive is not a trade off of giving and reciprocation; it is all of grace. The depth of His mind is too great for anyone to know. His wisdom is such that none can offer Him counsel.[37]

The climax of this doxology is verse 36; it is a statement of both creation and providence: "Because out of Him, and through Him, and unto Him are all things; to Him be the glory forever, Amen." The doctrines of the fall and redemption are based on the concept of God here extolled. All things have their origin in His creation. In all of their existence they owe their being to God. All things are for His glory; therefore, they all serve the purpose of magnifying God. They move toward Him who is their origin, and even those that are damned have their meaning in Him (Colossians 1:15-20; Acts 4:27, 28; 17:24-28; 1 Corinthians 8:6). The function of eternity is His praise.

CHAPTER 6

END NOTES

[1]The imperfect verb is used here to express an admittedly unattainable wish (Blass, DeBrunner and Funk, 359:2). The imperfect is also used to represent a repetitive wish. We have translated the word *anathema* with the word "damned" because it is used in the sense of final judgment.

[2]The word "Israelite" (9:4) is used in John 1:47, Acts 2:22, 5:35, 13:16, 21:28, Romans 9:4, 11:1 and 2 Corinthians 11:22. In every instance it is used as an ethnic distinction.

[3]The punctuation chosen in the translation in the text takes Romans 9:5 as (1) a statement of Christ's human nature and divine nature, and (2) an exclamation of praise used as a doxology of worship of Christ. The grammar standing alone would permit a punctuation that would allow the following translation: "Blessed be God over all, Amen" (Bruce, op. cit., p. 186). This translation would leave an unbalanced sentence. Paul has already used this doxology in the same way as we have translated it above (Romans 1:25). The doxology reflects Psalm 41:13.

[4]Blass, DeBrunner, and Funk, 304; 480:5.

[5]We should note Paul is not arguing the issue of free will and predestination. He is discussing the issue of works and faith. The attempt to make of this passage a proof text for Calvinism forces this passage into a discussion that Paul is not engaged in. The assumption in this use of the passage is that Romans 9 is a continuation of Romans 8:28-30. "In the example of Isaac's sons, it is in fact emphasized that the word of promise was spoken before the two children were born in order that God's selective purpose might stand, based not upon deeds but upon him who called. This election does not presuppose predestination as commonly understood, a choice by God prior to creation. If that were the case, the time at which knowledge of the choice was made known would be of no significance. The announcement of the choice must be made immediately after the decision; God's choice is determined in the midst of history." Johannes Munck, *Christ and Israel,* translated by Ingeborg Nixon (Philadelphia: Fortress Press, 1967), p. 42.

[6]Matthew Black, *The New Century Bible: Romans* (Grand Rapids: Eerdmans, 1981), p. 133.

[7]Thayer (p. 203) does offer some basic distinctions between mercy and compassion that are of value. Mercy means "to feel sympathy with the misery of another, esp. such sympathy as manifests itself in act, less frequently in word; whereas (compassion) . . . denotes the inward feeling of compassion which abides in the heart. A criminal begs (mercy) of his judge; but hopeless suffering is often the object of (compassion)."

[8]Paul has used a number of introductory formulas in presenting quotations from the Old Testament: "the word of God," "the promise," "this word of promise," "it is written," "the Scripture says," and others. All these are designed to show Paul's concept of Scripture. It is word of God; it is oracle; it has the authority of God. The word of promise bestows the blessing spoken in it. The law of God imposes moral obligation and brings divine judgment. Note 2 Timothy 3:16.

[9]It cannot be said that the "God of wrath" is an Old Testament concept and the "God of love" is the concept taught in the New Testament. In proportion, the New Testament says as much about the wrath of God as the Old Testament. In comparison, Jesus has more to say about judgment and the wrath of God than any other speaker recorded in the New Testament. This presumed contrast ignores the character of God's holiness which requires judgment against those who besmirch God's holiness. This view comes from an attempt to anthropomorphize God and to cast Him into man's image.

[10]The attempt to make Paul's use of the perfect tense verb an affirmation of a doctrine of personal predestination is gratuitous. The statement is intended to show God's

preparation of the vessels of glory for the glory they are to inherit. The perfect tense verb treats this preparation as an accomplished fact. The use of past tenses to describe future events is common in biblical literature, especially in prophetic literature.

[11]The parallel and interchangeable use of "beloved" and "elected" is shown up in the gospel accounts of the Father's witness of the Son. In Luke 9:35, Christ is called the "elected Son" (the best textual evidence supports this reading, which is adopted by the New International Version). In the parallel accounts in Matthew 17:7 and Mark 9:7, the Son is called the "beloved Son."

[12]Romans 1:28; 3:20; 10:2; Ephesians 1:17; 4:12; Philippians 1:9; Colossians 1:9, 10: 2:2; 3:10; 1 Timothy 2:4; 2 Timothy 2:25; 3:7; Titus 1:1; Philemon 6; Hebrews 10:26; and 2 Peter 1:2, 3, 8; 2:20.

[13]"Verse 4 gives a distinct NT meaning of the term; the usage at 1 Peter 1:9 conforms more closely to classical Greek (= the logical end of a process or action—its issue, consummation, perfection—and thus in philosophical writings its idea of chief good); cf. 1 Timothy 1:5: 'the end of the commandment is love'. So the 'end', the climactic development (practically 'perfection', 'perfecting') of the law is Christ." Matthew Black, op. cit., p. 138.

[14]Murray interprets this statement to refer to the termination of the law as the way of righteousness (op. cit., 11:50): "The view most consonant with this context is . . . that the apostle is speaking in verse 4 of the law as a way of righteousness before God and affirming the relation that Christ sustains to this conception. The only relation that Christ sustains to it is that He terminates it." The difficulty with this view is there was never a time that man could gain righteousness before God, by means of his own works, or obedience to the law (note Galatians 3:21, 22). See note 13 above.

[15]A full reading of the Old Testament shows that the way of salvation during this time was the way of faith (Romans 4). Moses' statement should not be construed to mean he offered Israel a system of works-righteousness and that they failed; so, God offered the plan of New Testament salvation. Salvation is the same in all ages; from the first offer of salvation, the plan of God has been the plan of grace. Israel needed to know that their relationship to God demanded holiness of life. Their holiness of life would be the product of grace, self-will, and discipline. It would do for them two essential things. First, it provided their identity with God. His holiness was their way of life. They were to live in obedience to the commandments of God. Second, it distinguished them from non-covenant peoples. It is clear that God provided forgiveness for Israel (both corporate and individual) by the fact that He provided the tabernacle and temple services with the sacrifices of atonement. They did not have to live under the threat of legalism, but their life in grace did call on them to manifest their uniqueness by holiness of life (Exodus 19:3-6).

[16]In the original setting, Moses reminded Israel that the word of the Lord had come down to them; it was not in heaven and was not in need of being brought down to Israel. He also reminded them the word of the Lord had not departed from them. It was not beyond the sea (the abyss) and did not need to be brought back. Even though Israel had departed from Sinai and was on the border of Canaan, the Word was near them.

[17]The translation of the Greek word with the word *abyss* is a transliteration of the Greek. This word is used as the equivalent of the Hebrew *Sheol*. "The abyss in this instance may most suitably be taken as the synonym of *sheol* and the latter is frequently in the Old Testament 'the grave.' " (Murray, op. cit., 11:53, note 10) The question here is "Who shall descend into the grave?" as if Christ were still in the sepulchre.

[18]Thayer, p. 562. The attempt of some to create a distinction of power or significance between *rhema* and *logos* cannot be supported from the etymologies of the two words nor from their use in Scripture. The sad result of this kind of reasoning is that it creates a canon within a canon. It implies some words of Scripture have greater authority and if possible, greater inspiration than others.

[19]The word *kerusso* is especially apt for this context. This term carries the idea of public proclamation: "to proclaim after the manner of a herald; always with a suggestion of

formality, gravity, and an authority which must be listened to and obeyed" (Thayer, p. 346).

[20]Thayer, p. 446.

[21]This emphasis is an appropriate answer to those who find in Romans 8:29, 30 and Romans 9:6-24 justification for a doctrine of salvation by decree, instead of justification by personal faith. Every "whosoever will" in Scripture is an absolute assurance to anyone of God's offer of salvation. Here, Paul's application intends to show the offer of salvation is open to men regardless of ethnic origin. Every "whosoever will" is God's assurance that salvation is provided for Jews and gentiles.

[22]We have seen this writing style earlier in Romans. This was a popular style of writing and speaking. It had been developed in philosophical circles. The speaker or writer carries his thought on by questions which he imagines to be in the mind of his hearer, whether antagonist, inquirer, or student. It is usually described by the literary designation *diatribe;* cf. Romans 3:1-3; 4:9, 10; 6:1-3; 9:19-24.

[23]Black op. cit., p. 139.

[24]Joachim Jeremias, *The Parables of Jesus,* translated by S. H. Hooke, (New York: Charles Scribner's Sons, 1963), pp. 144, 145.

[25]Murray, op. cit., 11:58.

[26]The psalmist clearly described the manner in which God speaks through the creation in Psalm 19:1-6. He followed with a description of the law of the Lord (vv. 7-14). It is a mistake to think, however, that he has described two different revelations. God is His own Revelator whether he speaks through the things created or through His law (cf. Romans 1:18-20.) So, the Apostle takes this passage as a general statement about God's revelation. His point is that revelation of the word of Christ has gone throughout Israel.

[27]Murray, op. cit., 11:66.

[28]Black, op. cit., p. 141.

[29]Such a literary device is known as *charaz.* "A favourite method was that which derived its name from the stringing together of beads *(charaz),* when a preacher having quoted a passage or section from the Pentateuch, strung on to it another and like-sounding, or really similar, from the Prophets and the Hagiographa." Alfred Edersheim, *Life and Times of Jesus the Messiah,* (Grand Rapids: Eerdmans, 1950), 1:449.

[30]Murray, op. cit., 11:79.

[31]Bruce, op. cit., 216: "The meaning may be that Israel's conversion will be the immediate precursor of the resurrection, to coincide with Christ's *parousia.*"

[32]Murray, op. cit., 11:81, 82.

[33]God had traditionally set aside man-made traditions to demonstrate His sovereignty and grace. In not allowing the covenant to pass to Ishmael (in human legal terms, Abraham's firstborn) and electing Isaac, in electing Jacob, the second born, to carry the covenant line, in choosing Judah as the tribe of the Messiah, in choosing David as Israel's second king, in choosing Solomon to succeed David, God showed His disregard for the laws of transfer created in human tradition. Man's rules are based on carnal criteria. God will not be bound by the dictates of such rules; He will remain sovereign over the transfer of His covenant. The grafting of a wild olive branch into a domesticated olive tree is God's way of demonstrating the fulfillment of His covenant under terms of His sovereignty and grace. Israel has assumed God could fulfill His covenant only through them and had become presumptuous.

[34]Blass, DeBrunner, and Funk, 483.

[35]The antagonism toward Jews that is often encountered in Christian church history is an assumption of gentile superiority over Jews. It is racism sanctified by religion, on the excuse that Israel deserves rejection and gentiles do not. It is a pharisaical presumption that gentile Christians are in Christ because they are now the covenant line—the new Israel. Paul will show the fallacy of this reasoning.

[36]Paul uses this word in a number of relationships: of the inclusion of the gentiles in

covenant, equal to the Jews (Ephesians 3:3-6; Colossians 1:26, 27); of the provision that all nations might believe on Jesus (Romans 16:25, 26; Ephesians 1:9); of the message of the gospel (1 Corinthians 2:7; 4:1; Ephesians 6:19; Colossians 4:3; 1 Timothy 3:9); of the incarnation of Christ (Colossians 2:2; 1 Timothy 3:16); of the resurrection (1 Corinthians 15:51); of the relationship between Christ and the Church as His bride (Ephesians 5:32); of the mysteries spoken in spiritual utterance (1 Corinthians 13:2; 14:2); of the mystery of iniquity in the working of antichrist (2 Thessalonians 2:7). Contrary to popular opinion, this word is not used exclusively of the Church, and it is not the equivalent of the Church.

[37]Murray, op. cit., 11:107.

CHAPTER 7

THE PRACTICE OF HOLINESS

ROMANS 12:1—15:6

The exhortations of Scripture are never arbitrary. The manner in which the Apostle Paul organized his epistles shows that there is reason behind the practices he urges in the name of holiness and obedience. We must also observe the concerns of practice in the Christian life are as broad as the concerns of mankind. So, here we read exhortations that concern relationships with members of the body of Christ, with those who oppress, with civil authority, and with those who have consciences offended by our practices.

We have designated this chapter "The Practice of Holiness." The tone for this section and the justification for the title are set in verse 2: "And do not be pressed into the mold of this present age, but be transformed by the renewing of the mind in order that you may demonstrate what the will of God is—the good and acceptable and perfect will." The will of God is that we should be holy (1 Thessalonians 4:3). The pattern of this holiness is the pattern of life in the kingdom of God: "For the kingdom of God is not meat and drink, but righteousness and peace and joy in the Holy Spirit" (Romans 14:17).

THE BASES OF THE PRACTICE OF HOLINESS
12:1, 2

There are two bases of exhortation to holiness. The first is a sound doctrinal commitment. The second is the presentation of the body as a living sacrifice.

A sound doctrinal commitment is fundamental to right practice. It is the consistent pattern of Paul in his epistles to attach doctrine and practice to each other, and to show that they are integral to each other. In this epistle Paul has laid a strong foundation in the previous 11 chapters. This foundation has dealt with the issues of divine revelation, sin, justification, sanctification, the nature of Christ, the work of the Holy Spirit, and the doctrines of grace and election. The practices that Paul now exhorts are based on those teachings.

The distinction we often use today between "faith and practice" is a modern distinction. It has no justification in Scripture, and it is arbitrary. How one lives must be determined by what he believes to be true. Therefore one's concept of God and salvation determine how he must live. Correctness of belief mixed with corruption in practice is the height of arrogance, or it is a perpetual battle of conscience and will. Correctness of practice with no understanding of correct belief leads to arbitrary regulation of life.

The second basis of obedience is the presentation of the body as a living sacrifice to God (12:1). This is the ground upon which all the exhortations that follow are based. Only on the assumption that the individual believer has offered himself in sacrifice to God, do these exhortations have true spiritual significance. The performance of man is of spiritual significance only if he has become a sacrifice to God. It is the sacrifice that renders the service spiritual.

The characteristics of proper personal sacrifice are given in the terms of Paul's exhortation. First, the act of offering a sacrifice is the act of a priest. The call to offer the sacrifice is here directed to the individual. In this way, Paul has established in practice the function of the priesthood of all believers. Individuals do have direct access to the altar of God. The Scriptures speak of believers' offerings before God as sacrifices of "a sweet smalling savor" (2 Corinthians 2:15; Philippians 4:18; cf. also Hebrews 13:15, 16). Peter draws from the Old Testament to describe this function of priesthood in the congregation of God (1 Peter 2:5; Exodus 19:6). That believers are priests of God through redemption is promised in Isaiah 61:6, and is celebrated in Revelation 1:6; 5:10, and 20:6.

Second, the incentive of this exhortation is "through the mercies of God." Paul is well aware that his ministry and the authority to exhort the congregation of God is a gift of God's grace to him. He wants the believers to know their response is a response in grace. The incentive of obedience in this case and in all cases of obedience is the awareness of the mercy of God. For Paul, mercy equals grace (Romans 9:23-29).

Third, the nature of the sacrifice is unique. It is a living sacrifice. Normally the concept of sacrifice calls for the death of the sacrifice. This sacrifice is called a "living sacrifice"; that is, a sacrifice that through its offering remains alive. Its being alive is a necessity if the exhortations that follow are to be fulfilled. This is a sacrifice of the body. In Christian theology the body is honored; it is not despised, as is the case in almost all other religious systems. It is a worthy sacrifice before God. It is the temple of the Holy Spirit and an instrument for glorifying God (1 Corinthians 6:19, 20). This body, in its being sacrificed, is rendered holy and, therefore, acceptable to God.

Fourth, Paul calls this offering the "reasonable service" of the believer.[1] By "reasonable" he means that the rendering of this act of worship is appropriate to reason; we might even say that it is logical.[2] The Scriptures never separate the mind of man from his soul (or spirit); so, reasonable service in this case arises out of the spirit of man. The offering of the body as a living sacrifice is an act of worship that reflects the nature of the inner man as verse 2 will show. The word translated "service" is never used in the New Testament, except in reference to the service of God (John 16:2; Romans 9:4; 12:1; Hebrews 9:1, 6). Its verb form is most frequently used of the service of God in worship (Matthew 4:10; Luke 1:74; 2:37; 4:8; Acts 7:7; 26:7; 27:23; Romans 1:9 and other passages). On several occasions it is translated "worship" (Acts 7:42; 24:14; Philippians 3:3; Hebrews 10:2). This entire exhortation is cast in the framework of worship. This act of worship is the foundation of the worship to be rendered in obedience to the exhortations which follow.

This action is coordinate with the spiritual conditions addressed in verse 2. The first part of this exhortation is negative: "and do not be pressed into the mold of this world order" (12:2). The "mold" of this age is represented in the value system of the world. This value system is variously expressed in terms of happiness, security, and success. This value system is developed in this age. The term "this world" is used in Scripture to designate the sin-cursed world order. It is the origin of cares that are destructive of spirituality (Matthew 13:22); it is already destined for judgment (Matthew 13:40); it is dominated by the god of this world (2 Corinthians 4:4); its wisdom and the disputers of this world reject the gospel of Christ (1 Corinthians 1:20; 2:6); its children are disobedient (Ephesians 2:2); its princes crucified the Lord of glory (1 Corinthians 2:8); it is called "this present evil world" (Galatians 1:4); and it is in darkness (Ephesians 6:12). The one thing most evident about the value system of this age is that God and His service are not first in the order of priority. Its viewpoint is temporal, because this age stands in contrast to the age to come—the kingdom of God, which is eternal. Worldliness is the adoption of the standards of this age as the criteria of happiness, security, and success. The believer must not allow himself to be pressed into the mold of these standards and patterns of behavior.

The second part of this exhortation is positive: "But be thou transformed by the renewing of the mind" (12:2b). The word which we have translated "transformed" is a very forceful word. It describes the change of form and appearance in Christ at His transfiguration (Matthew 17:2; Mark 9:2). It describes the transformation into the image of Christ when we behold His glory, being transformed from glory unto glory. The transformation stands in sharp contrast to the idea of conformity. Conformity is a product of being pressed into a given shape by external pressures. Conformity has no concern for internal character; its primary concern is outward appearance. Transformation is concerned with inner nature; outward appearance is important in transformation, but the outward appearance is the product of the change of nature that takes place in the inward man. By way of example, we may note the difference between a block of wood and a living tree. Any kind of wood may be shaped into specific form (such as a piece of timber, a child's toy, or a dowel). This shape comes from shaping by knives which are external to the nature of the wood. So far as shape is concerned, whether the wood is hard or soft is not important. However, an acorn produces a specific kind of tree because the nature of the tree is in the seed. External shape takes place because of the internal nature of the germ of life in the seed.

The transformation of which we speak takes place by the

"renewing of the mind" (12:2c). The term "renewal" (or its equivalent in verb form) is used to describe renewal through repentance (Hebrews 6:6), renewal of the inward man day by day (2 Corinthians 4:16), renewal of the new man in knowledge in the image of God (Colossians 3:10), and renewal in regeneration by the Holy Spirit (Titus 3:5). (These places and the text before us are the only places where this word and its cognates are used in the New Testament.) Here, "renewal" is a renewal of the mind. "Mind" is used here to represent the inner nature; it comprehends all aspects of man's spiritual (or immaterial) nature. It especially relates to spiritual understanding. All redemptive provisions for renewal of the character of man contribute to the believer's transformation into the image of the glory of Christ—repentance, regeneration, sanctification, beholding the glory of Christ and glorification. The transformation described here has as its goal the believer's glorification.

The purpose of this transformation is to demonstrate what the will of God is: "that you may prove what the will of God is—the good, and acceptable and perfect" (12:2d). The believer so sacrificed and so transformed becomes a display of what it means to do the will of God. The will of God for man is holiness of nature and behavior (1 Thessalonians 4:3; 5:23; 1 Peter 1:16). The description that follows the designation of God's will is designed to describe the nature of God's will; it is good, acceptable (pleasing) and perfect. These are qualities in the character of God; so His will reflects His nature.[3]

The idea of sacrifice is inseparable from the demonstration of the will of God. This connection should not imply that doing the will of God is unpleasant. God's will is not designed to make His children miserable. God's will is good, pleasant and perfect, exactly as God himself is. To be in God's will is to be in a peaceable relationship with Him; it is to be in His presence, approved and reconciled.

The doing of the will of God is the subject of the two applications which follow in Romans 12:3—15:6. These two verses dominate all the applications of holiness given here.

THE PRACTICE OF HOLINESS IN RELATION TO OTHER MEMBERS OF THE BODY OF CHRIST
ROMANS 12:3-8

Paul understood his office to be a gift of God's grace to Him; therefore, the exercise of that office took place in the grace of God. By the expression "the grace that was given to me" Paul refers to his authority and function as an apostle of Christ (1 Corinthians 3:10; 4:6, 7; 9:1, 2; 15:8-10). So, here he speaks in the spirit of grace in which he had been called. His address is directed to the members of the body of Christ generally and specifically to the recipients of this letter. They are the ones who are in Christ. Paul gives in this passage instructions on how to conduct oneself in relationship to other members of Christ's body. The most fundamental awareness is, "Do not think more highly of yourself than you ought to think" (12:3a). As a generalization this prohibits conceit or arrogance. More precisely, this exhortation warns the believer against thinking of himself as holding a function in the body of Christ that God has not given him. The way the believer is to think of himself is in accordance with the function in the body that God has given him: to "think with sound mind as God has measured to every man a measure of faith" (12:3b). The "measure of faith" here does not refer to saving faith, as Paul developed this idea in earlier chapters. It refers to the distribution of spiritual functions in the body of Christ. This expression is the same as "the grace that is given to me" (v. 3a), "gifts according to the grace given to us" (v. 6) and "according to the proportion of faith" (v. 6). Paul's point is: Whatever one does in the body of Christ, he does it by the gift of God's grace (1 Corinthians 4:7), and he does it as an act of faith in God who had placed all believers in their proper function in Christ's body (1 Corinthians 12:1-12, 28-31). It is arrogance to think the power and authority of the office rests in the office holder. The office function must be carried out in a sense of dependence upon God; so that the office function is a demonstration of the Spirit and of power (1 Corinthians 2:1-5; 2 Corinthians 10:3-5). To attempt to exercise an office (or body function) to which the Holy Spirit has not appointed one is to usurp the function of another member of the body, and it is to act beyond the measure of faith given by God.

Verses 4 and 5 describe the analogy of these spiritual functions with the body. Paul begins with a simple statement about the physical body: "For just as we have many members in one body, and all the members do not have the same function, so the many are one body in Christ" (12:4, 5a). Multiplicity and diversity are essential for the health and functioning of the physical body. The same application must be made to the body of Christ.

This passage should be studied in conjunction with 1 Corinthians 12 and Ephesians 4:7-13. The first principle of membership in the body of Christ is that the body is one: "So the many are one body in Christ and members one of another" (12:5). In this analogy, Paul emphasizes that the body is organic; that is, it is a living body existing by lifeflow from one member to another, or one cell to another. This stands in sharp contrast to a mechanical device. Though a mechanical device may have many parts, there is no lifeflow from one part to another. The multiplicity of members is fully recognized; the diversity of their functions is also recognized. The element that offsets individualism is the differing functions are members not just of the same body, but members of each other. In the physical body the most widely separated parts of the body receive the same blood flow and are participants in the same nervous system. This must be understood clearly if there is to be health, harmony, and efficiency in the body of Christ. It is fundamental that we know how this can happen; it can happen only in Christ. The term "in Christ" is used commonly in Paul's writings to describe the mystical union in which believers are joined to Christ, the Head of the body (Ephesians 1).

In practice, this means we recognize the diversity of gifts in the body of Christ, and that we function in the appointed role that God had given us: "having gifts differing according to the measure of faith given to us" (12:6). First, this diversity is God appointed (1 Corinthians 12:11). Second, the function in the body is a gift of God's grace. It is not the product of seeking, natural ability, or training. Natural ability and training may be used of God, but they are not the origin of a divine call or appointment. This is the significance of the Greek word *charisma*. This word refers to what has been received by gift. Third, these gifts are to be exercised in faith: "according to the proportion of faith" (12:6). That is, they are exercised in faith that God will "give the increase" (1 Corinthians 3:6-8).

In verses 6-8, Paul applies these instructions to the exercise of certain specific gifts. *Prophesying* is a special function of ministering in the church for edification, exhortation, and comfort (1 Corinthians 14:3). It is occasionally used in the delivery of a predictive prophecy. Functionaries in the eaarly Christian community were called prophets (Acts 13:1; 11:27, 28; 21:9). Paul lists prophets as second in the order of ministers in 1 Corinthians 12:28. Much of 1 Corinthians 14 is taken up with instructions concerning the exercise of this spiritual gift. Prophets are associated with the apostles in the foundation of the church (Ephesians 2:20; 3:5). The person who is to exercise this function must do so only under terms of divine appointment, and in dependency upon the Lord for the prophetic message.

The second function Paul names here is *ministering* (12:7). The word for ministering is the same word used of those appointed to serve tables in Acts 6, though there is no indication Paul is using this word here as a technical designation of office. It (or its noun form) is used generally of ministering to the temporal needs of people (Acts 6:2; 11:29; 19:22) and of ministering the Word (Acts 6:4; and 2 Corinthians 3:3). The noun form is used of an office in 1 Timothy 3:10, 14. The point of the statement is that whatever function of ministry is placed upon a believer, he is to exercise it in faith.

The third ministry Paul lists is *teaching*. The office of teacher is listed third in the order of spiritual gifts in 1 Corinthians 12:28, 29. An office with the formal title "teacher" is not frequently mentioned in the Acts and the epistles; though Jesus is often addressed by such a title. We have noted the reference to teachers in 1 Corinthians 28, 29; this office is also mentioned in Ephesians 4:11. Teachers are listed among the ministers at Antioch (Acts 13:1). Paul refers to himself as a teacher of the gentiles (1 Timothy 2:7; 2 Timothy 1:11). James warns that the teacher is placed under special responsibility which should not be sought after lightly (James 3:1). We note again that the teacher is to exercise his ministry in response to divine appointment and in the exercise of faith.

The fourth ministry listed here is *exhortation*. The word used here is the root from which New Testament students have developed the word *paraclete*. Most frequently it is applied to the work of the Holy Spirit, especially as it is represented by Christ in John 14:15-21; 15:26, 27; and 16:5-16. We draw on these references only to show the breadth of the meaning of the word "exhortation." The word in its verb form and noun form is variously applicable: comfort, exhort, counsel, advocate, intercessor, and helper. In the ministry of the church, the word is used in the exhortation of believers to spiritual duty (Acts 11:23; 14:22), in the comforting of believers (2 Corinthians 1:4-6), and in prayer to God (2 Corinthians 12:6). As a term of consolation the word is used in many places in Scripture. This word is not used in its noun form to designate any specific office in the New Testament. It is clear from the nature of the applications that it is a weighty function, and demands great dependency upon God. This role must also minister in dependency upon God and the measure of faith that He has given.

The fifth function listed here is *giving* or *sharing*. This is not a frequently used word in the New Testament; it is applied both to the imparting of spiritual benefits (Romans 1:11; 1 Thessalonians 2:8) and material benefits (Luke 3:11; Ephesians 4:28). In this context it seems best to take this as the giving of material benefits. We know that such sharing was an important part of Paul's emphasis in ministry (Galatians 2:10; 2 Corinthians 8, 9). Here Paul does not continue his parallel of "according to the measure of faith," but states the manner in which giving is to be done. It is to be done with simplicity, that is without pretense or ostentation. This word is also used to express liberality (2 Corinthians 8:2; 9:11, 13). In all of these uses the quality of sincerity is fundamental.

The sixth order of ministry in this list is *the one who exercises rulership*. The word for "rulership" is used in the New Testament to refer to those who are "over you in the Lord" (1 Thessalonians 5:12), of those who rule well in their own houses (1 Timothy 3:4, 5, 12), and of elders who rule well (1 Timothy 5:17). It is also used in the sense of maintaining good works (Titus 3:8, 14). By definition, the word means to be placed over a thing or a body of people, to be a superintendent, to preside over, or to care for. The quality of ministry that is essential in this function is earnestness. The word carries the connotation of eagerness. The phrase "in earnestness" may also carry the meaning of exercising government promptly.

The seventh order of ministry given here is the *giving of mercy*. The word for "to give mercy" is a word of action; its emphasis is upon actions designed to relieve misery, even when that misery has been brought on by the victim's own actions. The quality of ministry necessary here is cheerfulness, as distinct from hesitancy and begrudgingness. The pattern for the extension of mercy has been set by our Lord Jesus (Luke 23:34; Ephesians 4:32).

Many of these functions (which are sometimes called gifts or offices) are simply the transfer of spiritual graces. This is important. All believers are called on to do all of these things. There are those who are especially appointed for these functions and who minister in them according to God's call upon them. None of this excuses any believer from the spiritual services named in this list. One cannot pass off his duties as a believer on the excuse that he does not have a particular gift.

MANIFESTATIONS OF LOVE
12:9-12

Holiness is love (John 17:20-26; 1 John 4:7-21). It is this union of love and holiness that dominates Paul's presentation of spiritual living in Romans (cf. 1 Corinthians 13). The first quality of love is that it be free of *hypocrisy* (12:9). The word also suggests an openness of love in its manifestation and expression. Love also makes certain ethical judgments: "being horrified with the evil, and cleaving to the good" (12:9). The word for "cleave" suggests tenaciousness. It is used in the sense of being bound to a master (Luke 15:15) and being joined to the Lord in spiritual union (1 Corinthians 6:17). There is no justification of immoral behavior because it is performed in the name of love. Love is bound by the ethics of holiness.

Love dominates the personal relationships of the believer. In the immediate context Paul applies this to close personal interaction as in the body of Christ. Love in tenderness and in deference to one another: "in brotherly love being tenderly affectioned to one another, in honor preferring one another" (12:10). This exhortation to love in the body of Christ takes its pattern from the exchange of love in the family, particularly the tenderness of devoted parents toward their children. In the preferring of others, the pattern is amplified in Philippians 2:3, 4.

Love is earnest, diligent, eager to manifest itself and is not reluctant (12:11a). These qualities are complemented by spiritual zeal: "being fervent in the Holy Spirit, serving the Lord" (12:11b). The origin of holy fervor is the Holy Spirit; the use of the definite article with the reference to "spirit" suggests the Holy Spirit is intended. This is the pattern of service to be rendered to the Lord.

Love manifests itself in joy, patience, and prayerfulness: "rejoicing in hope, being patient in tribulation, and persevering in prayer" (12:12). The hope here refers to participation in, and anticipation of, the kingdom of God. Though all aspects of the promises of God have not yet been fully realized, the believer rejoices in those promises with the same assurance as if they had been fulfilled. This hope prepares one for patience even though he still lives under circumstances of oppression and affliction. The Scriptures do not encourage the believer to think he has immunity to sickness, poverty, persecution, disappointment, or any oppressive tactic of Satan. The Scriptures do encourage the believer to learn patience while he endures these tribulations (Romans 5:3-5). An essential provision for rejoicing and patience is prayer. The word which we have translated "persevering" carries the meaning of constant readiness and continuousness. In prayer, the believer keeps his hope alive by rejoicing, and he turns his tribulations into patience. Paul gives the same threefold exhortation to the Thessalonians (1 Thessalonians 5:17).

Love manifests itself in material things: "sharing in the needs of the saints, pursuing hospitality" (12:13). We have noted earlier Paul's zeal to care for the material needs of believers (Galatians 2:10; 6:10; Romans 15:27; 1 Corinthians 8, 9). Other New Testament references place the same kind of emphasis on believer's meeting the needs of other believers (James 1:27; 2:15, 16; Matthew 25:35, 36; 1 John 3:17, 18). Love seeks to entertain the stranger (Hebrews 13:2). The pattern of communion in the body of Christ breaks the barrier of acquaintances and receives strangers as brothers and sisters. Such a grace is required of those who would exercise the office of bishop (1 Timothy 3:2; Titus 1:8). This is listed in 1 Peter 4:9 as a necessary grace among believers.

Love is to be manifested toward those who do not act or think kindly toward the believer: "Place a blessing upon those

who persecute you; bless and do not place a curse upon them"
(12:14). This injunction cannot be satisfied with isolation from
the persecutor, or with the attitude, "I wish him no harm."
Love is never passive. This injunction calls on the oppressed
believer to seek the well-being of his persecutor. This is the
exhortation of our Lord (Matthew 5:38-45); it was also His
practice in His unjust trial and crucifixion (Luke 23:34).
Stephen made this prayer his own when he was being stoned
(Acts 7:60).

Life is experienced in a community of emotions: "Rejoice
with those who rejoice; weep with those who weep" (12:15).[4]
This injunction stands at the beginning of the applications in
the Christian community. The sharing of rejoicing and weep-
ing is to occur with those of low estate and those of high
estate. The sharing of joys and sorrows should not be impeded
by economic, social, and governmental caste systems. So, as a
follow up of this exhortation, Paul urges believers to "be in
harmony of thought with one another, not thinking in an
arrogant way, but associating with humble people; do not
become wise in your own estimation" (12:16). The believing
body is to think of itself as one in a sharing of emotions, and
in the sharing of thoughts about each other. There is no room
for conceit. There can be no allowance for division of fellowship on the basis of low estate and high estate.

With verse 17, the Apostle makes applications of the rule of
love in situations arising between the believer and his antagonists.
This was touched on in verse 14. Now, however, Paul devotes
several verses to our relationship with oppressors. Probably
the reason for coming to this subject at this point and his
giving it this much attention is that he wants to place this
exhortation in direct connection with what he has to say about
magisterial authority (Romans 13:1-7). It is essential for the
believer to know that abusive acts must be dealt with at the
personal level (which he addresses in 12:17-21), and at the
legal and official level (which he addresses in 13:1-7).[5]

Paul's first injunction in this relationship is twofold. First,
we are enjoined from paying back evil with evil. Second, we
are called on to think and act honorably before all men
(12:17). To pay back evil with evil is to become an evildoer. In
addition to the sinfulness of the act, this kind of behavior
reflects deeply rooted emotional sins—roots of bitterness that

poison the soul. This attempt to carry our personal vengeance is a usurping of the rights and authorities of the magisterial authority, and the judgment of God. Of the second (and positive injunction), we should observe that the believer's actions have an impact on both the believing community and the unbelieving. In relation to evil deeds, the believer is to respond in a way clearly honorable—praise worthy—in the eyes of all men. It is important for the world to see the believer responding to wrongdoing even personal injury, in a way that honors Christ. This is also unassailable by the standards of the world.

Paul follows up this standard with the exhortation that if possible, and as much as we can, to live at peace with all men (12:17). Paying back evil with evil does not make for peace; it creates a spiral of spite for spite. Acting honorably under terms of injustice and abuse does contribute to peace. Even if the wrongdoer is not shamed into right behavior, the believer remains at peace in himself. It is not possible to take personal vengeance without cultivating the hatred out of which vengeance arises. The first obligation of the believer is to remain at peace in himself. In this kind of action the believer contributes to the peace of the community. Paul here recognizes that there are some men so bent on evil that they will not be at peace, especially with godly men. The pursuit of peace is coordinate with the pursuit of holiness (Hebrews 12:14).

Verse 19 is an amplification of all Paul has just said. The amplification here deals most particularly with our attitude toward God when we endure wrongdoing against ourselves: "Do not avenge yourselves beloved; but give place to wrath, for it is written, 'Vengeance is mine; I will give retribution,' says the Lord" (12:19; Leviticus 19:18; Deuteronomy 32:35). The first part of Paul's statement reflects the rules of conduct dictated by God to Israel; there they are also an amplification of what it means to be holy before God (Leviticus 19:1, 18). Our Lord urged this same pattern of behavior; He also attaches these principles to holiness of life (Matthew 5:38-48). It should be noted that the rule "an eye for an eye" was never a permission for personal vengeance. Those who had created this permission had corrupted the Word of God; it is this corruption of the Word that Jesus corrected in the passage from Matthew. The first injunction here forbids attempts at personal vengeance. In place of this attempt, Paul urges the believer to have patience in tribulation and give place to wrath; that is, leave room for the wrath of God to work. That this refers to the wrath of God is implied by the fact that the definite article precedes wrath; it is "the wrath" which is to be yielded to. The person who attempts to work out his own vengeance is actually usurping the authority of God to bring the sinner to account. This interpretation is confirmed by Paul's quotation of Deuteronomy 32:35: "vengeance is mine; I will give retribution." In the Deuteronomy passage the way of God's fulfillment of His wrath is spelled out: "In due time their foot will slip; their day of disaster is near and their doom rushes upon them" (Deuteronomy 32:35b, *NIV*). What Paul is asking believers to do is to believe God will exercise judgment and to allow this judgment to work.

The believer's attitude cannot be a passive attitude allowing him to sit back and watch for the vengeance of God to be fulfilled. The believer is called on to become active in contributing to the well-being of his enemies: "If your enemy hungers, give him food; if he thirsts, give him drink" (12:20a; Proverbs 25:21). He contributes to the material and spiritual well-being of his enemy. This is more than simply turning the other cheek, and it is more than token behavior. In fact, the imperative verbs in these exhortations are present imperatives; they may be translated for emphasis, "Keep on giving him food . . . keep on giving him drink." The reason for this behavior is also a quotation from Proverbs: "For doing this you will heap burning coals on his head" (12:20b; Proverbs 25:22). Feeding your enemy and giving him drink is not a subtle form of vengeance; this idea violates the entire idea in the minds of the Scripture writers. Vengeance is never the object of pure action. The object of this behavior on the part of the believer is stated in verse 21: "Do not be conquered by the evil, but overcome the evil in the good." The evil referred to here is the evil of verse 17. Such oppression conquers only if it provokes good men to become evil in retaliation. If this occurs, good men have been overcome by the evil done to them and the evil which they allow in themselves. Evil does not conquer, even if good men die rather than become evil. The answer is that the evil can be conquered by goodness. The definite article is used to refer to "the good." The good that is meant is feeding and giving drink to the oppressor. The aim is to shame the evildoer, and the hope is he will repent. The believer has in this way turned an enemy into a brother. This is not always the outcome; some enemies remain enemies and do reap the vengeance of God. In this case, the believer is vindicated by God's judgment. The believer who refuses to stoop to retaliation also gains the respect of the world, by showing right behavior in the face of injustice.

SUBJECTION TO CIVIL AUTHORITY
13:1-7

This passage appropriately follows what Paul has just said about personal vengeance. All citizens must distinguish between personal execution of vengeance and governmental execution of vengeance. Believers are to be exemplary in their attitude and behavior toward civil authority. They are to let the processes of government and judgment work. It is God's will to provide in society a system by which evildoers are brought to judgment, even if their victims are personally forgiving toward them. God has ordained civil authority to serve the purpose of an orderly society and the preservation of right behavior.

Paul's statement is not an endorsement of any personal ruler. Neither is it an endorsement of any particular kind of government. These words were written under the rulership of the Roman Empire. God's ordination of government does not dictate the form of government that must be, but it does dictate the purposes which government must serve. God's ordination of government does not exempt governments and nations from the judgments of God. God still judges evil in individuals, and in nations.

Paul's opening statement establishes the ground upon which he will make the applications contained in this passage: "Let every soul be subordinate to the governing powers; for there is no power except by God, and the powers that exist are established by God" (13:1). Paul uses the term "soul" (*psuche*) to designate persons. He is universal in this injunction. It is an obligation of believers and unbelievers to be in subjection to government. Believers have a special obligation to be examples in good citizenship. He describes government as being the "higher powers" (KJV), and as being ordained by God.

This ordination is described in two ways. First, there is no power except that which God sustains. Paul's implication is that government by society was established in the order of creation. Second, the powers being placed by God are held in their establishment by God's providence. They have been appointed and are fixed by God's decree (note the perfect passive participle). Having been established, this government has a providential ordination. Paul is prepared to instruct believers in their attitudes and behavior.

The first application Paul makes is that resistance of government is a resistance to what God has ordained: "So that the one who opposes the power (of government) resists that which has been established by God; and the one who resists shall receive to himself judgment" (13:2). Paul's statement is a general one; he speaks of those who see government as wrong and oppressive. They establish a pattern of resistance to its authority. Paul says that these people resist what God has ordained: that is, the government which exists under divine providence. In this statement Paul does not elevate government to divine law. Resistance is stated in terms of opposing the institution ordained by God. Paul does not sanctify all governments do or all laws they pass. It is appropriate that wrong judgments and wrong legislation be opposed, but it is not appropriate that government itself be opposed. One of the aspects of government that God has ordained is the authority to bring the wrongdoer into judgment: "Those who resist shall receive to themselves judgment" (13:2b). The judgment referred to here is judgment by the government, not the judgment of God. The KJV translation "damnation" is not justified in this context.

God has placed this authority in government in order to provide for order in society and the common good of its citizens: "For the rulers are not a terror to the good work, but to the evil" (13:3a). This is the function God has ordained in both legislative and judicial process. Paul drives this truth home by a simple question: "Do you wish not to be afraid of the power? Do that which is good and you will have praise from the same" (13:3b). The obedient citizen has a right to expect freedom from fear of his government, and commendation for doing right. Paul further adds that the government "is the minister of God to you for good" (13:4a). The term "minister" is a frequently used word. It is the same word that is used in Romans 12:7 (note the various uses there). Here the word means that governmental authority does God's service in this area.

The ruler also exercises punitive powers, and this also is a fulfilling of God's ministry: "If you do evil, fear. For he does not bear the sword for nothing; for he is a minister of God, an avenger for the purpose of wrath upon the practicer of evil" (13:4b). God has ordained governmental authority for the support and praise of good; with the same force and words, Paul says that it is God ordained in the execution of punishment. The consequence is that if one does evil, he has need to be afraid. Paul symbolizes all punitive authority by the figure of the sword; the ruler does not carry a sword in vain. The sword is an instrument of death. The state and its officers have authority from God to carry the sword (in our day other instruments of enforcement and execution) for its purpose, namely, to kill, if necessary, in enforcement or punishment.

For the reasons just given, and especially for divine ordination, all citizens should obey the authority. It is especially important for the believer in Christ: "Wherefore, it is necessary to be under submission, not only on account of wrath, but also on account of conscience" (13:5). Paul appeals to two levels of consideration for obedience. The first is the fear of punishment; fear is a legitimate restraint to violation. The believer ought to have a higher level of consideration for government—his conscience. The believer's sensitivity to what is right and wrong should prevail over fear. The believer's awareness that the government is in place under divine ordination should be a part of his conscience. It is incongruous for a servant of God to disregard the authority of another servant of God.

The Apostle makes a specific application of these principles to the matter of the payment of taxes: "For on account of this you also pay taxes, for they are ministers of God attending on this very thing" (13:6). There would be many among the believers in Paul's day who would question whether believers ought to pay taxes in support of the Roman empire or its subordinate levels of government. People of Jewish (especially Palestinian) background would have come into their Christian commitment from a background of resistance of Roman authority. Paul makes it very clear that all the reasons he has given come down to this point; pay taxes. He introduces another word for "minister" here; it is a word closely associated with worship service. Perhaps his intention is to show this duty as a matter of spiritual concern. Paul extends this statement into a series of injunctions: "Pay to all that which is owed; to whom custom is owed, pay custom; to whom tax is owed, pay tax; to whom fear is owed, give fear; to whom honor is due, give honor" (13:7). Paul has in mind two kinds of taxes by his use of the two words "custom" and "tax." The latter is the word that was used when certain of the Jews questioned Jesus about the payment of taxes to Rome (Luke 20:20-26). "The 'tribute' corresponds to our term 'tax,' levied on persons and property (cf. Luke 20:22; 23:2); 'custom' refers to the tax levied on goods and corresponds to customs payments."[6] The other duties are matters of respect which are appropriate to good citizenship and especially to the profession of holiness. This interpretation of the believers' relationship to government is consistently supported in the New Testament. The story concerning Jesus and the question of payment of tribute represented His teaching, and it also represented the teaching of the church at the time of Luke's writing. Jesus' concession to the payment of a tax that Peter had foolishly committed to is supportive of government (Matthew 17:24-27). The Apostle Peter exhorts, "Show proper respect to everyone; Love the brotherhood of believers, fear God, honor the king" (1 Peter 1:17, *NIV*).

THE DEBT OF LOVE
13:8-14

Perhaps what Paul has just said about the discharge of debt by the fulfillment of obligation suggested to him the way he would introduce the next series of exhortations: "Owe no one anything, except to love one another" (13:8). The term for debt or owing another speaks specifically of failing to discharge one's obligations. The believer cannot afford to contract debts that he cannot discharge by love. This injunction applies to all forms of obligations that men contract that place them under duress of loyalty and personal dependency upon men. This could be financial obligation unduly and irresponsibly extended; it could be "trade-offs" in business or politics; it could be social loyalties that restrict the exercise of spiritual graces. The only legitimate bondage that the believer can afford is the indebtedness of love. By putting life in this kind of commandment Paul shows that it is moral obligation.

As moral obligation, love is equated with the entirety of the law of God: "For the one who loves another has fulfilled the law" (13:8b). The term "has fulfilled" indicates the filling up of the meaning of the law. The interpretation of the law of God in terms of the love of God is inherent in the statement of Moses: "Hear, O Israel: The Lord our God, the Lord is one. Love the Lord your God with all your heart and with all your soul and with all your strength. These commandments that I give you today are to be upon your hearts" (Deuteronomy 6:4-6, *NIV*). This statement shows a direct association of this one commandment and all the other commandments. Our Lord made this connection explicit in His answer to the inquiry concerning the greatest commandment (Matthew 22:34-40). When He had given the two commandments of the love of God and the love of neighbor, He concluded, "All the Law and the Prophets hang on these two commandments" (Matthew 22:40, *NIV*). James says that to love one's neighbor as one's self is the fulfilling of the "royal law" (2:8).

The Apostle intends the law of love be applied to specific ethical issues; so, he cites four of the ten commandments: "Thou shalt not commit adultery; thou shalt not murder; thou shalt not steal; thou shalt not covet" (13:9a; Exodus 20:13-15; Deuteronomy 5:17-21). This statement is intended as a summary of the commandments cited, and the order is that which is found in the Septuagint in Deuteronomy 5:16. "These summaries were well known . . . Such summaries were no doubt useful for catechetical purposes as well as for reference."[7] Paul shows that he does not intend to give a full quotation of the Decalogue by his remark: "and if there is another commandment . . ." The commandments he does cite deal with interpersonal relationships. They range from the violent and overt to the inwardness of covetousness. All of them (whether overt or covert) are treated as violations of the rights of one's neighbor. Even covetousness that is never acted on is an evil attitude toward the neighbor who has what we illicitly desire. Some sins, such as adultery, have come to be called "victimless crimes"; this is particularly said of adultery between two "consenting adults." Paul shows that adultery is abusive of the body (1 Corinthians 6:12-20).[8]

Even though Paul does not quote all the commandments, he intends to enforce all of them: "And if there is any other commandment, in this word it is summarized, 'Thou shalt love thy neighbor as thyself' " (13:9b; Leviticus 19:18). Paul intends to say that even those commandments relating directly to one's relationship to God in worship (the first four) are also summarized in the relationship of love toward one's neighbor. Jesus made the same summarization and application in His response to the rich young ruler (Matthew 19:17-20). It is impossible to conceive of a right relationship with God without a right relationship with one's neighbor. This is especially true when the commandments are translated into love. It must be noted that these commandments are negative; this is appropriate. Sin must be defined and prohibited; it must also be interfered with. Negative statements best serve this purpose. It is a very shallow concept of holiness that conceives of negative commandments as legalism per se.

Paul turns all of these negatives into the single positive statement of love. In this citation of Leviticus 19:18, Paul is in direct line with Jesus' use of the same statement (Matthew 5:43; 22:39). By adding the dimension of love, the Scriptures enjoin us to give life instead of take life, to give material things instead of coveting, to preserve virtue instead of defiling the body. In this dimension love is the giving of oneself to the wellbeing of one's neighbor. The measure of love called for here is "as you love yourself." To love oneself is essential for loving others. Low self-esteem and a hateful attitude toward oneself is not only personally and emotionally destructive; it is an impediment of our love of others. Jesus defines what it means to love your neighbor as yourself: "Therefore all things whatsoever ye would that men should do to you, do ye even so to them: for this is the law and the prophets" (Matthew 7:12). By His equating this rule with the law and the prophets, Jesus also equates it with loving one's neighbor as oneself. In specific application Paul has already suggested honoring one another in brotherly love (12:10). He will in Romans 14 discuss believers' care for one another in matters of conscience. He calls on believers to consider others better than themselves and to seek the interest of others as well as their own (Philippians 2:3, 4). In Galatians 5:14 and 15, Paul uses this principle as the ground to rebuke the Galatians for "biting and devouring one another." To understand this rule of conduct in these applications removes it from the oppressive legalisms some indulge in when they attempt to understand it. Paul's closing statement on the application of this rule is harmonious with the statements of Jesus: "Love does not do evil to the neighbor; love is the fulness of the law" (13:10; cf. Matthew 22:40). It is appropriate that we see love in this manner; the regulations of the law are, in fact, details of conduct called for if one is to love. This viewpoint also keeps love and the practices of holiness integral to each other. Love cannot do evil; in the very act, love is destroyed. Love cannot do wrong toward a neighbor, even in the name of holiness or righteousness.

The perspective of this obedience is the return of our Lord. The nearness of His return makes a special demand upon believers to live as those on the threshold of the fulfillment of the kingdom of God: "And this [that is, *do this*] seeing the time that your hour to arise out of sleep is already; for now our salvation is nearer than when we believed" (13:11). By the clause "and do this"[9] Paul intends to add these eschatological exhortations to the preceding. It is Paul's assumption that they do see the times in which they are living. He adds this dimension to the understanding of the times; "this is your hour, and it is upon you." The meaning of "your hour" is fulfilled and defined in the term "salvation." We need not assume this is a rebuke of the Roman believers; it is a general statement that lethargy cannot be tolerated. The dawning of the day of salvation prohibits sleep. There is a warning in the statement that "our salvation is nearer than we believed." It is possible for believers to be affected by the worldly attitude expressed in 2 Peter 3:4, "They [that is, scoffers] will say, 'Where is this "coming" he promised? Ever since our fathers died, everything goes on as it has since the beginning of creation' " (*NIV*). Peter states the question in extremes, but the issue is the same; does the fact that the Lord has not yet returned mean He delays His coming? Paul's answer is that whatever have been the perceived delays, the time is shorter now than when we believed on the Lord (cf. 2 Peter 3:3-10). Paul uses the word "salvation" in the same sense that Jesus used the word "redemption," and he uses it in the same context of warning of the times: "And when these things begin to occur, stand up and lift up your heads, because your redemption is drawing near" (Luke 21:28). Here, as in other texts, Paul shows the dual relationship that the believer has with the kingdom of God. The believer is now in the kingdom; "your hour already is." Yet there is a fulness of realization of the kingdom which is yet to be, but it is nearer now than it was when we started our trek toward heaven.

The evidence of the nearness of our salvation is that "the night is far spent [It is almost over!], and the day is at hand" (13:12a). The night stands for this world order (this age) which is characterized by the deeds of the night (v. 13; cf. John 1:5; 3:19; Ephesians 5:18) and is governed by the "rulers of the darkness of this world" (Ephesians 6:12). The day stands for the age that is to come, the day of salvation. The day is the light; it is characterized by the deeds of the light (v. 14; 1 Thessalonians 5:1, 4-8; Galatians 5:8, 9). Paul says that this day is at hand; he uses the same verb here that John the Baptist and Jesus used when they said, "The kingdom of God is at hand" (Matthew 3:2; Mark 1:15). The full force of this verb is that the day has come, and it is now present. The believer is already in the day of his salvation.

This position, in relation to the day of salvation, calls for living according to the day: "Let us, therefore, cast off the works of darkness, and let us put on the armor of light" (13:12b). Paul explains the works of darkness in verse 13, and he explains the armor of light in verse 14. He places his demands here in the strongest terms: "Throw off the works of darkness." The believer's relationship with darkness is to be one of renunciation. His relationship with the light is to be one of complete commitment—to be clothed entirely by the armor of God (Ephesians 6:10-18). He cannot live in "twilight" (Ephesians 4:20-32; 5:8-21).

Paul amplifies what he means by the works of darkness: "Let us walk respectably as in the day, not in carousing, not in drunkenness, not in sexual impurity and sensuality, not in strife and jealousy" (13:13). By the use of the word "respectably" Paul appeals to the fact that these standards are also the standards of honorable society. Though the religious systems of the pagan world encouraged these kinds of behavior, there were many in those societies that realized the debauchery of such deeds as Paul lists. In these works of darkness Paul lists the external sins of the flesh as carousing, drunkenness, and sexual corruption. He also lists, with equal condemnation, such sins of the spirit as strife and jealousy; these also were works of the flesh.

In a very significant turn of his figure of speech Paul commands, "But put on the Lord Jesus Christ, and do not make provision [forethought; planning] for the flesh, with the aim of fulfilling its lust" (13:14). Instead of saying, "Put on the armor of light," Paul says here, "Put on the Lord Jesus Christ." His intention is to show that to put on one is to put on the other. The Lord Jesus Christ is Light. He may be described in the figure of armor; in such a case His nature is presented in figures of speech that agree with various pieces of battle gear (Ephesians 6:10-18). It is equally appropriate to describe Him in terms of spiritual graces—the characteristics of light (Ephesians 4:17-32).

The final exhortation to make no provisions for the flesh provides an important insight into the conception and birth of sin. The word for "provision" carries the connotation of taking foresight for a thing, planning for the doing of a thing. James notes the same kind of thing in his analysis of sin: "But every man is tempted, when he is drawn away of his own lust, and enticed. Then when lust hath conceived, it bringeth forth sin; and sin, when it is finished, bringeth forth death" (James 1:14, 15). Those who are of the day and have put on the armor of Light must not make any allowances for a return to the darkness.

PROBLEMS OF CONSCIENCE
14:1-12

Religious and cultural backgrounds shape the consciences of people. This shaping often occurs before the individual comes to Christ. This shaping of conscience often continues to influence the behavior of the person after he comes to Christ. Many times this development occurs in the early years of one's life in Christ. The influence of this shaping may be a highly respected leader in the convert's community of faith, or it may be the pattern of life in the entire community. Very often this influence will be the convert's attempt to follow a lifestyle that is opposite his life before he came to the Lord. Such shaping of conscience may remain with the individual believer through-out his life. One thing is clear from all of these possibilities of influence; not all believers will have the same sense of restrictions in behavior. This creates problems of fellowship, because each believer feels his way of life is right. He probably feels it is ordained of God. This was the situation Paul addressed in Romans 14:1—15:6.

The issues at Rome seem to have arisen because some of the believers in Rome had come out of a Jewish background and others had come from a pagan background. However, the restrictions that were apparently causing trouble were not purely Jewish; no Mosaic restriction demands vegetarianism, yet this seems to have been one of the problems in Rome. So other influences had come into the picture. Paul addressed a similar situation in Corinth; that is, the subject of 1 Corinthians 8. In Corinth, the issue was the problem of eating foods sacrificed to idols. Though the provocative issues differ in these cases, the fundamental spiritual issues are the same.

Paul opens this discussion with a direct command: "The one who is weak in the faith, receive into your fellowship, but not for argumentative judgments" (14:1). Paul uses the word "weak" (or infirm) to describe this person; it is clear from what follows that he is describing the people who are bound in their consciences in the matters of eating and the celebration of holy days (vv. 2, 3, 5, 6). The Apostle calls this a weakness "in the faith." It is weakness of faith because it brings on this person doubts about his acceptance in Christ. His sense of security in Christ is inhibited by his restrictions of conscience. He is apt to be hurt in his own spiritual life and confidence toward Christ if he sees other believers doing things that he sincerely feels are sinful. It is clear that Paul treats this as an infirmity in faith. It is also clear that Paul regards such a person as a brother in Christ, and he does not "look down" on him.

We have no way of knowing what proportion of the Roman Christians were affected in this manner; however, this exhortation suggests they were the minority among the Roman believing community. We judge this because Paul's exhortation is addressed to those who are to receive the person who is weak in the faith. Apparently, the majority of the church in Rome was not bothered by these restrictions. So, Paul says they are to receive the "weaker brother." He is to be received into the full fellowship of the body. "The word is used in the papyri of 'receiving' into a household . . . . Here it is not only receiving fellow-Christians with a 'weak' faith into the household of faith, but taking them as full partners."[10] The person is to be received, but he is not to be received into arguments and strife about his restrictions. He is to be received into fellowship, not argument.

The differences Paul first describes are dietary: "One believes that he can eat all things; and the weak eats vegetables. The one who eats all things, let him not treat with contempt the one who does not eat all things. And the one who does not eat, let him not judge the one who eats all things, for God has received him" (14:2, 3). In describing those who have no religious restrictions on food, Paul says they believe they have the freedom to eat all things.[11] Others feel restricted in diet to vegetables alone. It is clear that this restriction did not arise from the Mosaic code, and it did not arise out of traditional Judaism. Not even the strictest Pharisees required vegetarianism. It is possible these people found biblical defense of their restriction in Genesis 1:29. On the other hand, Paul treats this as a seriously held limitation on behavior. He treats it as a position held in Christ (v. 6).

Paul develops two instructions for this situation. First, the one who eats is not to despise (treat with contempt) the one who does not eat. He has already said to receive him into fellowship. He must not be received as less than a brother or even only as a "tolerated" brother.

Paul is equally strong in his second instruction; the one whose conscience prohibits him from eating certain foods must not judge the one who eats all things. The act of judging implies that the person who is judged is considered not to be a brother. In answer to this, Paul says, "God had received him." The word "received" here is the same word used in verse 1; so, Paul reminds those who judge their brother that God has received the judged brothers into His fellowship. The uniformity of this teaching on judging is clear from its distribution in the New Testament (Matthew 7:1-5; James 4:11, 12).

The Apostle extends his instructions to show the presumption of judging. The likelihood is that he intends both sides of such a dispute to understand their judging as presumptuous: "Who are you, the one who judges another man's household servant? To his own master he stands or falls, for the Lord is able to make him stand" (14:4). Not one presumes to judge the servants of another man; if one were to be so presumptuous, both the servant and the master would rebuff him. For the sake of illustration, Paul uses the term here for household servant; this makes the service rendered and judged to be intimate and personal. Certainly in such services as this, the master alone determines whether a servant stands or falls. The presumption of the judge is thus emphasized because he has intruded into another man's house. Paul immediately turns his application to the spiritual: "The Lord is able to make him stand."[12] In the process of judging we imply the one who is being judged is not a proper servant of God, if a real servant at all. The weak brother may also raise questions of the strong brother's fulfillment of other spiritual graces. The "weaker brother" tends to judge the "strong" as bringing illrepute on the household of God; he may even question whether he is truly a brother. On the other hand, the "strong" may judge the "weak" as not being a worthy servant of the Lord. He may even judge that the weakness is a weakness in other spiritual graces. We may all be comforted with the fact that it is the Lord who makes all His servants to stand.

The controversy at Rome included restrictions on the observance of holy days: "One judges one day above another, and another judges every day alike. Let each one be fully assured in his own mind" (14:5). On the assumption that the background of this problem was Judaism, the most likely understanding of this statement is that it refers to prescribed days in the Mosaic code. However, as we noted the dietary restrictions went beyond the requirements of the Mosaic law, it is entirely possible these restrictions did as well. There was in Rome probably a mixture of Jewish observance of holy days and superstitious observance of days (Galatians 4:10). Paul's answer does not rebuke either party in this difference. He urges that whatever one does here he must do it in faith, being fully persuaded that his conduct is approved of God.

The differences Paul has mentioned must be resolved within the relationships of the body of Christ and by the practice of life. The first relationship to the body of Christ is that the restriction or liberty is taken "in the Lord." "The one who exalts a day, in the Lord he exalts it: the one who eats [all things], and he gives thanks to God" (14:6). In each side of this controversy the participant conducts his life in Christ; he feels that what he does honors the Lord. On the matter of the weekly Sabbath, it would have been easy for believers from a Jewish background to feel that there had been no annulment of the Mosaic Sabbath. Without denying the day of the Lord's resurrection, they would still feel compelled to celebrate Israel's deliverance from Egypt (Deuteronomy 5:12-15). On the other hand, believers who had no personal Jewish heritage would identify only with the celebration of the day of the Lord's resurrection. This would be a more significant day of worship for them than the seventh day. Paul makes a similar observation about foods. Even though there are differences of opinion concerning dietary restrictions, each person eats with thanksgiving to God for the food. This is especially evident in the table blessing which is probably the significance of the statement, "He gives thanks to God."

The second principle of relationships within the body is that "no one lives to himself and no one dies to himself" (14:7). Later Paul will emphasize how our behavior affects others and is potentially damaging to them, but here his primary interest is to show our subjection to Christ in life and in death: "If we live, in the Lord we live; if we die, in the Lord we die. Therefore, whether we live or whether we die, we are the Lord's" (14:8). For Paul, this means two things. First, to live or to die is not the primary issue for the believer (cf. Philippians 1:20-26; Acts 20:22-24; 21:13, 14). Both life and death occur in the Lord, under His care. His care has been established for the believer in His redemptive work (v. 9). Second, the Lord is sovereign over life and death. He is sovereign over the life and death of the unbeliever by creation. His sovereignty over the life and death of the believer has the added dimension of redemption (v. 9). In his correspondence with the Corinthians, Paul extends the application of this truth: "So, let no one glory in men. All things are yours, whether Paul or Apollos or Cephas, whether the world, or life or death or the things that are or the things about to be, all are yours; and you are Christ's and Christ is God's" (1 Corinthians 3:21-23). The conclusion drawn from both of these points is that both life and death are stewardships. The issue of the celebration of days and of the eating of certain foods is secondary to this stewardship.

In the two applications immediately above the redemptive work of our Lord is central: "For unto this end, Christ died and He lived in order that He might be the Lord both of the living and of the dead" (14:9). The past tense "and He lived" is designed to emphasize the resurrection of Christ, not His mortal life. His rulership over life and death places Him in rulership over the living and the dead (John 11:25, 26; 1 Corinthians 15:45-48). By this rulership He redeems and He is Lord. Paul extends this truth to a charge against the presumption of judging. To the weak he asks, "Why do you judge your brother?" (14:10a). To the strong he asks, "Why do you despise your brother? (14:10b). Both questions emphasize brotherhood, and demand that neither believer question whether the other is his brother.

These questions bring Paul to a warning to both parties in this controversy: "We shall all stand at the judgment seat of God" (14:10c). This is the appointed destiny of every man (Hebrews 9:27). The assurances of redemption are very clear; there is now no condemnation, and there will be none at the judgment bar of God (Romans 5:1; 8:1, 31, 34). Christ is our Intercessor and Surety (Romans 8:34; 1 Corinthians 1:30). We are nevertheless judgment-bound creatures.

Paul appeals to Scripture to climax this statement of judgment: "For it is written, 'As I live,' says the Lord, 'Every knee shall bend to me, and every tongue shall confess to God' " (14:11). Paul draws this statement from two sources in Isaiah. The introductory words "as I live" (Isaiah 49:18) give the words that follow the force of a divine oath; by His own life God pledges this. Paul attaches this vow to the statement of judgment drawn from Isaiah 45:23. In using these statements Paul combines references to the Lord (Jehovah) and God. The Apostle has clearly shown throughout Romans that the title *Lord* is to be ascribed to Jesus (Romans 10:9). The effect of this union of these terms here is to show the judgment which God has appointed to the Son is the judgment of God. Our Lord identified His right to judge on two grounds; first, He has life in Himself and is sovereign over the giving of life (John 5:21). Second, the Father has placed all judgment in the Son (John 5:22-27). At Athens, in his speech at Mars Hill,

Paul warned of judgment by the Man whom God has appointed and raised from the dead (Acts 17:31). Paul can freely mix his references to judgment as the judgment of God or the judgment of Christ.

This judgment will accomplish God's eternal purpose of creation to bring all things together under one Head, Christ (Colossians 2:19, 20). What is said here is that every knee shall bow in submission to God and every tongue shall confess to God (Philippians 2:10, 11). The issue is not whether one will worship God; it is whether he will worship as a reconciled worshiper or as damned.

The believer is judgment bound exactly as the unbeliever. Though there is no insecurity of redemption for the believer, there is an accountability for the things done in the flesh: "Therefore everyone of us will give an account of himself to God" (14:12). Our Lord warned of such accountability (Matthew 12:36). Paul places the judgment of works done in the Lord at the day of judgment (1 Corinthians 3:10-15). He describes the day of judgment as the judgment seat of Christ in which we give an account of the things done in the body, that is the things done in mortal life (2 Corinthians 5:10).

INSTRUCTIONS FOR HARMONY
14:13-23

Paul is now prepared to show how the principles discussed in 14:1-12 can be used to allow people of differing consciences to live together in harmony. His first statement is a carry over of the immediately preceding discussion: "Therefore, let us no longer judge one another" (14:13a). The first thing that must be done to provide harmony is to stop judging one another. In place of this, Paul suggests a positive kind of judging: "But rather judge this, not to put a stumbling block or a rock of offense before your brother" (14:13b). Each believer has an obligation to every brother not to be an occasion of spiritual danger to a brother. This danger rests in both sides of the controversy. The so-called weaker brother can certainly disrupt this harmony and offend others by harsh judgments, especially if those judgments deny the brotherhood of another in Christ. The so-called stronger brother can also disrupt the body by treating people with contempt simply because they are more restrictive in their consciences than others.

There are certain principles that are basic in this approach to the problem at hand. The first is an awareness of the nature of uncleanness: "I know and am persuaded in the Lord Jesus that nothing is unclean in itself, except to the person who considers a thing unclean; to that one it is unclean" (14:14). Paul speaks with great force in making his statement. He emphasizes his assurance of knowledge by two strong words of persuasion. The effect is to show that this persuasion had been arrived at earlier and was confirmed by subsequent reflection. He adds to this force by saying that this persuasion was "in the Lord." This places Paul under the obligation of integrity enforced by the lordship of Christ. Paul reflects an awareness of the Mosaic heritage by his use of the word "unclean" (variously translated as "common" and "defiled"). Peter had used the same word in his refusal to eat the food offered him in his vision at Joppa (Acts 10:14). Paul is confident of the cleanness of all things because God made all things, and all things belong to Him (1 Corinthians 11:25). That which in itself is acceptable can be made unclean. One way to make a thing unclean is to consider it unclean. For whatever reasons, a food is made unclean in the conscience of a brother in Christ (it is immaterial whether these reasons "make sense" to others), it is defiled for him. He does not have the liberty to eat this food, and he will have trouble accepting (as brothers) those who do eat that food. He does not have power to change the nature of the food, but the power of his own conscience defines sin for him.

This observation leads Paul to another point of instruction for harmony: "If on account of food your brother is injured, you are no longer walking according to love" (14:15a; cf. 13:8-10). We should understand that Paul is talking about spiritual harm being done in a believer's life when he uses the word "injure" (KJV "offense"). An insistence on the exercise of a personal liberty at the expense of a brother's spiritual health cannot qualify as "in honor preferring one another" (12:10) or loving "your neighbor as yourself" (13:9, 10). There is another serious implication of such action; such a violation of another's conscience may destroy a brother: "For food do not destroy that one on behalf of whom Christ died"

(14:15b). By placing the phrase "for food" at the beginning of this sentence Paul emphasizes the trivial nature of this exchange: food for a soul; my liberty above Christ's death. To destroy a brother for whom Christ died is a trivialization of Christ's blood. The Apostle offers a similar warning to the Corinthians (1 Corinthians 8:11). Paul does not question the good conscience of the person who practices his liberties, but he warns, "Do not let your good be blasphemed" (14:16). A believer's good conscience in the eating of foods is certainly an acceptable way for him to live. He is doing that which he considers good. He should not let that become an occasion of accusation and division in Christ's body.

There are other reasons for Paul's instructions; they deal with the nature of the kingdom of God: "For the kingdom of God is not food and drink, but righteousness, and joy and peace in the Holy Spirit" (14:17). This statement cuts both ways. On the one hand, eating certain foods does not make one any better. On the other hand, abstaining from certain foods does not make one any better. Neither condition enhances one's participation in the kingdom of God: "But food does not bring us near to God; we are no worse if we do not eat, and no better if we do" (1 Corinthians 8:8). Though Paul has directed his instructions to food, we must not forget part of the issue here is the question of holy days. The same principles that have been given in relation to foods apply here. Observance or non-observance of these things in no way enhances or damages one's position or spirituality in the kingdom of God.

The real nature of the kingdom consists in spiritual graces, all of which are in the Holy Spirit. Paul names righteousness; this is a right relationship with God in faith, justification, regeneration, and the pursuit of holiness. Peace is the nature of the kingdom of God; it is established in reconciliation, provided in the blood of Jesus. Peace is also a relationship of brothers in the kingdom (12:16). Joy is a spiritual grace; it represents the gladness of believers in their relationship with God and with each other. As this verse shows, its origin is the Holy Spirit. The phrase "in the Holy Spirit" is the essential qualifier for all the graces listed here. It is in the Holy Spirit that the Father's gift to the kingdom is fulfilled (Luke 11:11-13; Acts 1:4, 5; Romans 8:22-25). It is in and by the Holy Spirit that the kingdom is constituted (Acts 1:6-8; 10:37, 38). The Holy Spirit does in the church the things Christ did in His physical presence among the disciples during His ministry.

As a climax of his statement about the kingdom, Paul pronounces a blessing: "For the person who in this way serves Christ is pleasing to God and approved by men" (14:18). The manner of service that Paul speaks of here is the kind of service represented in the nature of the kingdom of God. To serve God in righteousness, peace, and joy in the Holy Spirit is to please God. This is life in harmony with God's nature and the nature of His kingdom. To serve God in this way directs the believer's attention away from meats and drinks. Certainly, if we are no better or worse for eating or not eating, it is inappropriate for us to attempt to serve God by such restrictions. These things cannot commend us to God, but life in the Holy Spirit does commend us to God. This is well pleasing in His sight. Paul also notes that this kind of life gains approval among men. Orderly society, even if it is not committed to biblical religion, does approve of the kind of dignity represented in godly living. It is important that believers be aware of their need of human social approval (Romans 13:3; 1 Timothy 3:2, 7).

Paul adds that believers are to contribute to the peace of the community of faith and to the building up of the spiritual well-being of the rest of the body of Christ: "pursue the things of peace and the things that edify one another" (14:19). The corporate interests of the wholeness of the church are essential in spiritual duty. This supercedes a mechanical code of behavior. It also supercedes a destructive insistance on one's liberties. Those believers who feel obligated to do everything they are free to do are immature and they do not contribute to the peace of the body.

Earlier Paul had warned against destroying the one for whom Christ died (v. 15); now he warns of destroying the work of God: "For the sake of food, do not destroy the work of God" (14:20a). Again, the Apostle shows the distorted value system that would exalt food above spiritual things. The work of God referred to here would seem to be (that is, from the context) the kingdom of God. To elevate food above this, whether by abstinence from certain foods, or by insistence on eating all foods, is to trivialize the kingdom. Beginning with this initial observation, Paul summarizes the principles of harmony for the body of Christ. All believers should realize that all things are clean (v. 14). However, it is easier for some believers to accept this mentally, than emotionally and in conscience. So there are still those who think of certain foods as unclean. A weak conscience in relation to a thing renders it evil to the person of such sensitivity: "All things are clean, but to the one who eats with offense, it is evil" (14:20b). The person who presses his conscience beyond itself and eats what his conscience forbids is casting a stumbling block in his own way and is in danger of falling spiritually. Such a person may be prompted to do such a thing simply because of the insistence of others, and not because he has a free conscience in the matter.

The Apostle suggests a code of conduct for all the body of Christ: "It is good neither to eat flesh, nor to drink wine, nor [to do] anything in which your brother stumbles" (14:21). The eating of flesh may refer to sacrificed foods as it clearly does in 1 Corinthians 8. On the other hand, it may refer to a total abstinence from meat. From verse 2 we observed that some in Rome were by religious commitment vegetarian in diet. At a later point, there developed in Colossae an ascetic order that created rules such as "handle not, taste not, touch not." Paul calls this order a false humility which will perish with the using (Colossians 2:16-25). If such were in Rome, it was in its beginning stages. Paul's words are not as sharp toward the Romans as his words are to the Colossian error. The specific things that are mentioned here are not the most important; the most important thing is that we should not do anything that creates spiritual danger or harm to a weaker brother.

This means that some liberties must be held privately: "Your faith which you have, have it to yourself before God; blessed is the man who does not judge [condemn] himself in that which he approves" (14:22). The individual's personal faith before God is his basis for a personal sense of freedom in practice. There are times and circumstances in which this must be held privately and before God. Paul does pronounce a blessing upon the person who has liberty in the things that he examines and finds acceptable. The significance of the word translated "approves" is that the approved things have been examined. Paul is by no means giving a blanket approval of all kinds of behavior; his words require an examining attitude on the part of the believer. To indulge in actions that have not been examined is disastrous.

Paul closes this chapter with a final warning to believers: "But the one who doubts if he eats is condemned because it is not of faith; and whatever is not of faith is sin" (14:23). The word translated "doubt" means to make a distinction—in this case a distinction between clean and unclean. The implication in this case is that the person wavers between two opinions. To eat food (or to neglect Sabbath observances) under such conditions of doubt is to bring oneself under condemnation. The translation "damned" in the KJV is too strong a word here. The reason he is condemned is that he is doing what he cannot do with a clear conscience, even though the restriction does not arise from the Word of God. Paul's statement that whatever is not of faith is sin means that those actions which do not arise from a clear conscience—a sense of acceptance—are sinful.

THE EXAMPLE OF CHRIST
15:1-6

This passage continues to give exhortations to the believers, especially the strong. The center of these exhortations is what Paul says about Christ in verses 3 and 4. In the first exhortation here Paul emphasizes his own duty toward its fulfillment: "We, the ones who are strong, ought to bear the infirmities of the weak, and not to please ourselves" (15:1). It is always the case that the strong should share their greater strength with those who are weak. Every loving family practices this, and so does every caring society. Those who are strong (whether in material wealth, political power, social prestige, knowledge, healing arts, spiritual insight, and stamina or any other area) have a moral and ethical obligation to share their strength with the weak. So this is not an unusual burden, but it is still a duty. The infirmities Paul is talking about are the kinds of weaknesses that he has just elaborated (Romans 14). Paul's language acknowledges that this is truly a weight—a burden. To put it mildly, bearing this burden is not convenient; it may even be irksome. But our main object in life is not to please ourselves; Christ did not!

So in the fulfillment of this spiritual grace Paul exhorts

believers, "Let each one of us seek to please our neighbor for good for the purpose of edification" (15:2). The nature of this verb emphasizes that this commitment to pleasing one's neighbor is to be the pattern of his entire life.[13] This is not pollyannish good. The aim is spiritual; each believer has an obligation to contribute to the spiritual strength of all other believers. The word "edification" means to build up, to strengthen, to encourage. The Apostle put this view of life in practice in his own ministry. Though he was free, he made himself all things to all men in order that he might win some (1 Corinthians 9:19-23); he sought to please others in order to save them (1 Corinthians 10:33).

These exhortations can exist at the social level and may be observed in the social level. Witness the outpouring of sympathy and action when news breaks about widespread disaster. This is significant, but it is not the primary point of Paul's thinking. His primary point is that this is the Christian way of doing things because of Christ: "For even Christ did not please Himself. But, just as it is written, 'The reproaches of the ones who reproached you fell on me' " (15:3; Psalm 69:9). The pattern of Christ's life was to please His Father (Hebrews 10:5-7; Psalm 40:7, 8). Christ's purpose in coming was redemptive; so it involved Him in bearing the enmity which men held against God. To please His Father He must bear reproach. Jesus faced this when he saw the contempt for the house of God in Judaism (John 2:13-17; Psalm 69:7-9). Jesus faced this contempt throughout His life on earth by His being made sin for us and being judged for our contempt against God (2 Corinthians 5:18-21).

The pattern of discipleship is to transfer the manner of Christ's life to the disciple's life. The Scriptures have been given for this purpose: "For whatever has been written has been written for our instruction in order that through the patience and the comfort of the Scriptures we might have hope" (15:4). This statement not only shows us the purpose of Scripture (to give us instruction), but also the way Scripture works. In order to show the latter, Paul speaks of the Scripture as he would a person. The Scripture conveys both patience and comfort. Each of these words is important in Christian experience. Patience has the full range of meaning in such matters as endurance, steadfastness and perseverance.

Comfort has the full range of meaning in such matters as encouragement, counsel, and help. The Scripture, by its nature, provides this equipment for the believer. Paul calls attention to persons and events in the Scripture that are helpful in these matters (Abraham and David in Romans 4; Israel in 1 Corinthians 10:1-13). He describes the qualities of the Word in 2 Timothy 3:16, 17. The purpose of the Scripture in providing these graces is to give us hope. The Scripture is the origin of our faith and it is the source of the cultivation of our faith (Romans 10:14-17).

Verses 5 and 6 are a benediction in which Paul by prayer bestows on the Romans the same graces that the Word imparts: "The God of patience and comfort give you the same mind in one another according to Christ Jesus in order that with the same mind and with one speech you may glorify the God and Father of our Lord Jesus Christ." The attributes of grace that come to the believer from the Word are the qualities of grace existing eternally and perfectly in God. So, He is called the God of patience and comfort. The aim of this prayer is the unity of the brotherhood. That unity is manifested in one mind, in one speech (literally one mouth), and one purpose. This purpose is that the body of believers should glorify God. Their witness and lives are to manifest the glory of God. This benediction calls to mind the high priestly prayer of our Lord, in which He prays the Father to unify all believers that the world may know that God sent His Son and believe on Him (John 17:19-23).

The trinitarianism of Paul's theology is interwoven throughout his teaching. It bursts forth with special significance in his utterances of worship as here: "that you may glorify the God and Father of our Lord Jesus Christ."

CHAPTER 7

END NOTES

[1]The term "reasonable" appears in a number of translations as "spiritual." This Greek word is appropriately translated "spiritual" in 1 Peter 2:2 ("spiritual milk of the word"). The KJV translates the phrase the "sincere milk of the word." The basic meaning of this word relates to reason and reasonableness. In Scripture reason has its origin in the spirit

of man. It would seem that the term "reasonable" is the best choice in this translation. This translation of this passage respects the etymology of the word and the biblical doctrine of the nature of man.

[2]Thayer, 379.

[3]Some have misunderstood and misused the KJV translation of this verse. They have interpreted this statement to list "levels" of the will of God. They have created the terminology of the so-called perfect will of God and the so-called permissive will of God. The Bible does not accept these distinctions as valid for believers' behavior. The Scriptures certainly do not permit a believer to choose the "permissive will of God" as an alternate level of obedience in place of the "perfect will of God." The scriptural answer to this idea is, "Therefore, to him that knoweth to do good and doeth it not, to him it is sin" (James 4:17).

[4]The infinitive is used here as an imperative. Blass, DeBrunner and Funk: 389.

[5]See Murray, op. cit., 11:137, 138.

[6]Ibid., 11:156.

[7]Black, op. cit., 162.

[8]The term "adultery" is used in the Ten Commandments as the general term to prohibit illicit sexual relationships. It is prohibitive of adultery and fornication. For this reason the citation of 1 Corinthians 6:12-20 is justifiable even though the term "fornication" is used in that text.

[9]Blass, DeBrunner and Funk: 442:9; 490:5; cf. also *NIV* translation.

[10]Black, op. cit., p. 165.

[11]The "word-for-word" order here is "he believes to eat all things." The word "believe" means "to have the confidence to risk, to feel equal to . . ." Blass, DeBrunner and Funk: 397:2.

[12]It is possible the Apostle is still using the term "Lord" in reference to the lord or master of a household. This is not likely since the Apostle does not use an expression such as "his lord" to correspond to "his own lord" used earlier. The consistent and early view of this statement is that it refers to either Christ or to God. The textual history of this passage would seem to confirm this view.

[13]Blass, DeBrunner and Funk: 332:1.

CHAPTER EIGHT

CONCLUSION

ROMANS 15:7—16:27

We have termed this chapter the conclusion for three reasons. First, Paul is wrapping up the development of doctrine he has presented throughout the book. Second, he is explaining his own ministry and his plans for extension of his ministry. Third, he closes his letter (as is characteristic of Paul) with a series of greetings to individuals. We do not wish to imply that this section of Romans is unimportant. Very significant points are covered here and they amplify much of what Paul has said earlier.

THE BLESSINGS OF GOD FOR GENTILES
15:7-13

The problems of differences of conscience (Romans 14:1—15:6) most easily arose when Jews and gentiles came into the same communion in Christ. The amount of time Paul spent on this problem shows its difficulty of resolution. As we have noted, a similar problem arose in Corinth (1 Corinthians 8) though probably with considerably different background. This problem arose out of the fact that God's will was to save the lost—Jews and gentiles. The route of revelation (through the Jews) and the instrument of revelation (the law and the prophets) was misinterpreted by both Jews and gentiles. Many of the Jews assumed that the ceremonial-prophetic laws were permanent. Many who accepted Christ continued to claim the necessity of observing these laws. They not only observed them themselves, but they insisted that gentile converts observe these laws.

On the other hand, many of the gentiles who came to

Christ considered the patterns of Jewish piety irrelevant for gentiles. Many came to Christ by way of the Jewish allowance for proselytes. They would have an appreciation for the Jewish background of Christianity. Others came to Christ directly from pagan religions; they had no history in Judaism. Both groups of gentiles would find the proscriptions of Judaism difficult to observe.

Paul had begun his discussion of the problems of conscience with the exhortation that the strong and the weak receive each other in full fellowship (14:1-4). Now he moves into his explanation of God's mission to the gentiles with the same appeal: "Wherefore, receive you one another, even as Christ has received you, for the glory of God" (15:7). He urges all who are in Christ to receive each other. Their fellowship must override their differences—even differences as wide as being Jewish and being gentile. The pattern and the reason for receiving each other is Christ. The expression "even as" means believers are to behave toward each other as Christ has behaved toward them. If Christ has received both Jews and gentiles, then Jews and gentiles are to receive each other in the same way. Paul applies this reasoning to forgiveness of one another (Colossians 3:13). This is the pattern of receiving each other. It is also the reason: receive others because Christ has received you. The reason is based on grace; both Jews and gentiles were received by grace. So the common ground that both Jews and gentiles share is their unworthiness and the grace of God in Christ. The purpose of this fellowship is the glory of God. God is glorified by the unity of the body of Christ. Grace manifested in holiness produces unity.

The unity of all mankind in redemption is God's plan of salvation, and each step in the revelation of redemption serves this purpose. The promise, the law, and the Messiah were given first to the Jew, but there has always been the follow-up expression "and also to the gentiles" (Romans 1:16; 2:9, 10). Now Paul fits the ministry of Christ into this pattern as the minister of salvation to both Jews and gentiles: "For I say Christ has become the Minister of circumcision on behalf of the truth of God in order that the promise of the fathers might be confirmed that the gentiles glorify God for His mercy" (15:8, 9a). Christ conducted His own ministry in primary ministry to the Jews (Matthew 16:24); He sent His apostles in mission to them (Matthew 10:6). At the same time, He ministered to a Roman centurion (Matthew 8:5-13), to the Syro-Phoenician woman and her daughter (Matthew 15:21-28), and to the woman of Samaria (John 8:1-26). He himself gave the commission that the disciples should go "unto the uttermost part of the earth" (Acts 1:8). Paul and Barnabas demonstrated this order of ministry (Acts 13:46-48). The leadership of the early church recognized this order and this promise at the Jerusalem council (Acts 15:12-18).

Christ's coming and His ministry are the fulfilling of God's promise to Abraham (Matthew 1, 2; Luke 1, 2; Galatians 3:16; Genesis 22:18; 26:4; Acts 3:24-26). In this light, He came not to destroy the law but to fulfill it (Matthew 5:17; Romans 10:4). He is the highest declaration of the truth of God and confirmation of God's faithfulness in all of history, since He is the Incarnation of the Word (John 1:14). He ministers on behalf of the truth of God.

Christ's purpose was not designed to terminate on the Jews. The universalism of His ministry appears in the visit of the Magi from the Far East (Matthew 2:1-12), in His commendation of the faith of gentiles (Matthew 8:10; 15:28), in His promise that people from all corners of the earth would gather at the table of the Lord in the kingdom (Matthew 8:11, 12), in His declared mission to call sinners to repentance and not the righteous (Luke 5:32), and in His commission of the church (Acts 1:8). He is the pinnacle of God's purposes to save the gentiles; in this salvation they glorify God for His mercy.

By the citation of a series of Old Testament promises, Paul shows that God decreed salvation to the gentiles from the beginning. Paul has already shown this in the nature of the Abrahamic promise (Romans 4:16-18). Now he calls other scriptures to witness. The first is from a hymn of praise to God on the lips of the king: "On account of this I will confess you among the gentiles, and I will sing praise to your name" (15:9; Psalm 19:49). This messianic psalm sees the Messiah King singing praise to God in the midst of a congregation of gentiles saved and drawn into His kingdom. "While David may have thought only of Yahweh's fame spread abroad, his words at their full value portray the Lord's anointed [50], ultimately the Messiah, praising Him among—in fellowship with—a most of Gentile worshippers."[1]

The second Scripture witness is from another hymn, the Song of Moses: "Rejoice, O Nations, with His people" (15:10; Deuteronomy 32:43). Here the gentiles are invited to join the nation of Israel in their song of victory over their enemies. By joining in the hymn of praise, the gentiles are joined to the covenant community. The brief Psalm 117 provides the next biblical witness: "Praise the Lord, all nations. Let all the peoples praise Him" (15:11; Psalm 117:1). In the rest of this psalm the people of praise are the objects of God's love and they inherit His faithfulness forever. Both the psalmist and Paul want us to see that God's redemptive blessings are shared with all the peoples of the earth. The biblical picture of the kingdom of salvation is that it reaches from sun to sun and pole to pole. Paul climaxes his citations of Scripture with Isaiah 11:10—"A root shall be out of Jesse, the One who will stand to rule the gentiles; in Him shall the gentiles trust" (15:12). Paul's source for the quotation is the Septuagint. This quotation comes from one of the most significant Messianic prophecies in Isaiah. It describes the nature of the kingdom of the Messiah. This statement identifies the gentile nations as full participants in the kingdom.

Paul closes this collection of Scripture quotations with a benediction: "And the God of hope fill you with all joy and peace in faith so that you may abound in hope in the power of the Holy Spirit" (15:13). This statement probably comes from worship patterns already established in the early Christian community. In the blessing cited in verse 5, we noted Paul's trinitarian emphasis in worship. There he emphasized the Father and the Son. In this blessing he emphasizes the Father and the Holy Spirit. It is the power of the Holy Spirit that provides the abundance of grace and hope.

PAUL'S MINISTRY AND PLANS
15:14-33

In Romans 1:8, Paul had commended the Roman believers for their faith and the good reports of them "all over the world." Now he speaks even more specifically and emphatically: "And I myself, my brothers, am persuaded concerning you, that you yourselves are full of goodness, being filled with all knowledge, able also to admonish one another" (15:14). Paul almost labors the points of emphasis in this statement, but it reflects his confidence in the Roman believers. Many of them he knew and he knew their labors in the Lord (Romans 16:3-16). He knew these people were able to receive such a weighty letter as he was writing. He knew also many of the things he would say were already being taught in Rome. Aquila and Priscilla had instructed Apollos (Acts 18:24-28).

Paul felt compelled to write these things because of his calling to minister to the gentiles: "And freely I wrote to you some things as reminding you again because of the grace that has been given to me by God" (15:15). Paul had not visited Rome, and he may have felt some would think him bold to write to the believers there; so, he explains his reasons here. First, he is aware of his boldness in writing them, though he will not grant that he was presumptuous to write. Second, by using the past tense ("I wrote") is referring to this letter; he had not written them an earlier epistle.[2] Third, his purpose is to remind these believers of truths in which they had already been instructed. The most important point of this statement is that Paul was fulfilling his apostleship to the gentiles. He wrote to the Romans on account of the grace that had been given him by God; this is Paul's way of referring to his calling in Christ (Romans 1:5; 12:3; Galatians 1:1, 2). Paul has a full sense of authority from God to do what he is doing in writing this letter.

The Apostle conceived of his work as an apostle to be an act of divine worship: "In order that I might be a servant of Christ Jesus to the Gentiles, ministering in priestly service the gospel of God in order that the offering of the gentiles might be acceptable having been sanctified in the Holy Spirit" (15:16, *NIV*). In describing himself as a servant (minister) of Christ, he uses a term of worship. Here it means to serve in a worship function. This worship function is explained in the rest of the verse. First, he is presenting the gospel in the role of a priest. This does not violate the biblical insistence on the priesthood of all believers. Paul described the ministry of the new covenant as the offering of a sacrifice of a sweet smelling savour to God. He also noted that the odor of the sacrifice was an aroma of death to some and an aroma of life to others (2 Corinthians 2:14-16). In this sense the presentation of the gospel is a priestly function, and it is open to all those who know Christ. Second, he is preparing the fruit of his ministry as an offering to God. The offering that he is presenting to God is the gentiles; they are made acceptable because they have been purified in the Holy Spirit. In themselves they were unclean, and unworthy of being an offering before the Lord. Paul cannot cleanse them, but the Holy Spirit has.

It was not necessary for Paul to defend his apostleship among the Roman believers. In the conclusion of this epistle, however, Paul did have occasion to review the nature of his ministry. He tells us some important things about his work and calling. It was not egotism for Paul to review his work with satisfaction, especially when he gives all glory to Christ for what has been done: "Therefore I have pride in Christ Jesus in the things pertaining to God; for I dare not speak of anything that Christ has not accomplished through me in word and in work in the obedience of the gentiles" (15:17, 18). His satisfaction lies in the things that Christ has done, not the things he has done, as if he had any power in himself (1 Corinthians 2:1-5). Paul always describes himself as an instrument of Christ's work (1 Corinthians 3:5-7). There is another side of this statement; Paul will not speak of what has been accomplished in the ministry of others. This is not the product of jealousy; it is the fact that Paul will not usurp the labors of others to verify his apostleship. He felt that his calling in Christ impelled him to preach the gospel where others had not (v. 20). The verification of Christ's work through Paul lies in the fact that the gentiles had obeyed Christ.

Paul's apostleship was confirmed by the demonstrations of power in his ministry: "In the power of signs and wonders in the power of the Spirit of God" (15:19a). Paul makes a similar appeal to the church in 2 Corinthians 12:12. In most places where the New Testament uses the word "signs" it uses it to refer to miracles. The combination "signs and wonders" is always used to describe miraculous intervention. It seems to be used in a technical manner in order to convey this meaning.[3] Paul's purpose in making this appeal here is to show the origin of His commission—Christ—and to show the origin of the miracles that accompanied his ministry—the Spirit of God.

The terms of Paul's appointment as an apostle dictated that he minister the gospel among the gentiles (Acts 9:15). In obedience to this, his conduct of ministry had taken him among the gentiles: "So that from Jerusalem even as far as Illyricum I fulfilled ["fully preached," *NIV*] the gospel of Christ" (15:19b). By this statement Paul gives the "circle" of his ministry. Though he was initially formally sent out from Antioch in Syria, he regarded the origin of the preaching of the gospel to be Jerusalem (Acts 1:8). The Roman province of Illyricum bordered onto the province of Illyricum; so, this statement probably means that he had preached as far as the border of Illyricum. The point of the statement is that Paul's ministry had been predominantly conducted in gentile areas and in areas not previously touched by other ministers of Christ. Paul uses the word "fulfilled" to speak of his preaching the gospel; his purpose is to emphasize that in his preaching he had declared "all the counsel of God" (Acts 20:27). Paul was determined that he would not inherit the labors of other men: "For we do not want to boast about work already done in another man's territory" (2 Corinthians 10:16, *NIV*).

In accordance with the understanding of his calling, Paul sought a ministry beyond the travels and ministry of the other apostles: "It has always been my ambition to preach the gospel where Christ had not been known" (15:20, *NIV*). The word translated as "known" means *to be named*. A review of Paul's ministry in Acts shows that he did extend the gospel into areas where Christ had not even been named. Paul understands this to be in fulfillment of prophecy. He was the instrument by whom God fulfilled the promise: "Those who were not told about him will see, and those who have not heard will understand (15:21, *NIV*; Isaiah 52:15). The Isaiah passage predicts the revelation of the suffering Servant of the Lord to the gentiles. They had regarded Him as despised and had not seen His servant-Messiah nature. Paul is, by Christ's grace, an instrument of this revelation to those who did not understand.

Earlier, Paul had told the Romans of his plans to visit them and the hindrances that had arisen (Romans 1:13). He refers to these plans and frustrations again: "For this reason also I have been hindered many times from coming to you" (15:22). Now he projects other plans in relation to his ministry among them. From Romans 16:1 we understand this epistle to have been written from the area of Corinth; Cenchrea was the port town of Corinth. Paul's understanding of his ministry there was that for the time being it had been fulfilled (15:23a: "having no place in these regions"). He recalls that for many years he had longed to visit them (15:23b). So he proposes now to visit them as he proceeds to Spain (15:24). He had expressed his plan to go to Rome when he was still in Ephesus (Acts 19:21). A visit to Spain from Rome would be reasonable and it would follow already established travel routes in the Roman empire. Paul describes his plans here within the framework and expectations of acceptance by the Roman believers. He would expect them to send him on his way with help and goodwill (15:24).

The immediate plans of Paul are to go to Jerusalem: "But now I go to Jerusalem to minister to the saints" (15:25). The ministry he had in mind was to take the offering he had been collecting among the gentile churches. The offering was for the poverty stricken believers in Jerusalem. Chapters 8 and 9 of 2 Corinthians were taken up with Paul's preparation for this collection. Some of Paul's comments here reflect the same things he had said to the Corinthians. He indicates that the believers in Macedonia and Achaia had been glad to contribute to this offering (2 Corinthians 8:1-7, 10-12). The offering was taken to relieve poverty (15:26: "for the poor saints in Jerusalem"). Concern for the poor was a prominent aspect of the believers in Acts (Acts 4:32-37; 6:1-7). and had been taught by both John the Baptist (Luke 3:11) and Jesus (Matthew 25:31-46). The Apostles at Jerusalem had urged Paul to make this concern integral to his ministry, and he indicated this had been the pattern of his ministry (Galatians 2:10).

Paul considers the ministry to the poor in Jerusalem to be an obligation of the gentiles: "They are their debtors" (15:27). The debt was incurred because the gentiles had received spiritual things from Jerusalem; so it is reasonable the gentiles should minister their "carnal things" to them: "For if in their spiritual things they have fellowshipped the gentiles, they ought also in carnal things to minister to them" (15:27). Paul regards the gospel as having come to the gentiles by way of Jerusalem; he had received the blessing of the Jerusalem church in his ministry among the gentiles (Galatians 2:9). In this way, Jerusalem had entered into the fellowship of the Spirit with the gentile believers. It became the obligation of the gentiles to share their material goods ("carnal things") with the Jerusalem saints. Paul uses the word for ministry here that he had used in describing his own ministry (15:16).

Paul's plans were to complete this collection, to proceed to Jerusalem and then to go to Rome: "Therefore, when I have completed this, and have delivered this fruit to them, I will go by you into Spain" (15:28). By the figure of speech ("this fruit") Paul shows that he regards such a collection and ministry as this is to be spiritual fruit of ministry. Paul expresses confidence he will get to Rome and that it will be under the blessings of the Lord: "I know that when I come to you, in the fulness of the blessing of Christ I will come" (15:29).

The Apostle shows concern for his reception in Jerusalem, and with good reason (Acts 21:10-14). So he urges the Roman believers to join him in the ministry and burden by praying for him: "I exhort you, brother, through our Lord Jesus Christ, and through the love of the Spirit, to join with me in prayers on my behalf to God" (15:30). The incentive of prayer Paul appeals to is their union with Christ, and the love of the Holy Spirit. The aim of the prayer is that he would be received well in Jerusalem: "In order that I may be delivered from the disobedient in Judaea, and that my ministry to Jerusalem may be acceptable to the saints" (15:31). Two concerns face Paul. The first is that the unbelieving Jews will not have their way when he arrives in Jerusalem. He knows their enmity against him and he knows deliverance can come only by the intervention of God. The second concern was that he and his mission would be well received by the believers. It may seem strange that he would voice this concern, but his earlier experiences in Jerusalem had not been entirely pleasant—even in his relationship with believers (Acts 9:26-30; 15:5; Galatians 2:1-5).

Paul's final reference to his proposed visit to Rome shows how much he looked forward to the visit: "In order that when I come to you in joy through the will of God I may be refreshed by you" (15:32). He had expressed the same hope in Romans 1:11-13.

The Apostle climaxes this review of his plans with another benediction: "The God of peace be with you all. Amen" (15:33). This is one way Paul closes out his epistles (1 Corinthians 16:23; 2 Corinthians 13:14; Galatians 6:18, and others). Paul continues this epistle by commending Phoebe to Rome, and by sending personal greetings to many of his personal acquaintances. These are taken up in Romans 16.

PERSONAL GREETINGS
16:1-16

The first statement Paul makes in this chapter is the commendation of Phoebe: "I commend to you Phoebe, our sister, who is a servant of the church in Cenchrea" (16:1). The word for "commend" is a formal word of introduction; so, this statement is more than a social greeting. She is commended on the grounds that she is a sister and also a servant of the church at Cenchrea. The word for servant is the same as the word for "deacon." We probably do not have sufficient evidence to conclude she was in a formal order called "deacon" or "deaconness." The fact that the word is used here in the masculine may imply it was a formal order. This word apparently is used in this way in Paul's address to the "bishops and deacons" in Philippi (Philippians 1:1) and in his instructions to Timothy (1 Timothy 3:8-13). All of this falls short of proof that Phoebe should be called a "deaconness." There is no question that she stands out as a minister (servant) in the congregation in Cenchrea. This is the only indication in Scripture that there was a congregation in this city; it was actually a neighboring town—more like a suburb in modern terms—of Corinth. In fact, this was a port town to Corinth. Though we have no other record of this church, there is no reason to think there was not a church there distinct from the congregation at Corinth.

Paul asks further that they receive Phoebe and give her help in Rome: "That you receive her in the Lord in a manner worthy of the saints, and that you help her in whatever matter she has need, for she has been a helper of many and of me" (15:2). It would seem Paul was especially interested in contributions to her continued ministry as a helper of people. The word for "helper" indicates a person set over others; it is the feminine form of the word "superintendent."[4] The help she rendered may have been in an official capacity. It is likely, however, that it was in the pattern of Lydia at Philippi (Acts 16:11-15). Paul very carefully mentions her help to him.

The word "salute" or "greet" stands at the beginning of verse 3-16. It is characteristic of Paul's letters that he includes such a list of greetings at the end. (Ephesians is an exception.) The people greeted were people of Paul's acquaintance and people in the church that he was writing. Since Paul had never visited the believers in Rome, we conclude that these were people whom he had known and ministered to (or with) in other places. This is not hard to imagine in view of the prominence of travel throughout the Roman empire.

The first greeting is extended to Priscilla and Aquila; Paul calls them "my fellow workers in Christ Jesus" (15:3). We know of their work with Paul in Corinth (Acts 18:1-4). They accompanied him to Ephesus and remained there after his departure (Acts 18:18, 19). While they remained in Ephesus, they instructed Apollos and commended him to the churches in Achaia (Acts 18:24-28). The Apostle also notes that they risked their lives for him (15:4). They were well known throughout the gentile churches, and the churches gave thanks for their ministry to them (15:4). Paul also sends greetings to the church in their house (15:5). He mentions a church which met in their house in Asia (1 Corinthians 16:19). This notation probably gives us insight into the nature of the church in Rome. Instead of their being a single congregation there that could be called the "church in Rome," the church probably consisted of "house churches" scattered throughout the city. Notice that Paul does not address the "church in Rome" in his opening remarks; instead, he greets "all who are in Rome who are loved by God and called to be saints" (1:7, *NIV*).

Epaenetus is distinguished for the endearing address ("my beloved") and for the fact that he was the first to come to faith under Paul's ministry in Asia ("the firstfruits of Asia," 15:5). Mary is distinguished in that she "labored to the point of exhaustion for you" (15:6). Paul knew something of the history of the church in Rome. Two kinsmen (that is by family) of Paul were among the believers in Rome; they are Andronicus and Junia. Paul notes three other things of interest about them. They had been fellow prisoners with the Apostle. They were well known among the Apostles. This probably indicates they had come to know the Lord in Jerusalem, or at least had ministered there as disciples. Finally, Paul notes that they had come to know the Lord as Savior before he did.

There is a series of greetings which are given with little elaboration in verses 8-11. The series includes Amplias ("my beloved in the Lord"), Urbane ("our fellow worker in Christ"), Stachys ("my beloved"), Apelles ("approved in the Lord" —tested and approved), the ones "out of Aristobulus" (probably meaning those of his household), Herodion ("my kinsman"), and the believers from Narcissus' household ("those of Narcissus in the Lord"). Verse 12 addresses three women: Tryphena, Tryphosa and Persis. All of them are distinguished for their labor in the Lord. Paul uses the same word here that we noted in verse 6, which emphasizes exhausting labor. The fact that Tryphena and Tryphosa are paired may suggest they were sisters.

Paul greets Rufus with a special personal note (15:13). He extends the greeting to "his mother and mine." Most likely Paul means that Rufus' mother had been like a mother to him. Paul also describes this brother as "the chosen in the Lord." He may be the son of Simon of Cyrene who was commandeered to carry Jesus' cross and who had a son by the name of Rufus (Mark 15:21). In verse 14 Paul sends greetings to a group of brothers. He names Asyncritus, Phlegon, Hermas, Patrobas and Hermes; then he adds "and the brothers which are with them." This may be another church group or house church (cf. v. 5). A similar grouping is named in verse 15, except that the latter group includes two women: Julia and the sister of Nereus. A number of commentaries suggest Julia may have been the wife of Philologus. Paul not only greets these by name, but also "all the saints that are with them." It is likely this greeting also represents a church group among the Roman believers.

It is noteworthy that Paul does not send greetings to Peter in this list. In the light of Paul's deference to Peter on other occasions (cf. Acts 15:6-11; Galatians 2:1-10, and notwithstanding the clash of Peter and Paul—Galatians 2:11-18) it is not likely that Paul would have ignored him, if he had been in Rome at the time of this writing. The assumption of some that Peter founded the church in Rome has no biblical or other sound historical foundation. It is also contrary to his apostleship as the apostle to the circumcision (Galatians 2:8, 9). If he had established the church in Rome and if he was the recognized leader (bishop or pastor), it is not likely that Paul would have ignored him in this list of salutations.

Verse 16 exhorts believers to "salute one another with a holy kiss." Such a warm personal greeting was in use among Jews in the time of Jesus; the omission of it was considered an affront (Luke 7:45). The significance of this greeting is shown in the hurt in the voice of Jesus when Judas used it to betray the Lord (Luke 22:47, 48). The father's greeting of the returned prodigal shows the acceptance of this rite and its depth of feeling (Luke 15:20). Paul gave the same exhortation to the Corinthians (1 Corinthians 16:20; 2 Corinthians 13:12) and to the Thessalonians (1 Thessalonians 5:26). Peter speaks of this greeting as the "kiss of love" (1 Peter 5:14). Obviously, no moral connotation is intended in this exhortation, but a great depth of love is intended. Though we do not wish to make this formal greeting morally binding or essential to the expression of love and fellowship, we must not enshrine aloofness and alienation by the abandonment of the practice. One may not practice this greeting because he does not identify with it culturally, but he must not avoid it because he is emotionally estranged from his brother.

Paul closes this list of salutations by a reference to all the churches: "All the churches of Christ salute you" (16:16b). Paul thinks of the unity of all congregations with each other under the common titles which they bear. Here he uses the title "churches of Christ." In other references he uses the title "church of God." The point of union, the basis of fellowship and of greeting is that all such congregations are of and in Christ.

A number of commentaries offer additional suggestions on the identity of these people. The most that can be done is to draw from comparisons with these names with what we know of society and government in that day. "We can note, however, that the names in Romans 16 represents names out of both Jewish and pagan traditions. The intermixture of these names shows that social, religious, and racial barriers were crossed in the fellowship of the church at Rome. It would be unreasonable to suggest that these barriers were crossed without problem; the earlier chapters of Romans deal with some of these problems. This list, and the manner of Paul's handling of the problems, demonstrate that the commitment of the church under God's will was to erase these barriers to the fellowship and service."[5]

The women who are mentioned here give us insight into the role of women in the early Christian community. Phoebe had distinguished herself as a servant of the church in Cenchrea, and now goes with commendation to Rome. The Book of Acts tells us of Priscilla's ministry with her husband and with Paul. Four women are commended as women who worked hard in the Lord: Mary, Tryphena, Tryphosa, and Persis. Julia and Nereus' sister were participants in a group of saints, probably referring to a congregational body. The church at Rome probably represented a picture of what was going on in the church generally at the time of this writing.

WARNINGS ABOUT EVIL TEACHERS
16:17-20

Some of the epistles of Paul were taken up almost entirely with answering false doctrine; in fact, some were prompted because of false doctrine. Romans certainly does not fall into this category. Very little attention is given to false doctrine or teachers of false doctrine. Romans is a straightforward statement of Christian doctrine. If the believers in Rome (or anywhere) would accept this body of teachings, false doctrine would by this acceptance be denied. However, Paul does seem to have some degree of apprehension about false teachers, as is seen in this short section of exhortations. It is significant that Paul does not even hint at the nature of the controversy involved in this warning. He seems to be more concerned with the spirit in which these people troubled believers.

Paul's first warning is to assess the manner in which these people conduct their work: "I exhort you, brothers, mark the ones who cause dissensions and offenses contrary to the teaching which you have learned. Turn aside from them" (16:17). Paul is the only writer in the New Testament that uses the word we have translated "dissensions." He warns the Corinthians that their carnality produces dissensions (1 Corinthians 3:3). He lists this evil among the works of the flesh (Galatians 5:20). Here their disruption is in relation to the teaching that the Romans had received. The singular doctrine that is referred to is the whole fabric of Christian doctrine. These people create division by opposing the body of Christian doctrine. Paul appeals to the believers on the fact that the doctrine that was being challenged is the doctrine that they had learned. Their acceptance of this doctrine is appealed to.

Paul's instruction is very simple; "turn aside from them." They are not to attend their teaching, and they are not to have fellowship with them. Paul's attitude here is much sharper than that seen in Romans 14 and 15 where he dealt with problems of conscience. There he urged continued fellowship, and attempts on both sides of the issue to understand and accept each other. Here Paul sees no reason for continued association. Paul has shown similar severity in other places in Romans (2:1-5; 3:8; 6:1-3; 9:19, 20).

In verse 18 the Apostle tells us why he urges such drastic action: "For these do not serve our Lord Christ, but [they serve] their own bodily appetites, and through beautiful words and flattery they deceive the hearts of the innocent." The term "bodily appetites" may refer to gluttony (cf. Philippians 3:19 where the same expression occurs). It stands in contrast to any idea of spirituality. Their god is not the Lord Christ, but their own bodies. So their speech is not in demonstration of the Spirit and power (1 Corinthians 2:4). Instead of the Spirit and the gospel, they use their own beautifully tuned words and flattery; they turn these words against the doctrine and call it into question. Their purpose is to deceive the hearts of the simple or innocent.

Paul is particularly concerned with the reports of the believers in Rome. He has mentioned earlier how their good reputation has spread throughout the church. He does not imply that these false teachers had gained a footing in Rome, but he does wish to spare them of damage from these teachers (16:19). Paul also wishes to provoke them to alertness. He urges wisdom on them, but not the wisdom used by the deceivers: "I wish you to be wise for purposes of good" (1 Corinthians 14:20); noting the advice of our Lord in Matthew 10:16. In matters of evil, Paul wishes the believers to be without guile, certainly not "worldly-wise." Our Lord commended the faithful believers in Thyatira because they had not known the "deep things of Satan" (Revelation 2:24). Paul commends the same kind of simplicity to the Philippians (Philippians 2:15).

In a brief, but powerful word of encouragement, Paul directs the attention of the believers to the return of Christ:

"And the God of peace shall crush Satan under your feet shortly" (16:20a). The title "God of peace" appears to come from the benediction language of the early church. In each place where Paul uses this title, he reflects a benediction or blessing use (Romans 15:33; 2 Corinthians 13:11; Philippians 4:9; 2 Thessalonians 3:16). The promise Paul issues here is a reflection of the promise given in Genesis 3:15 in which God promised that the seed of the serpent would be bruised by the seed of woman. Satan is described in Revelation 12:9 as the "ancient serpent called the devil and Satan" (cf. Revelation 12:14, 15; 20:2). The devastation of Satan is shown by the word "crush"—to break into pieces. The imminence of this event is described in the same kind of language used in direct references to the return of Christ, especially in the Book of Revelation (Revelation 2:5, 16; 3:11; 22:7, 12, 20); the events in the Book of Revelation are also described with this language (Revelation 1:1; 22:6). We feel confident in saying that this is a promise of the return of our Lord. The language carries the idea of suddenness and quickness, which is probably uppermost in the mind of the Apostle.

Paul closes this section of his epistle with a benediction: "The grace of our Lord Jesus be with you" (16:20b). It serves as a kind of climax of the promise Paul had just made. It reemphasizes the origin of the victory. This entire verse—the promise and the benediction—is designed to assure the Roman believers against the designs of the false teachers described in verses 17 and 18.

ADDITIONAL GREETINGS
16:21-23

The salutations which are extended here are from people who were with Paul at the time of his writing this epistle, or who were closely associated with Paul in his ministry. The first is Timothy, "my fellow worker" (16:21). He is first mentioned in Acts 16:1, and is frequently in the company of Paul subsequently. In verse 21, three are mentioned and described as "my kinsmen," most likely referring to family relationship to Paul. There is a Lucius mentioned in Acts 13:1, though there is no way of knowing if the two are the same. A brother by the name of Jason was prominent in Paul's ministry in Thessalonica (Acts 17:5-9). The proximity of Thessalonica to

Corinth makes it reasonable to associate the Jason of Paul's greeting with the Jason in Acts 17. Sosipater is mentioned only here in Scripture.

The greeting from Tertius is direct: "I greet you, I Tertius, the one who has written the epistle in the Lord" (16:22). Tertius is not mentioned by name in any other reference in the Scripture. However, Paul's use of a secretary (*amanuensis*) in the writing of the epistles is well established. He notes that he writes the salutation by his own hand, which indicates the epistle itself had been written by another (1 Corinthians 16:21; Galatians 6:11; Colossians 4:18; 2 Thessalonians 3:17). Tertius, the one who had served as secretary for this epistle, joins Paul in fellowship of ministry to the Romans. It was not possible for him to remain aloof from the Romans as he transcribed such an epistle as this.

Gaius is described as Paul's host and the host of "the whole church in Corinth" (16:23a). In writing the Corinthians, Paul mentions he had baptized Gaius (1 Corinthians 1:14). There is every reason to identify the Gaius of these two references as the same. Since he served Paul as his host, it was appropriate that he would join the Apostle in saluting the believers in Rome. The statement that he was host to the whole church may mean that the church at Corinth met in his house. On the other hand, the language would also allow that he entertained the "whole church" (that is, any who traveled through Corinth in ministry, or transfer or displacement). If this is the case, he would necessarily have been a wealthy person. Gaius is mentioned in Acts 19:29 and 20:4. These are not likely references to this person.

Erastus is described as the "chamberlain of the city" (16:23b). The word for "chamberlain" may be translated as trustee or treasurer. When Paul left Ephesus determined to go to Jerusalem, he sent Timothy and Erastus to Macedonia (Acts 19:21-23). At a later point Paul notes in his correspondence with Timothy that Erastus has remained at Corinth (2 Timothy 4:20). This, and the reference to Gaius above, would indicate that the believers were to be found in positions of wealth and influence even in such cities as Corinth. Quartus is mentioned only here in Scripture.

DOXOLOGY
16:25-27

The doxology before us is an expanded doxology. It probably was used in brief form throughout the church. Paul,
however, wished to elaborate on the praise of God. In doing
so he offers us some important insights into his theology. For
the most part he repeats material that he has already included
in the epistle. The doxology is instructive for us because it
shows how Paul incorporated his theology into his prayer life.

The basic doxology appears in verse 27: "To the only wise
God be glory forever, Amen." Verse 25 is an elaboration on
the nature of God. Verse 26 expands the concept "mystery"
which is introduced in verse 25.

God is praised as "the One who is able to establish you."
The instrument of this establishment is Paul's gospel ("my
gospel"). He further identifies his gospel as "the preaching of
Jesus Christ" and the "revealed mystery." Throughout his
writings, and especially in Romans, Paul treats the preaching
of Jesus Christ as the gospel—the word of God (Romans 10).
This gospel stands at the head of Romans as the gospel
preached beforehand to Abraham (Romans 1:2) and which is
the power of God to salvation (Romans 1:16, 17). The content
of the gospel is the preaching of Jesus Christ. The gospel
itself is the product of divine revelation; it was not available to
man by means of investigation (1 Corinthians 2:7).

The mystery that was revealed was hidden in ages past, yet
it was present in the words of the prophets. Israel found it
quite easy to treat the words of their Scripture as the final
step in divine revelation. God ordered the opening up of the
Scriptures in process of the fulfillment of times in order for
the law to serve its purpose (Galatians 3:15—4:4). The full
significance of "the writings of the prophets" (16:26) could
not appear until Christ, the fullness of the promise of God
and incarnation of the word of God, appeared. The lifting of
the "silence" and the revelation of the mystery have occurred
by the command of God. His purpose in making this revelation known is that all nations should come to the obedience of
faith. Paul closes out this epistle with this appeal to God's will
that all men—Jews and gentiles—should know Christ in
redemption.

This elaborated praise is due "the only wise God." Glory is offered him by Jesus Christ. The offering of this praise is the function of eternity.

CHAPTER EIGHT
END NOTES

[1]Derek Kidner, *Psalms 1-72: Tyndale Old Testament Commentaries*, D. J. Wiseman, General Editor (Downers Grove, IL: Inter-Varsity Press, 1973), p. 96.

[2]This is an "epistolary aorist" used specifically to refer to material in the current writing. Blass, DeBrunner and Funk: 334.

[3]This phrase (either "signs and wonders" or "wonders and signs") appears in the following places: Mark 13:22 (speaking of the signs and wonders of false christs and false prophets); John 4:48; Acts 2:22, 43; 4:30; 5:12; 6:8; 7:36; 14:3; 15:12; 2 Corinthians 12:12; 2 Thessalonians 2:9 (speaking of the lying wonders of the antichrist); Hebrews 2:4.

[4]Thayer, p. 549.

[5]R. Hollis Gause and Beulah Gause, *Women in the Body of Christ* (Cleveland, TN: Pathway Press, 1984), p. 66.